CT/Woolstens/£14.95
13.4.82

T

The Multinational Motor Industry

GEORGE MAXCY

CROOM HELM LONDON

© 1981 George Maxcy
Croom Helm Ltd, 2-10 St John's Road, London SW11

British Library Cataloguing in Publication Data

Maxcy, George
   The multinational motor industry.
   1. Automobile industry and trade
   2. International business enterprises
   I. Title
   338.8'87   HD9710.A2

   ISBN 0-7099-0312-X

Typeset by Jayell Typesetting · London
Printed and bound in Great Britain by
Biddles Ltd, Guildford and King's Lynn

CONTENTS

TO BETTY

TABLES

PREFACE

This book is an industry study of multinational enterprises. Despite the mountain of literature describing and analysing these organisations, the results have been somewhat disappointing. In part, this is because the studies have almost invariably been concerned with multinational enterprises in general, and the latter differ so much in their characteristics and consequences from industry to industry that any overall assessment tends to be inconclusive. Focusing on a particular industry should make the task easier and more rewarding.

Part One seeks to present, in a straightforward way, what economists have been saying about multinational enterprises, and to provide a theoretical framework for the subsequent examination of the motor industry. In Part Two the international growth and development of the industry is traced from the first foreign direct investment in 1902 to the present, highlighting the issues raised in Part One. Underlying and shaping these developments are the conditions of production and these are treated in Part Three followed by a look at certain aspects of the industry in six contrasting countries. The final chapter states the conclusions.

I am grateful to a number of people at the Society of Motor Manufacturers and Traders for their help, especially Wilfred Bucknall, to Colin Gonze of the International Metalworkers Federation, to the Motor Vehicle Manufacturers Association, Washington, DC, and to the vehicle manufacturers themselves. I must admit, however, that I found the latter very reticent about the multinational aspects of their activities. Understandable perhaps but frustrating for the researcher.

Ian Bowen, John Dunning and Sanjaya Lall read an early draft of Part One and I am indebted to them for their comments. Most of all I would like to thank Garel Rhys, who read the entire manuscript, for his encouragement and suggestions.

Finally, I must express my appreciation to the Houblon-Norman Fund for a grant towards the expenses incurred in writing the book.

PART ONE

ECONOMICS AND THE MULTINATIONAL ENTERPRISE

1 THE NATURE OF THE MULTINATIONAL ENTERPRISE

The essential and unique characteristic of the manufacturing multi-national enterprise (MNE) is that it owns and/or controls resources engaged in production outside the country in which it is based. Because of this its behaviour is likely to be different from that of a purely national company. But this feature, by itself, is not sufficient to account for the great interest and concern aroused by MNEs since the second world war, rather it is the combination of multinationality and certain other characteristics, which may be found in national and multinational firms alike, that is responsible. Paramount among these is the huge size of the typical MNE. In the motor industry a dozen giant enterprises produce the great bulk of the world's output of vehicles outside the Communist countries and, for the year 1976, their consolidated sales ranged from General Motors' 47 billion (thousand million) dollars to Volvo's 3.6 billion.[1] Related to size is the oligopolistic structure of the industries from which most MNEs have originated, together with the emphasis on product differentiation and extensive advertising associated with such an industry structure. Of great importance also is the fact that MNEs are generally found in industries dominated by advanced technology. They account for the bulk of research and development expenditures in these industries and they are the major innovators.[2] Much of their economic power is derived from this. In short, MNEs are typically very large organisations owning and/or controlling an international network of productive resources, and operating in high-technology industries, oligopolistic in structure.

That network is normally established by means of direct investment abroad by the parent company and involves the transfer of a 'package' of resources — technical and managerial knowledge along with capital. Control over the use of these resources remains firmly in the hands of the parent company, located in a particular country, managed and owned predominantly by citizens of that country. The MNE may straddle the globe, employ hundreds of thousands of people from many lands; nevertheless, it has a nationality. It is American, British, German, Japanese or whatever.[3] Moreover, in many respects, the MNE behaves in the same way as a national firm in that it attempts to do on an international scale what the large, purely domestic concern does on a country-wide basis. Whatever their differences, the two types of firm belong to the same species, and a look at the large national firm with regional subsidiaries reveals much concerning the nature of the MNE; helps to explain why it behaves as it does, and why its activities have led to a certain amount of unease and controversy.

The goal of the national firm is increased profit and growth for the organisation as a whole as reflected in the consolidated balance sheet of the parent company. The latter organises and co-ordinates the activities of the group, based on a common strategy which may at times be contrary to the sectional interests of individual subsidiaries. This normally involves, for internal accounting and control purposes, the setting of 'transfer' prices on intra-firm transactions, and may sometimes require the allocation of markets between subsidiaries. For cost and administrative reasons, research and development activities are centralised and usually located near the national headquarters. It is taken for granted that the head office makes all the major investment decisions and has the final say on what products are to be made, which subsidiaries are to make them and the techniques and equipment to be used. When a new plant is under consideration it is, of course, the parent company that settles on the location, taking into account any geographical differences in wage rates and other costs, as well as possible financial inducements offered by national, regional or local authorities to establish the plant in a particular area. When a site is chosen, the company does not feel obliged to recruit and train the management from the surrounding area, or to give preference to local suppliers of materials and parts, although it may do both on grounds of efficiency. Nor does it see any reason to enter into joint ventures with local firms, or to offer shares in the new subsidiary to the local inhabitants. They are welcome, however, to buy stock in the parent company. There may be protests from businessmen with firms threatened by the increased competition, but the superior performance of the nation-wide firm is generally welcomed as being beneficial to the region as a whole. In its relationship with the government, the national firm recognises, of course, the sovereignty of the nation-state in which it is established, submits to its laws and regulations, but does not hesitate to use what political influence it has in furtherance of its goals. It also seeks, through advertising and selling expenditures, to influence people's tastes, habits and cultural attitudes, as well as to create an overall climate of opinion congenial to business interests.

When the large national firm goes multinational it tries to behave in much the same way, that is, as if national boundaries made no

difference. But intra-firm transactions and the allocation of investment
or sales, which formerly had little or no effect on the home economy,
now directly affect the tax revenue, employment, balance of payments,
level of income and the economic development of each country in
which the MNE is established, including its home country. Inevitably,
powerful nationalistic interests and emotions are aroused, and the firm
finds itself involved in new, perhaps unexpected, tension and conflict
over behaviour it had always taken for granted. Moreover, it may be the
target of a more general resentment against what is regarded as foreign
exploitation, unwarranted interference in host country affairs and the
undermining of indigenous culture and development.

In general, the problems are more numerous and acute in the case of
developing countries. Apart from social and political factors, this is
largely because the host nation is poor, with an overriding desire for
industrialisation and economic development, and its attempts to
influence the actions of the MNE to further this aim often conflict
with the company's goal of profit for the parent company. Many
developing countries offer financial and other inducements to attract
foreign investment, but at the same time a growing number are insisting
on joint ventures with local concerns or with the government as
partner. Once the foreign subsidiary is established it usually finds itself
under pressure to train and promote nationals to management posts, to
purchase materials and components from local suppliers and to export
to earn at least enough foreign exchange to pay for its imports. There
may be limitations on royalties and other payments made to the
parent company, as well as price controls and restrictions on the remission of profits. Its intra-firm transactions are likely to be viewed with
suspicion and, as the burden of servicing foreign investment grows, there
may be demands for the gradual 'fade-out' of foreign ownership or
threats of nationalisation. It is all a far cry from doing business at home,
but MNEs are adaptable organisations, and they have generally been
able so far to cope with the demands made on them by host governments and still return satisfactory overall profits on their activities in
developing countries.

More serious from the standpoint of the MNE is the view of some
critics, both inside and outside developing countries, of the impact
these organisations have in general on economic development. Their
economic argument centres on the belief that neither the products
supplied by most MNEs, nor the techniques used to produce them
locally, are suitable for poor, developing countries. In this view, what
the mass of the population needs is a more productive agriculture to

provide a better diet, facilities to meet basic sanitation and health needs, low quality and cheap consumer goods, furniture, housing and, of course, more jobs. What it gets from the local affiliate of the MNE are the same sophisticated consumer goods bought by the average family in the affluent home country, produced by capital-intensive techniques designed for high-wage economies. High-powered advertising and selling pressures create a demand for these goods and help to destroy indigenous tastes and culture. The great inequality of incomes existing in most poor countries enables a small minority of the population to buy these products, manufactured on a small, inefficient scale for local consumption. The relatively high wages often paid by MNEs to their workers, and the high returns often obtained by local businessmen and resource owners associated with the foreign affiliates, reinforces this inequality of incomes and perpetuates the demand pattern. And, in the short run at least, the fortunes of the subsidiaries and the groups allied with them are, to a large extent, dependent upon the continuation of this income inequality. The consequence is that the industrialisation that does take place is limited and, although GNP per head may increase, most of the people are no better off.[4] Some critics take this further and see the MNE as part of an international hierarchical and exploitive system under which the developing countries remain dependent on the rich developed nations, and the inequality between them is perpetuated.[5]

In reply it might be argued that, despite all the talk of 'unsuitable' products and the desirability of 'intermediate technology', governments of most developing countries offer considerable inducements to MNEs to manufacture the very same products locally, and insist that the latest and best equipment be used to produce them; that MNEs are the only organisations capable of transferring technology on the large scale needed to raise living standards, and that modifications *are* made in techniques and products to suit local conditions, if only as a result of adjusting to smaller scales of output. And, if the presence of MNEs leads to greater inequality of incomes, it is up to governments to make use of fiscal measures to bring about the desired income distribution. Some would dismiss the critics' case on the grounds that it is simply a reflection of a general prejudice against MNEs founded, for the most part, on xenophobia and half-baked Marxist, anti-imperialist propaganda.

In developed countries, the MNE has an easier time of it, the complaints are fewer and the attacks on it less fundamental. With MNEs of its own, each nation acts in both the capacity of home country and host country. As host to the subsidiaries of foreign MNEs, there is often concern over the policies of these companies with regard to future expansion, the introduction of new products, the allocation of exports and research and development. Behind this lies anxiety over jobs, the balance of payments and technological capability. A dim view is taken of the MNE which could expand the operations of its local subsidiary but chooses to do so elsewhere on the grounds that the climate for investment is more favourable. There is outrage if any MNE seeks to close down operations. The introduction of new products elsewhere is resented, as is any allocation of export markets that is unfavourable to the local affiliate. The more difficulties the host country incurs over its balance of payments, the more it monitors the export and import behaviour of foreign concerns in its midst. As for technological cap- ability, it is troubled by the fact that almost all research and develop- ment by MNEs takes place in the home country.[6] It fears that this might lead to a brain drain and an inability on its part to create and exploit new products. Largely because of this concern over technology, host countries tend to oppose the domination by foreign firms of what they consider to be 'key' industries and go to great lengths to ensure that at least one nationally-controlled firm survives in each such indus- try. Unlike the situation in developing countries, the question of 'foreign exploitation' and 'monopoly profits' is, in general, not a major issue in developed economies.

In their capacity as home countries, the developed nations face the same issues as far as the policies of their own MNEs are concerned. In the United States this has led to strong attacks on these organisations by trade unions and politicians alleging that they have undermined the balance of payments, created extensive unemployment and exported America's technological superiority. Elsewhere there has been little criticism. Indeed, European governments tend to look favourably upon their MNEs, to give them support and to regard them as essential bul- warks against economic domination by American MNEs.

One other major and general problem faces the MNE in every country in which it operates, and that is the question of sovereignty. Its declared policy is to behave as a 'good citizen' in each country in which it is established, to observe its laws, regulations and customs and to comply with the policies of its government. This may involve the subsidiary in supporting policies contrary to those of its home country government, and in behaviour and practices that might not be accept- able or even legal in its home environment. On the other hand, when the nations involved pursue different policies, the home government may put pressure on the parent company to get its foreign affiliate to act in ways contrary to host country policies. In such cases the MNE, fully aware of the impossibility of serving more than one 'master', muddles through as best it can. In its dealings with governments, it knows that as a 'citizen' in its home country it can legitimately attempt to influence government policies without normally stirring up a storm of political protest, but it soon learns that if it presses what it considers to be its reasonable demands on host governments, it may lay itself open to charges of 'foreign interference' which, in certain notorious cases, have proved to be all too true.

In short, when a national firm with regional subsidiaries becomes a MNE and attempts to carry on 'business as usual', it finds itself embroiled in a bevy of new problems and often under attack from all sides -- radical intellectuals, nationalists, local business interests, trade unions, host and home governments alike. As to why any firm should choose to invest abroad under these circumstances, the answer must be that foreign investment can be very profitable, and also that such investment may sometimes reflect other motives on the part of decision makers in large organisations – the desire to increase the size of the enterprise itself, or the pursuit of power for its own sake. In any event, the international network and global outlook of the MNE gives it options and advantages that the purely national firm, no matter how large, does not possess; and also presents it with opportunities to bargain advantageously with national governments and trade unions, as well as to circumvent at times attempts to control its activities and to tax its profits.

To begin with, when the home market for the products of a firm becomes saturated and export outlets are limited or even shrinking, it can, without having to risk diversifying into unfamiliar products and processes, continue to grow and to increase profits by means of foreign direct investment. An important consequence of this is that it can spread the high and rapidly-growing costs of research and development, innovation and of acquiring specialised knowledge in general – technical, managerial and marketing – over a much larger output than its national, home-country competitors. At the same time, the MNE can exploit directly and more effectively, the very wide wage differentials existing between countries. To the extent that tariffs and other restrictions on trade permit, it can become more efficient, and more profitable, by 'rationalising' production on a global scale according to world-wide comparative advantage. Moreover, having production units in the world's major manufacturing nations enables the MNE to restrain foreign competition, in the form of exports or aggressive marketing on the part of foreign subsidiaries in its own home market, by the ability to retaliate in the home market of its overseas rivals.

The wider options of the MNE give it greater bargaining power in negotiations with national governments and trade unions. The national firm can, of course, only invest, introduce new products, produce in and export from the country in which it is established. The MNE may literally scan the world when considering where to locate a factory, has a choice as to where new models or products are to appear, and often controls duplicate sources of supply in different countries. Some significant part, if not the bulk of the resources controlled by the MNE, always lies outside the reach of the national government and the nation-bound trade union. These resources provide the MNE with alternatives and the very existence of these alternatives strengthens its bargaining power.

Lastly, there is the opportunity of minimising taxes, transferring profits, and shifting currency to take advantage of expected exchange rate changes, which is presented by the existence of the extensive 'international trade' between the various firms making up the MNE. Material, parts and components, finished goods, sometimes machinery and equipment, may move on a large scale between the parent company and its affiliates, and between the affiliates themselves. Estimates suggest that more than one-quarter of the value of all international trade in goods is of an intergroup character.[7] When these goods move from one country to another, they must have 'price tags' for the customs and tax authorities. Often these are intermediate goods for which no market exists which might indicate what the price should be. What is the price of a Ford Fiesta engine or a Volkswagen door in these circumstances? With no independent buyers and sellers involved, it has to be, within limits, what the respective companies say it is. Similarly, with intra-firm charges for technical and managerial services where the 'proper' price is considerably more difficult to determine, such pricing decisions, which all MNEs must frequently make, are subject to inducements to use 'transfer prices' to increase profits and to reduce risk and uncertainty.[8]

Tax rates on corporate profits generally vary between 35 per cent and 50 per cent and, if they differ between countries in which the MNE is established, it is possible to use transfer prices to minimise taxes for the enterprise as a whole by making a large part of the profits earned in high-tax countries appear in affiliates located in low-tax countries. Tariffs complicate the picture, for underpricing exports to save heavy import duties might land profits in a high-tax country. But this is elementary. There are tax holidays, tax havens, differences in definitions of taxable income, the principles that govern tax jurisdiction, and, in the home country, allowances for foreign taxation to consider. No doubt the tax departments of the MNEs do consider them — very thoroughly. It is conceivable that some profits may go round and round in ever-diminishing accounting circles until they disappear from the sight of all tax authorities.

Whether the possibility of minimising overall tax and tariff payments through the use of transfer payments is a significant advantage over national firms depends on the extent MNEs make use of them for this purpose, and how effective government authorities are in checking and controlling such practices. Not surprisingly, fully documented evidence on this is scarce, but the fact that the government of almost every developed country is now instituting checks on transfer pricing, following the lead of the US Internal Revenue Service, strongly suggests that MNEs do make such use of transfer prices, and on an appreciable scale.

Any tax advantage the MNE may gain in this way over the national firm may, however, be offset by the greater risk and uncertainty of operating overseas. But here too, transfer pricing has its uses and may be utilised to minimise any disadvantage by shifting profits to the parent company from countries with exchange restrictions, restrictions on the transfer of profits, or suffering from political and economic upheavals. The overpricing of exports to such countries or the underpricing of their exports may enable the MNE to get profits safely out. Related to this is the ability of the MNE to use its international network to move out of weak currencies into strong ones when exchange rate changes seem likely. MNEs as a whole have enormous short-term liquid assets, and much of the funds flowing internationally during periods of monetary crisis is of MNE origin. 'Leads' and 'lags' in making intragroup payments for goods and overhead services are one way in which this can be done by the MNE. Some would consider this to be speculation, others merely the exercise of prudence in the financial management of company funds.

Such is the nature of the MNE. A few hundred of these huge organisations play a major role, and an increasingly significant one, in international investment, production, trade, and in the generation and control of advanced technology. Their importance is aptly summed up in the words of the US Tariff Commission: 'Whatever one's views on the multinational corporation may be, it is beyond dispute that the spread of multinational business ranks with the development of the steam engine, electric power, and the automobile as one of the major events in modern economic history.'[9]

Notes

1. United Nations Economic and Social Council, *Transnational Corporations in World Development: A Re-examination*, Commission on Transnational Corporations, 4th Session, E/C, 10/38 (UN, New York, 1978), table IV-I, pp. 288-312.

2. Sanjaya Lall and Paul Streeten, *Foreign Investment, Transnationals and Developing Countries* (Macmillan, London 1977), p. 14.

3. There are admittedly a few significant cases of joint nationality, such as, the Royal Dutch/Shell Group and Unilever, both joint Dutch and British companies.

4. For a good brief presentation of this point, see H.W. Singer, *The Strategy of Development* (Macmillan, London, 1975), pp. 18-21. For a more detailed treatment, see Lall and Streeten, *Foreign Investment, Transnationals and Developing Countries*.

5. For example, Stephen Hymer, 'The Multinational Corporation and the Law of Uneven Development' in Jagdish Bhagwati (ed.), *Economics and the World Order – From the Nineteen Seventies to the Nineteen Nineties* (Macmillan, New York, 1972), pp. 113-40.

6. United Nations Department of Economic and Social Affairs, *Multinational Corporations in World Development*, E. 73.11.A.11 (UN, New York, 1973), p. 50.

7. United Nations Department of Economic and Social Affairs, *The Impact of Multinational Corporations in the Development Process and on International Relations*, Report of the Group of Eminent Persons, E.74.11.A.5 (UN, New York, 1974), p. 88.

8. Sanjaya Lall, 'Transfer-pricing by Multinational Manufacturing Firms', *Oxford Bulletin of Economics and Statistics*, vol. 35, no. 3 (1973), pp. 173-91.

9. US Tariff Commission, *Implications of Multinational Firms for World Trade and Investment and for US Trade and Labor*, Report to the Committee of Finance of the US Senate and its Subcommittee on International Trade, 93rd Congress, 1st Session (US Government Printing Office, Washington, DC, 1973), p. 78.

2   ECONOMIC THEORY AND THE MNE

Why Foreign Direct Investment?

> In South Korea, Taiwan and Indonesia we see promising markets
> and we see an attractive supply of cheap labour. (Henry Ford II,
> 1972)[1]

This is the first of the two major issues concerning MNEs which have
attracted the attention of the economic theorist. Essentially, of course,
firms invest abroad for the same reasons that they invest at home,
namely, to make profits and to grow. But the establishment of production facilities overseas raises questions not dealt with by hitherto
existing theories of investment. How can one explain the ability of the
national firm to expand across its borders and to compete successfully
in an alien environment against existing or potential host country concerns? Why does the firm prefer to produce and sell in a foreign country
rather than to supply that market by means of exports or by licensing
local manufacturers?

It is often said that firms decide to manufacture in foreign countries
because they wish to take advantage of lower costs of production, or
that they seek to reach markets protected by transport costs, tariffs
and other barriers to exports. These factors do, of course, enter into
foreign investment decisions but, in themselves, they are not a sufficient explanation as to why such investment takes place. If wages or
other factor costs in the host country are relatively low for the
foreign firm, they will generally be the same for domestic competitors.
Local production eliminates international transport costs and import
duties, but it still leaves the subsidiary with the task of competing
against domestic companies on their home ground. In doing so it suffers
from certain cost disadvantages.

Initially these arise from the essentially fixed costs the foreigner
must incur in order to acquire vital knowledge about the economic,
political, legal, social and cultural environment of the host country;
the kind of information that local businessmen possess merely by being
born and brought up there, or can easily obtain as nationals because
they know where to go and whom to see. The greater the difference in
national environments, the greater this handicap will be. Obviously the
establishment of a subsidiary in Japan by an English or American

company would involve considerably more initial costs of this nature than one set up in Australia or Canada. As well as its knowledge disadvantage, the foreign firm undergoes greater risks in producing abroad, and this can be viewed as an extra fixed cost to be offset by a higher rate of return than could be obtained from further investment at home. Once the overseas subsidiary is established, certain operating costs will be higher because it is located far from its decision-making centre. These arise from the need for international travel and communication, with its attendant delays and misunderstandings, particularly if there is a language barrier.

It follows that for foreign direct investment to take place the investing firm must possess some unique advantages which offset the disadvantages and enable it to operate profitably abroad. A number of such advantages have been put forward in the literature but most, and certainly the most significant, may be summed up as being derived from superior knowledge and large size.[2]

Superior knowledge takes the form of new products and new production processes, the ability to differentiate products and adapt them to local tastes and conditions, and a level of technical, managerial or marketing know-how above that of local competitors. Much of this enterprise-specific knowledge, which has been profitably exploited in one market, may be employed elsewhere at little or no additional cost. Certainly it would be much less than it would cost an indigenous firm to develop the knowledge itself. Yet without comparable knowledge, the latter finds it difficult to compete with the local subsidiary of the MNE.

Just as size confers cost advantages and market power, and serves as a barrier to entry in particular industries within national economies, so too does it favour foreign direct investment inasmuch as the local subsidiary of a MNE is part of an organisation that is likely to be much larger than its national competitors in most host countries. Hence the subsidiary, regardless of its own volume of output, benefits from economies of scale resulting from the centralisation of certain non-production functions such as R & D and finance in the hands of the parent company, and the reduction in the unit costs of these overheads as they are spread over the output of the entire MNE production network. It may even be able to secure technical economies of scale, which local competitors restricted to the domestic market cannot achieve, because of specialisation and exchange of components and finished products within the MNE system. In any event, there are likely to be important marketing economies provided by access to the

MNEs world-wide distribution network.

In practice the two types of advantage tend to be closely linked together. In the main, this is partly because superior knowledge in the form of successful innovation frequently calls for large-scale research and development expenditure and some control over price is needed to make this profitable, and partly because product differentiation is a highly developed form of competition in mature industries made up of a few large firms.

But explaining how the foreign-investing firm is able to compete successfully against host country rivals is only part of the story. It is an essential part, but not a sufficient explanation of foreign direct investment. Why does not the firm choose to exploit its unique advantage by licensing superior knowledge or by producing at home and exporting? It would seem more profitable to sell superior knowledge to a foreign firm to exploit in its own country unhandicapped by the extra costs the outsider would have to incur. That would account for licensing, which does occur on a large scale, but leaves foreign direct investment unexplained. The fact that such investment takes place at all implies that the potential licenser is unable to arrive at a satisfactory arrangement on price and other conditions of sale with possible buyers so that it becomes more profitable to exploit the knowledge himself. Part of the explanation of foreign investment lies in imperfections in the market for knowledge. Indeed, it may well be that much of a firm's superior knowledge, consisting as it does of the firm-specific experience and expertise of a management team, cannot be embodied in a licence.

In recent years theorists have taken further the idea that some of the firm's competitive advantages might not be marketable and produced what is believed to be a more comprehensive, systematic theory of foreign direct investment.[3] This makes use of the concept of 'internalisation', originally developed much earlier to explain the origins and equilibrium size of firms. Basically the idea is that undertaking certain types of transactions through the market is costly and inefficient and, where they can be organised and carried out at a lower cost within the firm, they will be internalised. Most manufacturing firms, for example, rely on independent selling outlets to distribute their products to buyers because the cost of using the market for these transactions is much lower than the cost of organising them themselves in wholly-owned retail outlets. However, under certain circumstances a firm may consider the latter course of action to be cheaper and more efficient, and so internalise these transactions.

Companies will tend to internalise transactions when the costs of finding a relevant price and of defining the obligations of both parties to a contract are high; when the risks associated with accepting such contracts are great, and, when there are taxes on market transactions. Such is the case in the international market for new knowledge where the products concerned are highly sophisticated and differentiated, and the technologies complex. Consequently the firm will generally prefer to internalise the knowledge in the form of foreign direct investment. Where the commercially exploitable knowledge takes the form of a simple patent involving a new technique which can be precisely specified, or a formula for a soft drink, the market and licensing or outright sale of the knowledge may be the firm's choice.

This approach retains the basic idea of earlier writers, namely, that a firm must possess unique assets in order to invest in overseas production. But it is more comprehensive and systematic in that it identifies the common source of the advantages and also indicates that foreign direct investment is part of the same process. Firms are larger because of horizontal and vertical expansion which internalises activities which could be or were performed by independent companies. Firms possess superior knowledge largely as a result of internalising research and development activities and building up a management team with expertise in producing and marketing the concern's products, rather than relying on the market for new ideas, products, processes and experienced personnel. It is the ability and willingness of the firm to internalise economic activities which are performed inefficiently or perhaps not at all by the market, that accounts for its exclusive advantages. It is the same incentive to internalise that explains, to a great extent, the firm's choice of foreign direct investment over licensing.[4]

This examination of what are called the *ownership-specific* advantages of the firm answers the basic question as to what makes foreign direct investment possible in the first place, and goes a long way towards explaining the foreign direct investment decision itself. But the complete explanation requires the introduction of conditions in host and home countries, the taking into account of what are called *location-specific* factors, some of which were briefly referred to at the beginning of this chapter.[5] Firms may be quite content to exploit their unique advantages by producing at home and exporting. The erection of a tariff or other barrier to such exports may trigger off foreign investment. Relatively low real wages are primarily responsible for so-called 'runaway plants'. Size of market, its rate of growth and the

presence of local competition will certainly influence investment decisions. So will government policy towards foreign investment, inducements to invest and the general 'climate of investment'. Not only is the
export or invest-abroad decision strongly influenced by such factors, so
too is the question of licensing. Where the host country market is small,
licensing may be preferred. On the other hand, there may be no possibility of licensing advanced technology in many developing countries
because indigenous firms lack the necessary skills to make use of it.

In short, the location advantages of countries must be taken into
account along with the ownership advantages of firms in order to
explain foreign direct investment. Taken together they determine
whether a firm will export, license or produce in a foreign country.

The Product Cycle Theory

The location-specific characteristics of countries are bound to change
over time and this will affect the investment decision. The product
cycle theory, developed mainly by Raymond Vernon, places foreign
direct investment in a dynamic setting and is of particular relevance to
any industry study concerned with growth and development.[6]

It was designed to modify traditional international trade theory
based on the doctrine of comparative cost and the assumption that
'superior knowledge' became readily available to producers everywhere.
Given competitive conditions the classical theory predicted that the
manufacture of new products would take place in the lowest-cost
location. By introducing innovation, scale economies, ignorance and
uncertainty, Vernon was able to give a more realistic explanation of
why new products are developed in certain countries, and to trace out
the consequent changes in the pattern of international trade and investment, taking the investing firm's competitive advantage for granted and
implicitly ignoring the option of licensing.

The product cycle theory starts with the assumption that firms in
all advanced countries are roughly the same in their access to, and
ability to understand, the growing body of scientific knowledge. However, the commercial use that they make of that knowledge is conditioned by demand and supply conditions in the market in which they
are located, for they are more aware of, and more responsive to, the
needs of that market and the possibilities of introducing new products
there than producers located in other countries would be.

Thus in the United States market, with its relatively high-income,
high-unit labour costs and plentiful capital, American producers are
likely to be the first to spot opportunities for new, sophisticated

products which would appeal to high income consumers, and labour-saving products that would appeal to American producers. On the other hand, in the European market, conditions may point to possibilities for material-saving and space-saving innovations, in which case European producers would tend to be the pioneers. In both instances, the producers would locate their initial factories in the market which they intended to supply with the new product. This may or may not be the lowest-cost location in the sense of factor cost plus transport costs to the market. In the early stages the product is likely to be unstandardised, with the manufacturer still wishing to remain flexible in his choice of inputs and in the making of modifications in the characteristics of the product. Hence he needs to be in close contact with customers, suppliers and even competitors and, during this period of uncertainty, these considerations weigh heavily in favour of locating near the familiar market, especially since the price elasticity of demand is relatively low for the new product as far as the output of individual firms is concerned.

As the product matures, these factors influencing location become less important. The basic features of the product become standardised despite the efforts of individual firms to differentiate their versions of it. Mass production becomes possible, economies of scale are achieved, and the firms become more cost conscious and better able to estimate costs with some precision. At the same time exports of the new product will be expanding. In the case of American innovators, exports of products with a high-income elasticity of demand and those substituting for high-cost labour will begin to grow rapidly to European markets and to other advanced countries. Once such a market reaches a size which makes local production feasible, the American producer would have to consider setting up a foreign subsidiary to supply that market. Any move abroad to one or more locations opens up more possibilities. There are bound to be differences in costs of production in the plants established in various countries, and this may lead to supplying third-country markets from a foreign location. It may also be that labour costs abroad are so much lower than at home that when a foreign plant achieves large-scale production, exports back to the home country may become profitable. Obviously, many influences other than pure cost considerations lie behind foreign investment decisions, such as, the threat of local competition in the importing country, the investment climate there, the anticipated loss of a market because of tariffs, a move abroad by a home competitor, ignorance of overseas costs and overestimation of the risks, as well as 'non-economic' factors. The conclusion drawn from empirical studies of such decisions is that, 'threat in general is a more reliable stimulus to action than opportunity is likely to be'. This is particularly so when domestic rivals counter the initial foreign investment made by one of their number by investing abroad themselves.

More speculatively, a third stage is envisaged when standardisation of the product is far advanced and the innovating firms have lost their advantages so that competition is based largely on price. Investment and production will then tend to move to the less-developed countries offering low labour costs.

In a later version, Vernon places the product cycle model squarely in an oligopoly framework.[7] The first stage, *innovation-based oligo-poly*, remains almost the same in its explanation of the source of innovation and initial production. More is said concerning European innovations which tend to be land-saving or material-saving, e.g., synthetic fertilisers and rayon, or represent cheaper versions of established consumer products. Much the same applies to Japan, also a source for products that economise on living space, such as, miniaturised electronic circuitry.

Stage two, *mature oligopoly*, has the same economic forces tending to push production overseas as innovational leads become reduced. However, the loss of this advantage may be replaced by economies of scale acting as a major barrier to the entry of new firms. Oligopolistic competition is the order of the day, with foreign direct investment tending to be bunched as rivals match each other's moves. This has been particularly noticeable in many developing countries which have been making use of import restrictions to promote local industry. Foreign firms have crowded in even though their anticipated sales have been far below that needed for efficient production. In a heavily protected market, with prices free to rise, profits could be made and potential gains in the world market shares of rivals contained. But the same pattern may occur without import protection. When the oligopoly advantage lies in product and brand differentiation, producing close to the market generally increases sales revenue and profits. The consequences for competitors in that market may induce them to follow the leader.

The third stage, *senescent oligopoly*, sets in when the firms are no longer protected by the innovational factor or economies of scale. The latter may present some difficulties for new entry, but the barrier is not high enough to bring stability for the leaders. Price competition becomes severe, costs become vitally important, and there is strong pressure to secure sources of cheaper materials and components. This leads to foreign investment in low-cost locations because of reluctance to rely on indigenous suppliers. Where strict quality standards or close delivery schedules are essential, it is uneconomic to be dependent on an un-controlled supplier, especially one in a foreign country. Beginning in the mid-1960s, MNEs farmed out all sorts of components to their foreign subsidiaries in low-cost locations.

However satisfactory this explanation may be for the investment behaviour of MNEs for most of their existence, Vernon himself admits that, 'By 1970, the product cycle model was beginning in some respects to be inadequate as a way of looking at the US-controlled MNE.'[8] For a growing number of firms with 'a global scanning capacity and a global habit of mind', the sequence of innovation and initial production in the home market, followed by exports and the step-by-step spread of inter-national investment and production no longer holds true. In response to world-wide opportunities and threats, such firms have developed complicated logistical networks of affiliates. The innovative stimulus may now come from any part of the MNE system, and the production response to it may take place wherever it is considered most appro-priate. The American influence persists, but US MNEs will scour the world in search of ideas, capital, labour, materials and markets, and even innovating investment need not take place in the home country. In other words, MNEs still have a nationality, but their activities are becoming more and more footloose.

Welfare Consequences of Foreign Direct Investment

This is the second major issue involving foreign direct investment which has engaged the economic theorist. Influenced by the concern expres-sed by many countries receiving such investment, most of the analysis has been directed at the welfare consequences for host nations. But the impact of MNEs on their home countries has not been ignored and, primarily because the operations of these organisations are global in nature, their effect on world welfare has received some attention. It is convenient to begin with the latter.

World

One of the major contributions of a world-wide enterprise is that its organisation becomes a pipeline for the transmission of knowledge and progress wherever they appear in the world. (Frederic G. Donner,

Chairman, General Motors, 1967)[9]

The best of all possible worlds, according to the classical economists, is a world of perfect competition, a world in which goods and factors of production – capital, labour, technology, skills, knowledge – are freely available everywhere at competitive prices. There is no place in such a world for MNEs. 'In a world of perfect competition for goods and factors, direct investment cannot exist . . . For direct investment to thrive there must be some imperfections in markets for goods and factors, including among the latter technology, or some interference in competition by government or by firms which separate markets.'[10]

But if MNEs cannot go to 'heaven' perhaps they can help the rest of us to move in that direction. Some economists think they can, some think not. Both use the classical model as the ideal against which the performance of the MNEs is assessed, and the key question is whether these organisations serve to decrease or increase the many and inevitable market imperfections of the real world. In one view, their ability to overcome tariffs and other barriers to trade makes for a more competitive world economy, and their direct transfer of capital, technology and other factors of production improves the international allocation of resources thus improving efficiency and world output. The opposing view stresses the oligopoly characteristics of MNEs and their ability to use their international networks to circumvent market mechanisms and government regulations stimulating competition. When they establish production facilities behind tariff barriers, they use their market power to restrict competition and obtain monopoly profits. Or tariffs may induce the bunching of investments by competing oligopolists so that each ends up manufacturing on an inefficient scale. Moreover, the integration of the production networks of the MNEs makes it more difficult for countries, particularly developing countries, to exploit their dynamic comparative advantages.

But even if it is accepted that, on balance, MNEs improve the allocation of resources so that world output is increased, it does not necessarily follow that world welfare is improved, although the economist tends to leave it at that because of the awkward and difficult problems this raises. Suppose, despite the increase in total production, some countries are left worse off? Or, even if no country is worse off, suppose all the additional wealth goes to the already-rich countries? Just to raise questions such as these is to reveal that welfare is regarded primarily as a national concern, that people rely on the government of the country in which they live to look after their welfare. And these national governments care little about the highly problematic effects of MNEs on world efficiency, but a great deal about how these organisations affect their own individual economies and the welfare of their own citizens. This has been particularly true of countries playing host to MNEs.

Host Country

The assessment of the welfare effects of foreign direct investment on host countries has been based on conventional marginal analysis.[11] The question asked is — what would be the economic effect in the long run of an *additional* £X of foreign investment on the recipient? The amount of extra investment would be small in relation to the existing foreign capital stock in that country and, of course, much smaller compared to its total real capital. With the capital comes superior knowledge and, when these are combined with local labour and other host factors of production, productivity is increased and the growth in output and real income is presumed to be greater than any possible alternative use of the domestic resources utilised by the foreign firm. It is the *difference* between the gross domestic product with the foreign investment and without it that matters when calculating host country gains from such investment.

We can never be certain as to what would have happened without the foreign investment, but without postulating an alternative an assessment of the consequences becomes impossible. In order to isolate the effects of foreign investment it is customary to assume that the host government maintains the economy in internal and external equilibrium, that is, it successfully uses monetary, fiscal and exchange rate policies to maintain full employment without undue inflation or serious balance of payments problems. It is also convenient to begin with some further assumptions; that the host country is able to get the foreign investment without inducements in the form of tax concessions, subsidies or tariff protection; that it is successful in maintaining effective competition in the industry in which the foreign investment takes place; and finally, that it is both willing and able to maintain a reasonably effective surveillance of the use made by foreign firms of transfer pricing, royalties and intra-firm charges for services.

Given these assumptions, the host country should stand to gain from inward foreign investment, if only because its government usually has the right under double taxation agreements to receive the first share of any tax on the profits of the local subsidiary of the MNE. These taxes are on the earnings of the foreign capital as such, and on the profits in excess of those earned by domestic firms springing from superior knowledge developed elsewhere. They represent a gain to the host government at the expense of the treasury of the home country of the MNE, which otherwise might be expected to tax the income of its citizens and enterprises wherever earned.

Other direct benefits from the foreign investment may accrue to local factors of production or consumers. For various reasons, the foreign firm may pay more than the prevailing wage rates, higher interest rates on borrowed money, or higher rents for land. Or it might supply goods at lower prices or make improvements in product quality without increasing prices. If this happens the subsidiary is, in effect, sharing some of the profits from its superior knowledge. In addition, welfare may be increased by the effect of the extra investment on the distribution of real income, real wages tending to rise as labour productivity increases with more capital to work with, and returns on existing capital tending to be reduced.

Supplementing these direct gains are the indirect benefits the host economy is likely to derive from the presence of foreign firms with high productivity. These external economies may be realised in various ways. The foreign firm may finance the training of workers, technicians and managers who subsequently move into indigenous enterprises. Self-interest may induce it to improve the efficiency of its local suppliers, customers, distributors and those servicing its product. Its example and competitive behaviour may lead to the adoption of improved methods on the part of rival and other domestic companies. These are not once-and-for-all gains but are a continuing influence for higher productivity throughout the host economy. Much importance is attached to these external economies which represent one way, and a very important one, of transferring technology from one country to another. Some would maintain that, as far as developing countries are concerned, they are the major benefit to be derived from foreign investment.

Unfortunately these external economies defy measurement. However, Harry Johnson put forward two reasons for believing that host gains from technical external economies are of 'commanding importance'.[12] The first is that economic development depends heavily on the international diffusion of advanced technology and managerial methods, and this diffusion takes place primarily through the activities of MNEs. The second is concerned with the economics of technological and managerial knowledge. The generation of such knowledge is an expensive business, but once it has been acquired it costs little to extend its application elsewhere. Hence buying knowledge is likely to be much cheaper and more efficient than spending time and scarce resources to learn what others already know. Better to welcome the MNE bringing in new knowledge from which local firms can learn than to exclude it in order to encourage national companies to invest and create the same knowledge themselves. Any local research should be devoted to inventing and innovating products and processes the foreigner does not possess.

Under the assumed conditions then, the host country's benefits from foreign investment seem impressive and the costs, in the form of profits and other remittances to the parent company, manageable. Once a foreign subsidiary is established and in operation, real GDP every year is at a higher level than it otherwise would have been. Out of that increase the host country takes part in taxes and perhaps receives part in higher payments to local factors of production or benefits to con-sumers. But most important of all are believed to be the external economies generated by foreign firms which, largely unintentionally, act as agents for the diffusion of technical progress and the stimulation of additional domestic investment which further raises real income. And it is out of that higher annual real income that the cost of the foreign investment can be met year after year in the form of interest, dividends, royalties and profits. A properly-run economy, it is main-tained, will normally ensure that the foreign exchange will be available to transfer the payments abroad. Only in exceptional circumstances will these payments be a burden to the host country's balance of payments, and primarily responsible for the devaluation of its currency to the extent that the consequent worsening of its terms of trade wipes out the gains from the foreign investment.

This unlikely possibility aside, the benefits should exceed the costs and the net benefit from the package of foreign capital and superior knowledge may well be of 'commanding importance'. One question remains — could the host country have obtained the contents of the package on some other, more favourable, basis, that is, with less than the real resource costs entailed by foreign direct investment? Marginal analysis has nothing to offer here and the treatment of the question in the literature has been little more than a discussion of the pros and cons of possible alternatives. No generalisations or conclusions have emerged from this other than the commonsense one that the host country ought to consider all the options open to it before deciding on foreign direct investment.

If the assumption of full employment is dropped, the benefits of foreign investment are likely to be much greater since the entire increase in output can be considered as a gain because the 'alternative' is no output. Moreover, the foreign investment will have multiplier effects on the host economy further increasing employment and incomes (just as any investment, domestic or foreign, has) and this must be credited to it. On the other hand, there are costs to consider as well if the foreign factory replaces native enterprises, and it is just possible that it might cause a net increase in unemployment.

If the other assumptions about the host country being run 'properly' are relaxed, the benefits of foreign investment will be smaller and the costs greater. A large increase in tariffs to induce foreign investment in manufacturing, together with a tolerance on the part of the government of monopoly or oligopoly conditions in the industry in which the investment takes place, may result in large price increases to consumers compared to the import prices prevailing before the tariff. If that happens, not only do the foreign concerns gain interest on their capital and rent on their superior knowledge, but also real income is transferred from consumers to these firms in the form of excess profits. A similar loss to consumers may occur in oligopolistic industries where economies of scale are important. The high tariffs may encourage the entry of too many foreign firms in relation to the size of the local market. Product differentiation and the financial strength of each of the MNE competitors rule out the price competition which might enable at least one firm to expand to an efficient size. Prices to consumers are high primarily because each firm is operating inefficiently on a small scale. In this case, real income to consumers is reduced more by inefficient production methods than by excess profits. The offering of excessive financial inducements to foreign investors obviously reduces the gain from taxing the profits of MNE subsidiaries. Moreover, the amount paid in taxes depends on the *reported* profits of these firms. If the host government's surveillance of the intra-company transactions described in the previous chapter is ineffective, profits may be understated for the benefit of the group as a whole. A badly-managed economy, with rapid inflation, an overvalued exchange rate and chronic balance of payments difficulties puts a premium on the use of these channels for the withdrawal of funds from the host country.

It follows that the welfare consequences of foreign direct investment depend crucially on correct host government policies and the ability of the government to carry them out. Moreover, it is assumed implicitly that the government represents all of its citizens and always acts in the 'national interest' and not in the interests of particular groups. On that basis, if the government can manage the economy with reasonable success, preserve competitive conditions, and keep a careful eye on MNE intra-firm transactions, inward foreign investment will almost certainly increase welfare, perhaps appreciably. On the other hand, the more these conditions are lacking, the less the net benefits are likely to be. And although foreign investment is generally assumed to be beneficial, economic theory clearly points to the possibility that a country may be worse off as a result of playing host to the subsidiaries of MNEs. If that happens, the remission of dividends and other payments abroad constitute a real burden on the economy, and incomes may be still further depressed by devaluation and deflationary measures brought about by the need to accumulate the foreign exchange required to service the foreign investments.

If one departs from this marginal approach and asks what would be the effect of a large-scale and sustained inflow of foreign direct investment, the traditional answer would be that this would appreciably raise average real incomes, with wages rising faster than property incomes. This conclusion is based partly on the grounds that there would be a major increase in the overall capital/labour ratio, and partly because there would inevitably be significant external economies since superior knowledge cannot be kept inside foreign subsidiaries indefinitely but ultimately becomes free and generally available in the host country. Again, this approach implicitly assumes that the host government consistently pursues the 'national interest' this time unaffected by a large and growing foreign presence and influence over the economy.

Home Country

> For years I thought what was good for our country was good for General Motors and vice versa.
> (C.E. Wilson, US Secretary of Defence, former President of General Motors, 1943)[13]

Using the same marginal approach and assuming as before that the government is able to maintain the economy in broad internal and external balance, theory suggests that home country welfare may be reduced by the overseas investment of the MNEs. To begin with the home gross domestic product will be less than if the investment had been made at home. Since full employment is assumed, the reduction in gross domestic product is given by the amount of profits that would have been earned on the additional domestic investment, part of which will go to the home government in taxes. This loss is at least partially offset by the profits earned overseas. But since these profits are *after* host country taxes, it is generally believed that they will be less than the *before tax* profit of that investment had it taken place at home. If profits before tax are the same abroad as at home and tax rates are the same in both places, say 50 per cent, then the home country is worse off by an amount equal to half the gross earnings of the foreign invest- ment by its nationals.

However, this frequently-used argument ignores royalties and the fact that most foreign investment is financed to a large extent abroad by debt issues and bank loans rather than by an outflow of domestic capital. Because of this leverage factor, foreign profits after tax may be less than before-tax profits at home, yet the home country may gain. Moreover, there is the possibility that intra-company transactions may be used to make profits appear in the home country headquarters of the MNE rather than in the accounts of overseas subsidiaries.

Investment abroad rather than at home will tend to reduce welfare through its effect on factor incomes. Shareholders and managers bene- fit to some extent at the expense of domestic labour which now has less capital to work with. Consumers too are likely to be somewhat worse off since more investment at home could be expected to increase productivity and lower prices under competitive conditions. On the other hand, if the foreign investment took place in low-cost locations and the products were exported back to the home country and sold at a lower price than similar domestic manufactures, consumers might be better off.

As far as externalities are concerned, it would seem that any benefits would go to the country in which the investment took place so that the home country might suffer losses on this score. However, it is argued that such losses are not likely to be significant, certainly far less than the gains to the host.[14] This is largely because, in most cases, the MNE occupies a dominant position in its industry at home so that most of the external benefits of its activities have already been absorbed by the home economy. Moreover, any losses may be offset to some extent by gains from 'knowledge sharing', which does not appear in the profits of an additional overseas subsidiary.[15] The rest of the group gets its own research and development cheaper because it is able to charge part of the cost to the new subsidiary. Also there may be some feed-back of knowledge useful to the group which is obtained at less than cost, and there may be gains from informal contacts with overseas managers.

On balance, theory does not seem to indicate much in the way of gains from foreign investment for the home country. And if the assumption is dropped that the government maintains the economy in internal and external equilibrium, with and without the foreign investment, welfare would very likely be reduced. Those made redundant by 'runaway plants' would tend to remain unemployed, this would have multiplier effects further depressing the economy, and the outflow of capital plus the displacement of home exports might lead to balance of payments difficulties, devaluation and a lowering of real income from the consequent worsening in the terms of trade.

Departing from the marginal approach, a large and sustained outflow of capital and knowledge would have an adverse effect on home country welfare. Labour would have less capital to work with and the technological superiority of that capital would be eroded so that real wages would tend to be depressed. It is considered unlikely that the foreign investment would so stimulate economic growth in host countries that the subsequent increase in demand for imports would more than compensate home labour for these losses from having less capital per head and loss of monopoly in the exploitation of knowledge.

Conclusions

As far as one can generalise, it does seem fair to say that, with certain qualifications, the main stream of economic theory suggests that host countries benefit from foreign investment and that source or home countries do not. This is particularly so when large and continuing flows of capital and knowledge are involved. As for world welfare, it is doubtful whether economists have anything useful to say yet about MNEs in general and world efficiency, let alone welfare.

The theory's great merit, with regard to host countries, is the stress it places on the wealth-creating aspects of foreign investment, uncontaminated by balance of payments, employment, or other considerations. The message is clear -- whatever else foreign investment may do, if it doesn't raise real income it should be rejected. Emphasis is placed on the role of the host government in ensuring that the country will share in the increased wealth. The significance of external economies is highlighted, and this is reflected today in host country preferences for foreign investment with 'linkages' with the domestic economy.

If the host country gains from foreign investment, it is perhaps worth mentioning that it does not necessarily follow that the home country must lose. Both may gain. The theory is not saying that foreign investment is a zero sum game, but it does encourage people to think again about something usually taken for granted, namely, that overseas investment is beneficial to the home country as well as to the investing firms.

Whatever the truth of the matter may be in regard to the gains or losses from foreign direct investment, no nation is willing to accept the view that the unhampered integration of the world economy by profit-seeking MNEs might so increase global efficiency and output that all countries would be better off in the long run. That argument carries even less weight with governments than did the case for free trade in the past. To a greater or lesser degree all countries, home as well as host, developed as well as developing, seek to influence the strategic decisions and behaviour of the MNE, sometimes by offering induce-ments, sometimes through legislation, official pressure and threats. Ultimately, of course, the state may exercise its sovereign power and use force against the MNE presence in its territory. The relationship between the nation-state and the MNE is the concern of the next chapter.

Notes

1. Richard J. Barnet and Ronald E. Miller, *Global Reach* (Simon & Schuster, New York, 1974), p. 307.

2. This approach was pioneered by Stephen Hymer, *The International Operations of National Firms: A Study of Direct Investment*, doctoral dissertation (Massachusetts Institute of Technology, 1960). Further developed by C.P. Kindleberger, *American Business Abroad: Six Lectures on Direct Investment* (Yale University Press, New Haven, Conn. and London 1969); R.E. Caves, 'International Corporations: The Industrial Economics of Foreign Investment', *Economica*, vol. 38 (February 1971), pp. 1-27 reprinted in J.H. Dunning (ed.), *International Investment* (Penguin Books, Harmondsworth, 1972); J.H. Dunning, 'The Determinants of International Production', *Oxford Economic Papers*, vol. 25, no. 3 (1973), pp. 289-336; and other writers.

3. P.J. Buckley and M. Casson, *The Future of the Multinational Enterprise* (Macmillan, London, 1976); John H. Dunning, 'Trade, Location of Economic Activity and the MNE: A Search for an Eclectic Approach' in Bertil Ohlin, Per-Ove Hesselborn and Per Magnus Wijkman (eds.), *The International Location of Economic Activity* (Macmillan, London, 1977), pp. 385-418; Neil Hood and Stephen Young, *The Economics of Multinational Enterprise* (Longman, London and New York, 1979), Chapter 2.

4. There are of course costs involved in internalisation. With the need to co-ordinate more activities, increased accounting and control information is required, and communications costs increase. There are also the costs of political discrimi-nation to take into account. And it must be borne in mind that as markets become less imperfect the net gains from internalisation will be reduced.

5. Dunning, 'Trade, Location of Economic Activity and the MNE', pp. 395-418.

6. R. Vernon, 'International Investment and International Trade in the Product Cycle', *Quarterly Journal of Economics*, vol. 80 (1966), pp. 190-207, reprinted in Dunning (ed.), *International Investment*.

7. R. Vernon, 'The Location of Economic Activity' in J.H. Dunning (ed.), *Economic Analysis and the Multinational Enterprise* (Allen & Unwin, London,

1974), pp. 89-114.

8. R. Vernon, *Sovereignty at Bay* (Basic Books, London, 1971), p. 10.

9. Frederic G. Donner, *The World-wide Industrial Enterprise* (McGraw-Hill, New York, 1967), p. 26.

10. Kindleberger, *American Business Abroad*, p. 13.

11. This approach was pioneered by G.D.A. MacDougal, 'The Benefits and Costs of Private Investment From Abroad', *Economic Record* (March 1960), pp. 13-35; for an excellent summary of the analysis applied to host and home countries, Harry Johnson, 'Survey of the Issues' in Peter Drysdale (ed.), *Direct Foreign Investment in Asia and the Pacific* (Australian National University Press, Canberra, 1972), pp. 1-6; for a critical view of the approach, Sanjaya Lall and Paul Streeten, *Foreign Investment, Transnationals and Developing Countries* (Macmillan, London, 1977), Chapter 3.

12. Harry Johnson, 'Economic Benefits of Multinational Enterprises' in H.R. Hahlo, J.G. Smith and Richard W. Wright (eds.), *Nationalism and Multinational Enterprise*, (A.W. Sijyhoff and Oceana Publications Inc, Leiden and Dobbs Ferry, New York, 1973), p. 169.

13. Heinz Karl Heider, *International Operations and Growth of the Firm: A Study of the Experience of General Motors, Ford and Chrysler*, doctoral dissertation (Cornell University Graduate School, 1975), p. 458.

14. Caves, 'International Corporations: The Industrial Economics of Foreign Investment', p. 5.

15. W.B. Reddaway, *Effects of U.K. Direct Investment Overseas, Final Report* (Cambridge University Press, Cambridge, 1968), pp. 326-31.

3 THE NATION-STATE AND THE MULTINATIONAL ENTERPRISE

I think the answer to your question 'What is it that makes a good citizen?' is simple. It is not whether you think you are a good citizen, it's whether people in that country think you are a good citizen.

(Harlow W. Gage, General Manager, General Motors Overseas Operations Division)[1]

The state and the MNE need each other to further their respective interests. However, the relationship is an uneasy one since the global aims of the MNE inescapably conflict at times with the purely national goals of the individual country. The MNE strives to increase the welfare of its shareholders and managers, by using foreign direct investment to expand the long-run profits and growth of the organisation as a whole. The state, on the other hand, seeks to enhance the welfare of its citizens by utilising foreign direct investment to increase incomes, create employment, support the balance of payments, raise the level of technology and skills, provide tax revenue and, at times, to serve political ends. All these goals are affected in one way or another by the MNE in its international allocation of activities, investments and markets and in its use of intra-company transactions in ways beneficial to itself.

In its policies towards the MNE, the state does not appear to have been unduly influenced by economic theory. Ironically, where theory tends to approve, host governments tend to be critical, and where theory tends to be critical, home governments give their approval, despite objections from trade unions and others. Beyond this, the main concern of governments, as far as purely economic issues are involved, has been the impact of foreign direct investment on the balance of payments, trade and employment. In this they have ignored the view of most theorists that the sole criterion of the desirability of foreign direct investment should be its effect on gross national product, that if it increases real income it should be accepted, regardless of its other economic consequences. If balance of payments disequilibrium or unemployment occurs, it is best taken care of by monetary and fiscal policies, together with appropriate exchange rate adjustments. But keeping a national economy in internal and external equilibrium by 'suitable' macro-economic measures is something that has eluded the best of governments and most, if not all, have stubbornly clung to the belief that foreign direct investment is a good thing if it improves the balance of payments and creates employment, and a bad thing if it leads to the reverse. As a result economists have sought to find out whether it is good or bad on these criteria.

Balance of Payments

> At the end of 1950, the value of General Motors net working capital and fixed assets overseas was about $180 million . . . By the close of 1965 this investment had increased to about $1.1 billion, or approximately six times the amount in 1950. This expansion was accomplished almost entirely from financial resources generated through General Motors operations overseas and through local borrowing which would be repaid out of local earnings. (Frederic G. Donner, Chairman, General Motors Corporation, 1967)[2]

Host Country

If one simply looks at money flows between parent companies and their overseas subsidiaries, foreign direct investment will almost always have an adverse effect in the long run on the balance of payments of the host country. The foreigner seeks to make a profit on his invest-ment and, if he is to be successful, more must come out than goes in, that is, the remission of dividends and interest must eventually exceed the initial sum invested. As a consequence, income payments by the host country in any one year on total past investments are usually appreciably more than the annual inflow of fresh capital. Only if the rate of growth of foreign capital (including reinvested profits) is greater than the return on investment (after tax) will the balance of payments show an improvement. However, such a state of affairs is unlikely to continue for long periods if only because it requires a continual increase in the amount of investment and, in all probability, an ever-increasing share of foreign ownership in the host country's total capital stock. It is not surprising then to find that actual host country remissions of profit and other payments to MNEs abroad are far in excess of incoming capital transfers from parent companies. This outcome has been accentuated in the past decade or so as MNEs have financed a growing proportion of their overseas investment by means of local borrowing in host countries. When this happens, the initial gain in foreign exchange to the host is relatively small and soon offset by the outgoing payments associated with the investment.

But of course these money flows are far from being the only effect foreign direct investment has on the host's balance of payments. Exports and imports are directly affected by the activities of foreign subsidiaries and this tends to swamp the effects of the money flows. Such is obviously the case when the subsidiary is established to produce for export to the home country or to third countries, and such investment of course has favourable effects on the host's balance of payments. Manufacturing investment, however, has tended to be of an import-saving nature and here the net direct trade effects are not necessarily favourable to the host country. There may be substantial savings in the import bill for final products, but this may be accompanied by large increases in imports of raw materials, components and complementary finished products, as well as in the machinery and equipment needed to establish local production. There is also the possibility that the cost of imports may be inflated by tied purchases or overpricing. Exports, on the other hand, may be non-existent because the goods are not competitive in world markets or are restricted by the parent company for overall policy reasons. And finally, some of the local resources employed by the foreign subsidiary may be taken away from activities that earn or save foreign exchange.

In addition to these direct trade effects, foreign investment influences the host's balance of payments through its effects on productivity, and the level of incomes and prices. If this leads to higher incomes, imports will increase, but beyond that relationship the analysis becomes complex, riddled with assumptions and bogged down by lack of data. Hence there is no evidence to support any useful conclusions regarding these dynamic, indirect effects yet their cumulative impact on the balance of payments may be highly significant in the long run.

The approach so far has implicitly assumed that the foreign investment is wholly-owned and that the only alternative for the host country is imports. Just as in the case of the welfare effect of such investment, the balance of payments effect cannot be determined without comparing what happens with what would have happened if it had not taken place. If, in the absence of foreign investment, domestic investment *of an identical nature* would have occurred, then the verdict depends solely on the money flows between parent and subsidiary, which sooner or later result in an adverse balance for the host country. The direct and indirect effects on exports and imports can be ignored in this case because they would have been the same whether the project were domestically-owned and financed, or foreign. More realistically, local investment would be bound to differ in a number of respects, such as, scale, efficiency, marketing policies and access to overseas outlets. Where domestic investment is a feasible alternative, it is the *differential* trade effect and not the total trade effect that is relevant. And if the domestic project had to be financed at the expense of investment elsewhere in the economy, the adverse balance of payments effect of the foregone investment would also have to be taken into account.

However, production by domestic concerns is often not possible, either because local savings are scarce or, more probably, the scientific, technical and managerial knowledge is lacking. When the alternative is no factory, then all the trade effects should be credited to the foreign investment, as well as the capital inflows and subsequent remissions to the parent company.

But the alternatives need not be limited to 100 per cent domestic or foreign projects. Various combinations of local and overseas finance and enterprise may be possible. Local companies may be financed by borrowing abroad, know-how may be obtained by licensing or management contracts, joint ventures may be established or turn-key projects purchased. Each of these would have different balance of payments implications. In any particular case, it may not be reasonable to consider some or any of them as alternatives. But to say that the balance of payments effects of foreign investment are favourable or unfavourable means nothing by itself. Favourable compared with what?

The relatively few studies that have been made of the balance of payments effects on host and home countries reveal how complex the subject is, and how sensitive the results are to the assumptions that must be made regarding what would happen without the incoming investment. Because of this there is no convincing evidence to support the view that foreign investment in general is a great help to the balance of payments or a great burden. One thing is certain, the direct trade effects are crucially important. If foreign investment is to improve the host's balance of payments in the long run, the trade effects must be favourable, and favourable enough to more than offset the foreign exchange costs of servicing the investment. Any attempt to go further than this by bringing in the indirect trade effects is defeated by an inability to deal systematically with the cumulative effects of foreign direct investment on productivity, prices and incomes.

Home Country

As far as money flows are concerned, sooner or later outward foreign investment has a favourable effect on the balance of payments of the home country for the reasons given in the preceding section. The inflow of dividends and other income payments will in time exceed capital outflows.

As with the host country, the direct trade effects dominate the outcome, and these in turn depend upon the assumptions made concerning the alternative. If British companies build plants abroad that would otherwise not exist, in all probability this will result in the displacement of exports from the UK, and hence the balance of payments will be adversely affected. On the other hand, if it is assumed that British firms establish factories overseas which would otherwise be built by indigenous enterprise or by competing foreign MNEs, the trade effects will be beneficial because of the shipment of material, parts, components, machinery and equipment associated with the investment. For the most part, these exports would be lost if the foreigner builds the plant. And in this case the favourable trade effects reinforce the income remissions over time of the investment.

Putting the host and home country conclusions together reveals the surprising possibility that the direct trade effects might lead to an improvement in the balance of payments of *both* countries. This could happen if the host country's only alternative was imports and the trade effects were strongly in its favour while, at the same time, the investment was defensive from the standpoint of the home country in the sense that if it did not invest in the host country, one of its foreign competitors would. In the long run this possibility may be less surprising, for there is a presumption that the indirect effects of foreign direct investment if they could be measured, would reflect dynamic changes in the economies of the home and host countries which would be likely to benefit both their balance of payments.

Employment

Host Country

It may be irrational for the governments of developed countries, enlightened as they are by the 'science' of economics in the art of maintaining full employment, to be sensitive about jobs and the MNE — but they are. Any intimation that the MNE is planning to reduce the level of activities of its local subsidiary, let alone to close it down entirely, quickly brings forth angry protests from the politicians on behalf of those facing dismissal. Moreover, sizable financial inducements are offered to secure new investment by MNEs and this is proudly justified in terms of the number of jobs to be created. Implied in this attitude is the assumption that the alternative is unemployment. The MNE is presented a strong bargaining card by governments over this issue.

In the case of regional and local unemployment, this attitude by governments has, under certain circumstances, the blessing of most economists. Macro-full-employment policy may not be able to overcome unemployment in particular areas without increasing demand to a level which results in an unacceptable rate of inflation. At the same time, domestic firms may not respond to inducements to invest in these depressed areas, while foreign enterprises do. In which case, the MNE is unequivocally increasing employment in the host country.

As far as developing countries as a whole are concerned, unemployment is so widespread, massive and intractable that MNEs are, in general, eagerly sought not only for the industrial jobs they can provide in their own plants, but also for the employment generated indirectly through their use of local suppliers and distributors, and the stimulus additional investment gives to the economy as a whole. But this increase in employment provided by the foreign investor may be offset to a greater or lesser extent by the displacement of local firms and craftsmen as a result of the superior competitive ability of the foreign subsidiary so that, in the extreme case, the employment impact may be negative.

Regarding this question, a 1973 UN Report on MNEs concluded, 'On the whole the net impact on the host countries is positive since extreme cases of the destruction of local industries and wholesale displacement of labour are rare . . . For the developing countries as a whole, the employment contribution of foreign affiliates is small in relation to the massive employment problem.'[3] The solution to the employment problem rests primarily with the developing countries themselves. The spread of MNEs can help, but not much, although their impact on the modern sector may be of significance, especially in small countries which have received foreign investment on a proportionately large scale, such as, Taiwan, South Korea and Singapore.

Some maintain that MNEs could make a more important contribution to the employment problem in developing countries if they did not normally use the same capital-intensive techniques developed in the advanced countries. What is needed, it is argued, is so-called 'intermediate technology', techniques more efficient than traditional methods yet remaining relatively labour-intensive. This question is discussed further in the section on technology.

Home Country

> The record is clear that the expansion of investments abroad creates more job opportunities in the United States — not less. (Thomas A. Murphy, Vice-Chairman, General Motors Corporation, 1973)[4]

When a MNE shuts down a plant in its home country and builds one abroad, it seems obvious to the dismissed employees that outgoing foreign investment creates unemployment. When a growing proportion of the MNE's investment takes place overseas, it appears plausible to conclude that employment is being reduced, that home country exports will be replaced by production abroad, and that cheap imports from MNE foreign subsidiaries will undermine domestic production for the home market. It is not surprising that trade unions soon come up with estimates of the number of 'lost' job opportunities resulting from overseas investment.

However, these estimates are quickly countered by those from the MNEs which show significant increases in home country employment as a consequence of investment abroad. The conflicting estimates are the outcome, of course, of different assumptions about what would have happened without the foreign investment. The unions assume that export markets for the products in question would have been retained and that domestic firms would have remained competitive with imports of these products. The MNEs assume that this loss of exports and increase in imports would have happened anyway, that it resulted, not from foreign investment, but from changes in comparative advantage which gave foreign rivals competitive superiority. Their case is that the foreign investment was defensive; that the decision to produce abroad enabled them to retain much of the market formerly supplied by exports and, in doing so, to increase home country exports of machinery, equipment, materials, parts and components to their overseas subsidiaries, thereby expanding employment at home. Without the foreign investment, these jobs in the export sector would be lost. As for imports of finished products from their overseas subsidiaries, they represent only a small proportion of the total of such imports, and if they were stopped the gap would be filled by foreign competition, not domestic firms.

Technology

Host Country

The ability of the nation-state to maintain and increase its economic and political power and influence in the world, and to raise the standard of living of its citizens, depends to a major extent on new technology. It can create this itself, largely by investing in education and in research and development, in order to develop new products, processes and organisational methods. But so costly has this become that no nation, apart from the United States, generates more than about ten per cent of the world's new technology, so that most countries are very much dependent on the importation and diffusion of foreign technology to achieve their major goals. This means that they must import the superior knowledge in the form of new consumer or producer goods, or license or otherwise buy the knowledge to enable their nationals to use it in domestic production, or accept foreign direct investment based on knowledge advantages. Each of these ways of acquiring new technology reflects the dependence of the nation-state on the outside world in this respect. Each method has its costs and benefits which are extremely difficult to evaluate and compare.

In the case of direct investment by the MNE, the transfer of technology is likely to be carried out more thoroughly than through licensing arrangements, and the affiliate has continuing access to the knowledge and managerial know-how of the parent company which undertakes almost all the research and development of the group.[5] In this lies much of the competitive advantage of foreign affiliates over local rivals owned by nationals. At times this may enable them to dominate a particular industry and this is most likely to occur in the newer, high-technology industries which are expanding in the world economy. If this occurs, the host country becomes dependent on the technological advances of the foreign parent company, and on its willingness to share those advances with its affiliate, for the growth and development of what is loosely called a 'key' industry. Such dependence gives rise to host country doubts and suspicions, especially when the home country of the parent concern is a major competitor in world markets in the same industry.

This uneasiness frequently results in the host country offering incentives to, or putting pressure on, the MNE to undertake more research and development in the local affiliate on the assumption that the flow of technology will be more assured and that greater benefit will be derived from the presence of the MNE as a result. There are good reasons for doubting the wisdom of such a policy from the host country standpoint. If trained scientists and engineers are in short supply, the affiliate can only increase its research and development by taking personnel away from the laboratories of domestic concerns thereby reducing indigenous knowledge creation. The existence of a 'brain drain' does not necessarily mean that there is a surplus of such people. The emigration may be prompted by higher salaries and better facilities to work with than by a lack of suitable openings in the host economy. In which case the situation becomes worse if affiliates start bidding for the services of the remaining scientific personnel. More important, control remains in the hands of the parent company. It decides the extent and direction of the research to be done by the subsidiary, and the disposition of the results. The new technology will be used for the benefit of the MNE as a whole, without *necessarily* providing any direct benefits to the host country of the affiliate generating the technology. The shift of some research and development from headquarters to an overseas affiliate makes no difference to the locus of control. For this reason the MNE is unlikely to reduce tension by consenting to undertake such work in a particular host country.

The issue takes on a new dimension in the case of developing countries. Some 98 per cent of all expenditure on research and development is done in the advanced nations. It is aimed at generating new and more sophisticated consumer goods and more labour-saving, capital-intensive machinery and equipment to produce them. There is a fair amount of agreement that much of this technology is largely irrelevant to the basic needs of the mass of the people in the developing countries. Yet governments, and small but affluent minorities in these countries want, or are induced to want, 'the latest', and MNEs often find it profitable to produce it for them locally. Affiliated plants make attempts, to a disputed extent, to adapt or modify the techniques and the products to local conditions and to smaller-scale production, but there is no systematic attempt to do more than this, to develop more suitable products and techniques. Presumably this is because the MNE does not think it would be profitable for it to do so, and local enterprise either shares this view or is unable to marshall the skilled manpower and resources to undertake the task. Consequently what technology there is is foreign technology, controlled by foreigners, and the few native engineers and scientists have little option as far as research jobs are concerned in industry but to work for MNEs, either locally or abroad. The dependence on foreign technology is complete and the host country may never develop the capability to generate technology.

It is not necessarily the dependence at this stage that matters, since all nations are more or less dependent in this respect and for good reason; it is the belief that the economy is locked into the *wrong* technology, and is without the research and development capacity to evolve an alternative. It has been suggested that the growing trend by MNEs since the mid-1960s to shift labour-intensive activities to developing countries as part of the internationalisation of their operations alters this conclusion. So far this has not involved the development of any new technology, merely the identification of labour-intensive activities suitable for transfer. The electronics industry is by far the most important in this field, but there is a wide variety of industries involved, including the motor industry. In doing this, 'the international firm is thus emerging as a major supplier of unskilled, labour-intensive technology, as well as capital-intensive technology'.[6] In the longer-run, it is maintained, the MNEs will *develop* new, labour-intensive technologies 'as soon as restructured incentive systems make them profitable'.[7] Such a development would greatly enhance the prospects of the newly-industrialising countries.

Home Country

Purely from a technological standpoint, the transmission abroad of existing labour-intensive techniques of MNEs, and even the investment to discover new ones of this type for this purpose, would probably be acceptable to the home country on the grounds that the developing countries are in desperate need of such technology, and that this would be in the world's interest. It is the transmission overseas of the latest, most sophisticated technology, that has aroused concern.

The source country for new and advanced technology has a comparative advantage in world trade in its high technology industries which, in all likelihood, will be dominated by MNEs. Will not the investment and production in foreign subsidiaries using that technology undermine the country's technological superiority, even though control over the technology remains with the parent company? The MNE maintains that it must produce abroad to forestall the rise of foreign competitors, and that the extra foreign sales on existing products provides the profits and the incentives to invest in further research and development and innovations. While admitting that in the longer run the diffusion of industry and technology cannot be prevented, the critics argue that the country should export high technology products, not high technology industries, that much of the resources now devoted to foreign investment, especially in developed countries, should be allocated to research and development into new products and cost-reducing processes at home. The country would then maintain its technical superiority, and the trade and employment dependent upon that superiority. What is required is a continually-rejuvenated home economy, not the steady drain of defensive foreign investment.[8]

Ownership and Control

Host Country

> In my view, one of our greatest challenges in the years ahead is to
> find ways to accomplish the objective of world-wide participation in
> the ownership of multinational businesses ... What we in General
> Motors would like to be able to do is to extend the opportunity for
> stock ownership participation to people overseas on the same basis
> as it is made available to people in the United States. If the situation
> around the world were as uncomplicated as it is for the Texas citizen
> who buys General Motors stock instead of trying to buy a share in
> the local assembly plant in Arlington, Texas, there would be no
> problem. (Frederic G. Donner, Chairman, General Motors Corpora-
> tion, 1967)[9]

Foreign ownership and control lie at the heart of the concern expressed
in host countries over the MNE. Whatever the actual impact of foreign
direct investment on welfare, the balance of payments, employment,
research and development and other aspects of the economy, it is the
knowledge that *foreigners* own and control the affiliates that makes the
nation-state uneasy. It is aware that equity ownership entitles the
successful foreign investor to an income stream in perpetuity, and that
major decisions are made in New York, London, Paris, Frankfurt or
Tokyo, which may not be in its interest but which it is more or less
powerless to influence. Important industries, even whole sectors of the
economy, may be so dominated by foreign firms that the nation-state
feels that its sovereignty is impaired. Harold Wilson, British Prime
Minister, clearly expressed this attitude in a speech in 1969.

> But there is no future for Europe, or for Britain, if we allow Ameri-
> can business and American industry so to dominate the strategic
> growth industries of our individual countries that they, and not we,
> are able to determine the pace and the direction of Europe's indus-
> trial advance, that we are left in industrial terms as hewers of wood
> and drawers of water while they ... enjoy a growing monopoly in
> the production of the technological instruments of industrial
> advance.[10]

How much more vulnerable the real 'hewers of wood and drawers of water', the developing countries, must feel, with little in the way of indigenous industry to prevent the MNEs from dominating much of their economies and hence affecting, directly or indirectly, their political systems and institutions.

One fairly general reaction of Third World nations has been to seek to influence the decision-making process by putting pressure on MNEs to share local equity ownership with nationals, and to increase the number of their citizens in senior management positions. Domestic stockholding in foreign subsidiaries obviously enables local investors to share in the earnings and reduces the future drain on the economy in the form of profit remissions abroad. Moreover, if it takes place at the expense of the sizable debt issues and bank loans now being made by host countries to foreign firms, it would not deprive domestic industry of any capital. Local shareholders must bear in mind, however, that a profit-maximising MNE would prefer, other things being equal, to have profits declared in wholly-owned subsidiaries rather than in partly-owned ones, and that it has some leeway in such matters. But however successful a policy of local share ownership may be in altering the distribution of income between host and home country, it is unlikely to give the former any real control over the decisions made by the foreign subsidiary. Shareholders everywhere tend to play a completely passive role as long as dividends are satisfactory, and to lack the cohesion and knowledge to challenge the management of their companies when they are not. Partly for the same reason, getting nationals into top positions in management, whatever its other merits, has little effect on the behaviour of foreign subsidiaries in the sense of inducing them to conform more closely to host country goals. In developed countries, nationals already occupy most of the senior positions in affiliates of foreign MNEs, yet this has failed to allay anxiety on the part of their governments over the loss of control to foreigners.

Much the same conclusion applies to joint ventures in Third World countries between local firms and MNEs. As long as the national firms and their managers receive a share in the profits which represents a satisfactory return on their investment and their contributions to the enterprise, it is highly unlikely that they will act as watchdogs in the national interest. And even if they wanted to, it would perhaps be no exaggeration to say that as a rule they rarely know what goes on in the giant international business in which they represent but a small part. Moreover, the superior technical, marketing and financial knowledge of the MNE, which gives it its advantage over host country competitors, generally enables it to dominate the joint enterprise even when it is a minority partner.

In short, economic man has no nationality and control lies with the owners of continuously up-dated technology and expertise, rather than with the owners of shares. This may be formalised in internal company arrangements which make certain that the MNE retains control of the joint venture. These may take the form of management contracts, provisions in licensing agreements which cover production, marketing and prices, or the precise delineation of the responsibilities and authorities of the local partner. The growing willingness of MNEs to enter into joint ventures with local firms, and even with host governments, may reflect a realisation that they are able to do so without losing control. Moreover, joint ventures enable them to control more local resources for any given amount of investment on their part, and are likely to gain them local support and political allies as well.

Some host governments in developing countries have reacted to this situation by seeking to limit the extent of foreign ownership by so-called fade-out policies which call for agreement in advance for the gradual divestment of foreign holdings, or by various forms of technical assistance agreements on the order of the various types of contractual arrangements being made between MNEs and Eastern European countries. Under the divestment proposals it is hoped that the foreign technology will be fully mastered by the time the host country firm assumes full control and ownership and the monopoly rents of the MNE are finally ended. Whether foreign investors will be willing to enter such agreements on any significant scale is questionable. On the other hand, they have entered into a growing number of East-West agreements and these have aroused considerable interest in developing countries, especially for contractual arrangements which reduce the MNE from the status of owner to that of contractor. These require the host country to provide the capital, to be responsible for marketing and to assume the risks. To be successful, the host country must possess personnel with the requisite technical expertise to be effective participants in the management and control of the enterprise while the technical assistance agreement is in operation.

Most host countries, however, have continued to welcome MNEs but have sought to control their behaviour, not primarily through ownership but through exercising their sovereign power to pass laws and regulations aimed at improving the terms and conditions of their dealings with MNEs, and to ensure that these organisations act in ways which further the country's economic development and welfare. Foreign investment proposals and licensing agreements are being screened and a more selective approach adopted. Foreign subsidiaries are encouraged or required to make use of national producers as suppliers, minimum export targets are laid down which must be met, price controls are imposed, percentage limits set for royalty payments, restrictive business practices attacked, transfer payments scrutinised and the performance of foreign firms monitored. Some observers doubt the effectiveness of such measures, others question the will or ability of host governments to apply them.

In developed countries, with powerful industrial firms of their own, the problem of ownership and control of foreign concerns in their midst has seemed much less pressing. Governments have been constrained from taking discriminatory action against them if only because this might place the overseas assets of their own MNEs at risk. In general control has been sought by attempting to maintain a national presence in key industries penetrated by foreign companies, and relying largely on competition to secure the benefits of their activities. Foreign take-overs of domestic concerns have been blocked, joint ventures discouraged, and support given to structural changes needed to create national companies able to challenge effectively the local subsidiaries of foreign MNEs. In addition, government officials have made formal and informal representations to individual MNEs to enlist their co-operation for particular policies in the national interest. All very gentlemanly, but not necessarily ineffective in the case of MNEs striving to be 'good citizens'.

Home Country

Because a growing proportion of the MNEs business is taking place outside the jurisdiction of the home government, the problem of control arises here too, despite the fact that nationals overwhelmingly dominate the board of directors and the top management of the parent company and own the vast majority of the shares. It is not *foreign* ownership and control that is the issue, but the potential ability of the parent company to make use of its overseas network in ways considered by the government to be against the national interest. Normally the foreign commercial activities of the MNE support the economic and political policies of the home government and vice versa, but this is not always the case. The American government's attempts to affect parent company decisions in such matters as the balance of payments, employment, trade with certain countries and arrangements limiting competition are well known. On occasions this has involved pressure on parent companies to influence the behaviour of overseas subsidiaries in ways contrary to the policies of host countries. 'A classic case was one in which the headquarters of a multinational enterprise received a communication from the U.S. Department of Commerce and one from the U.K. Board of Trade urging it simultaneously to increase its exports in both directions across the Atlantic.'[11] Such attempts to extend the jurisdiction of the nation-state beyond its geographical boundaries inevitably infringe on the sovereignty of other countries and represent in a dramatic and politically-explosive way, the general problem of control of the MNE.

Summary and Conclusions

A considerable body of opinion in both home and host countries is critical of the benefits of foreign direct investment. In home countries there is a feeling that jobs, exports and technological supremacy are lost to the host countries who receive the investment. At the same time many people in host countries believe that foreign investment brings them none of these benefits, that on balance it means fewer jobs, a burden on the balance of payments and technological dependence. Both cannot be right. It is possible both are wrong.

Despite this criticism, most home governments continue to encourage overseas investment by their own MNEs, and host governments for the most part not only accept foreign investment but offer inducements to MNEs to invest within their borders. However, the relationship between the nation-state and the MNE continues to be an uneasy one since the global aims of the MNE inescapably conflict at times with the purely national goals of the individual country.

Arguably the unhampered integration of the world economy in this way by the MNE might so increase global efficiency and output that all nations would stand to gain in the long run. But such a view carries even less weight with governments than did the case for free trade in the past. To a greater or lesser degree all countries, home as well as host, developed as well as developing, seek to influence the strategic decisions and behaviour of the MNE, sometimes by offering inducements, sometimes through legislation, official pressure and threats. Ultimately, of course, the state may exercise its sovereign power and use force against the MNE presence in its territory.

All of which poses problems for the MNE. No man can serve two masters and the MNE may have dozens. Simultaneously to further the often conflicting national interests of all of them would not only destroy its multi-nationality and the economic advantages attached to it but would clearly be impossible. Hence the political and social tension so often associated with the MNE as it strives to organise and co-ordinate its international network based on a common strategy, overriding national interests when it is considered profitable for the group as a whole. This tension is greatly heightened by the sheer size of the typical MNE, and by the fact that a significant part of the organisation, if not the bulk of it, lies outside the jurisdiction of any individual state, even of the home country of the corporation itself.

Does this means that the mutual interests of the state and the MNE will not be enough to prevent a major clash over the issue of control? Will the MNE undermine the sovereignty of the state, or will the nationalistic state emasculate the MNE? Economists are divided on this.

Some foresee a confrontation in which either the nation-state or the MNE will emerge as the dominant institution, but there is disagreement as to the identity of the victor. One view is that, 'The nation-state is just about through as an economic unit ... Tariff policy is virtually useless ... Monetary policy is in the process of being internationalised. The world is too small. It is too easy to get about.'[12] Freed from the restrictions and distortions imposed on production and trade by competing national governments, the MNE will be able to integrate the world economy along rational lines for the first time in its history, to maximise world efficiency, and perhaps to act as a bridge to the next stage in man's development − the world state. The MNE will then be matched by a multinational political organisation, the only kind capable of effectively controlling it.

In stark contrast is the view that it is the nation-state that holds the upper hand.

> I really do not see how the fact that the value of the world sales of an international firm exceeds the national income of say, Tanzania, − impairs in any way the ability of the Government of Tanzania to reject its application to set up a subsidiary in the country, to restrict and regulate its activities if it is set up, or to expropriate an existing subsidiary.[13]

Moreover, others argue that the nation-state has already begun to demonstrate that ability in its dealings with the MNE and will increasingly do so in the future.

For essentially unalterable reasons of both economics and politics,

the traditional approach to foreign direct investment — outright
ownership and full control of local enterprise — and thus the traditional framework of multinational corporate operations, have nearly
lost all relevance in *most* countries. In others, notably the industrialised nations, the MNE is likely to be subject to increasingly severe
restrictions, with respect to both its expansion and its future mode
of operation. In the socialist economies of the Eastern bloc, the
conventional form of foreign private direct investment has never been
a serious possibility.[14]

Already there are signs that the MNE is on the run in developing countries and on the defensive in the industrialised ones. Now that traditional
oil and mining concessions are no longer obtainable in the Third World,
firms are competing for the 'service contracts' that they formerly
rejected outright. Companies that bluntly refused to consider joint
ventures are busy seeking local partners at host country insistence. The
types of agreements and arrangements currently being made in Eastern
Europe by MNEs, tempted by the potential benefits and pushed by
competitive pressures, may profoundly alter the terms on which they
operate in future in developing countries. As for industrialised countries, the sheer scale of the operations of MNEs, the potential threat
they pose to the international monetary system, and the structural
changes their activities impose on national economies, are under
increasing challenge by governments, trade unions and public opinion.
If the MNE is to survive it must adapt to these drastic changes taking
place in the international environment and accept arrangements which
are not based on perpetual ownership and control of foreign assets.

Perhaps the truth, as so often happens, lies somewhere in between.
The Report of the United Nations study group on multinational
corporations came to this conclusion.[15] Its authors rejected the view
that the nation-state was dead and that the MNE would increasingly
determine and dominate the pattern of world production and trade;
and also the conclusion that economic nationalism would settle the
shape of things to come, drastically limiting the scope and influence of
foreign direct investment.

But although the nation-state was pronounced alive and well, the
authors were convinced that it needed help if MNEs were to be ade-
quately controlled, that a multinational approach to the problem was
essential. To that end they proposed the establishment of a United
Nation's organisation to regulate the flow of international investment
and production along the lines of GATT and UNCTAD in reference to

international trade. A General Agreement on Multinational Enterprise between governments was suggested which would be concerned with such matters as the harmonisation of investment incentives, double taxation, agreements, anti-trust legislation, controls on capital flows and dividend remissions and the question of extra-territoriality.

Critics would argue that these are just the kind of questions that nation-states, in different stages of development and seeking their own advantage in a highly competitive world, are unlikely to be able to agree upon. Nevertheless, work on MNEs (Transnational Corporations as the UN now prefers to call them) continues at the international level. The UN Commission on Transnational Corporations and the Centre on Transnational Corporations have been created, and efforts are being made to establish a code of conduct relating to these corporations.[16]

Notes

1. Jon P. Gunnemann (ed.), *The Nation-state and Transnational Corporations in Conflict* (Praeger, New York, 1975), p. 50.

2. Frederic G. Donner, *The World-wide Industrial Enterprise* (McGraw-Hill, New York, 1967), p. 109.

3. United Nations Department of Economic and Social Affairs, *Multinational Corporations in World Development*, E. 73.11.A.11 (UN, New York, 1973), p. 52.

4. *The Economic Impact of the Multinational Corporation*, statement by Thomas A. Murphy, Vice-Chairman, General Motors Corporation, presented to the Subcommittee on International Trade of the US Senate Committee on Finance (Washington, DC, 27 February 1973).

5. It has been estimated that in 1966 the research and development expenditure abroad by American MNEs represented only about four per cent of their total spending on knowledge creation. Edward Mansfield, 'Technology and Technological Change' in J.H. Dunning (ed.), *Economic Analysis and the Multinational Enterprise* (Allen & Unwin, London, 1974), p. 166. It is unlikely that the distribution of such expenditure has altered much since then, or that it is at all different for non-American MNEs.

6. G.K. Helleiner, 'Manufactured Exports from Less-developed Countries and Multinational Firms', *Economic Journal* (March 1973), p. 31.

7. Ibid., p. 33.

8. Robert Gilpin, *U.S. Power and the Multinational Corporation* (Basic Books, New York, 1975), pp. 207-13.

9. Donner, *The World-wide Industrial Enterprise*, pp. 98-9.

10. Quoted in Rainer Hellman, *The Challenge to U.S. Dominance of the International Corporation* (Dunellen, Cambridge, Mass., 1970), pp. 142-3.

11. R. Vernon, *The Economic and Political Consequences of Multinational Enterprise* (Harvard University Press, Cambridge, Mass., 1972), p. 185.

12. Charles Kindleberger, *American Business Abroad: Six Lectures on Direct Investment* (Yale University Press, New Haven, Conn., and London, 1969), pp. 207-8.

13. United Nations Department of Economic and Social Affairs, *The Impact of Multinational Corporations on Development and on International Relations*,

Report of the Group of Eminent Persons, E.74.11.A.5 (UN, New York, 1974), statement by Professor Edith Penrose, p. 149.

14. Peter P. Gabriel, 'The Multinational Corporation in the World Economy: Problems and Prospects' in R. Flanagan and A. Weber (eds.), *Bargaining Without Boundaries* (University of Chicago Press, Chicago and London, 1974), p. 5.

15. United Nations Department of Economic and Social Affairs, *The Impact of Multinational Corporations on Development and on International Relations*.

16. See United Nations Economic and Social Council, *Transnational Corporations in World Development: A Re-examination*, Commission on Transnational Corporations, 4th Session (E/C.10/38, UN, New York, 1978).

PART TWO

GROWTH AND DEVELOPMENT

When Russia and China and India and South America come into consuming power, what are you going to do? Surely you don't think that Britain and America will be able to supply them? Surely you don't visualise Britain and America as nothing but vast factories to supply the world! A moment's thought will make clear why the future must see nation after nation taking over its own work of supply. And we ought to be glad to help the work along.

(Henry Ford, 1930)[1]

4 THE BEGINNINGS

In 1902 the German firm of Daimler acquired a wholly-owned subsidiary in Austria and, unknowingly, became the first multinational enterprise (MNE) in the motor industry. Paul Daimler, son of the founder of the parent company, was appointed technical director of the Austrian Daimler Company, itself established in Wiener Neustadt in 1899 to manufacture motors and parts, particularly Daimlers. However, until 1902 its operations had been restricted to assembly as far as Daimlers were concerned. Paul Daimler brought a number of technical personnel with him from Germany and arranged for workers from the Austrian plant to be trained in Cannstadt, thus becoming responsible for the first transfer of technology within an automotive MNE. He designed and produced a number of Daimler vehicles in Wiener Neustadt, but in 1906 Ferdinand Porsche became chief engineer and subsequently links were established between the Austrian company and two French firms which reduced the Daimler share in the business to 25 per cent. In 1913 that share was sold to Karl von Skoda thus completely severing the link between the German and Austrian companies.[2]

With that sale went the Daimler company's claim to be a MNE in these early days, for its links with other firms seem to have been confined to licensing. The French concern, Panhard and Levassor, began regular production in 1891 under a Daimler patent. The English engineer Frederick Simms acquired all the patent rights of Daimler for the United Kingdom and the colonies (excluding Canada) in 1890. Subsequently he sold them to the British-owned Daimler Motor Company which began to produce cars in Coventry in 1897. Another Daimler licensee was the Daimler Motor Company founded in New York in 1888 which began manufacturing an American Mercedes in 1904.[3] The plant was closed in 1913 after a fire.

Fiat too was active as a licensee — Austro-Fiat in Vienna in 1907, the Fiat Motor Company in Poughkeepsie, New York, in 1909, and a plant in Russia in 1912. The American plant is of particular interest. It manufactured the complete car including the bodywork, except for some bearings and the rear axle housings which were imported from Turin. In 1916 the whole of its capital was purchased by the Italian company. Ironically, the first manufacturing subsidiary in the United States of a European automotive firm never produced motor vehicles.

Fiat at that time was fully occupied with government contracts and used Poughkeepsie as a buying agency for strategic war materials and components. In March 1918 it was sold to the Dusenberg Motors Corporation.[4]

Other early examples of multinationalism in the European industry concern French companies. In 1903, the Anglo-French firm Clement-Talbot was formed by Adophe Clement, who controlled the French tyre industry at that time, and Lords Shrewsbury and Talbot. The company produced cars on both sides of the channel, and in 1919 merged with another MNE, A. Darracq & Co. Ltd. The latter was of French origin but by 1914 it had become the parent company, owning S.A. Darracq, with its foundry and stamping plant in France. In the following year, Talbot-Darracq amalgamated with the English firm, Sunbeam Motor Company, by means of an exchange of shares to form S.T.D. Motors Ltd., a concern which struggled on with little success until 1935 when it was dissolved. Renault is said to have established two assembly plants in Russia before the Revolution,[5] but these were probably licensing arrangements rather than investments by the French company.

The first American firm to become a MNE was the Ford Motor Company when it established a Canadian subsidiary in 1903. This happened after the parent company had only been in existence for little more than a year, with an output of less than 2,000 cars. That it occured at all at that time was largely due to the initiative of a Canadian, Gordon McGregor, who was an experienced wagon manufacturer with a factory in Walkersville, Ontario. At a time when the wagon business was facing severe competition, he was quick to see the merits of the Ford car and the potential profits to be made by producing it in Canada. Because of the Canadian import duty of 35 per cent of the wholesale price, Ford cars selling for $800 in Detroit cost the buyer $1,000 in Toronto. Local assembly and manufacture of some parts, combined with the importation of the engine and other components from the United States at a rate lower than on complete cars, presented a profitable opportunity. Moreover, there were good prospects for Canada becoming an exporter of motor vehicles to British Empire markets as it had unilaterally established a broad British preferential tariff system and hoped for reciprocity.

Ford-US furnished no capital and not a great deal in the way of entrepreneurship. Basically, the contract, which gave McGregor the right to form the Ford Company of Canada, represented the sale of knowledge for a controlling interest in the new enterprise. The

American company agreed to furnish McGregor with all its Canadian patents free, to supply all plans, drawings and specifications for making its cars, and to contribute technical assistance. For this the Ford-US stockholders received 51 per cent of the shares of the new company, capitalised at $125,000. Of the total cash subscriptions ($56,250), over 60 per cent represented Canadian funds, with the remainder apparently being provided by Michigan friends of C.G. Bennett of the American company. A majority of the nine directors of Ford-Canada were to be stockholders in the parent company, and this group would elect a President and Vice President.

Typical of many foreign investments, there was an allocation of markets. The agreement specifically stated that neither company was to sell in the other's territory, and Ford-Canada was granted the sole right to make and sell automobiles throughout the British Empire, excluding England and Ireland because of a prior agreement with a British sales agent. Two economic historians, with access to the Ford archives, have summed up the arrangement as follows:

> Ford-Canada thus became the holders of a vast commercial empire outside the dominion – an impressive domain; but the stockholders of Ford-US retained control of the entire enterprise, which cost them not a penny in cash, which had no adverse effect on the balance of payments, but to which Ford-US had to contribute patents, highly-valuable designs, 'know-how' and technical assistance.[6]

Ford-Canada, like the parent company, was extremely successful, so that it was in a position to finance its own expansion in Canada and later overseas.

With its decision to set up a subsidiary company in England in 1911 to assemble cars made up of completely-knocked-down (ckd) units imported from America, the Ford Company consolidated its title as the first American MNE in the industry. This move owed much to the initiative of an Englishman, Percival Perry, who was responsible in 1909 for the establishment of a successful Ford selling branch in London and a dealer organisation throughout Britain. He was to be in charge of Ford-UK for many years. The investment decision was based mainly on savings in shipping costs. Cars had been shipped to London boxed complete, with the axles resting on the floor of the boxes, wheels placed loosely alongside. Significant savings in shipping space, and hence costs, resulted from sending the vehicles overseas in unassembled form. In addition, having a British company rather than a branch had certain tax advantages, and it was felt too that assembly by a British company would enhance the local reputation of the Ford organisation.

Again the investment package contained no cash and consisted basically of knowledge. The new company was financed entirely from profits earned in England. It had an initial capital of only £1,000 and its 200 shares were wholly-owned by the shareholders of Ford-US. Perry chose the site for the plant which was at Trafford Park on the ship canal on the edge of Manchester. He considered it a better centre for distribution than London and it contained a building suitable for assembly operations. Production started in 1911 and the proportion of local content slowly increased as bodies and other elements came to be furnished by local suppliers and by Ford-UK itself. This was done under Detroit's careful supervision. Ford-UK set up a purchasing department to buy parts from British firms – horns, lamps, wiring and soft trim. This new unit worked closely with Ford-US. With every item available in England, a comparison was made between its price and that for the same article in Detroit; if the quality was good and the cost less than that in Detroit plus transportation across the Atlantic, the local pro-duct was bought.[7] Manchester continued, however, to make an exact replica of the American car, the famous Model T. Sales, which included some exports to France, rose rapidly and reached 7,310 vehicles in 1913, making Ford by far the largest producer in England.

Although the decision to assemble cars and to make or buy some of the parts and components locally was made on purely economic grounds in the sense that it was not influenced by tariffs or other host government policies, nevertheless it took the McKenna duties, introduced as a war-time measure in 1915, to bring about complete manufacture in England. These amounted to 33 1/3 per cent on motor vehicles and parts from areas outside the Empire and 22 2/3 per cent from Empire countries. When it became clear that these duties would be retained in peacetime, Detroit declared in 1920, 'in the near future Ford cars sold in the UK will be entirely of local manufacture'.[8] The tariff made complete production of the Model T in England both essential and possible. Essential in the sense that the market would be lost otherwise. Possible because the locally-produced car could not compete with American imports without protection.

Throughout these developments, which were financed from retained profits in England, Ford-UK remained a wholly-owned subsidiary. The tiny initial capital had been increased before the war to £200,000 by the creation of 39,800 new shares which were not issued until 1915.

These went to Ford-US stockholders with the exception of 400 shares allotted to key English employees. Henry Ford bought up all the minority shares in 1919 so that the Ford family then had complete ownership of the British firm.

In addition to the establishment of production facilities in England, a second European assembly plant was opened in France in Bordeaux in 1913 as a response to growing French demand. During the war this, rather than the Paris branch, became the centre for Ford activities in France. Ford-UK regularly shipped ckd units to Bordeaux where the vehicles were assembled, largely for war purposes.

With annual sales reaching a quarter of a million units, and production facilities in the United States, Canada, England and France, the Ford Company was, by most definitions, a MNE before the first world war. Its success in establishing and operating production facilities overseas is in strong contrast to the experience of the European manufacturers. The explanation lies in the product. Ford-US had created a satisfactory car which met the large middle-income demand for private transport which existed in North America. The mass production methods it evolved to meet that demand gave the company technical superiority over foreign firms, and this enabled it to overcome the handicaps of producing abroad and to compete successfully for the relatively small, but growing, demand for such transport in foreign markets. The European manufacturers, on the other hand, concentrated on expensive, luxury cars, since the middle-income groups in each country were not large enough to support the scale needed to make possible the innovation and production of relatively cheap models. But this gave the producer no significant superiority in product or in production methods over similar small-scale, labour-intensive makers of high-priced, specialist cars in other countries. Without such superiority, foreign direct investment could not succeed.

Notes

1. M. Wilkins and F.E. Hill, *American Business Abroad: Ford on Six Continents* (Wayne State University Press, Detroit, 1964), p. 226.
2. Dr Hans Seper, *100 Jahre Steyr-Daimler-Puch A.G.* (Mally & Co, Vienna, 1964), pp. 28-34, and correspondence with the Daimler-Benz Company.
3. Gerald Bloomfield, *The World Automotive Industry* (David and Charles, Newton Abbot, 1978), p. 310. See also Friedrich Schildberger, 'Die Entstehung des Industriellen Automobilbaues', *Automobil-Industrie* (January 1969), pp. 55-62.
4. Michael Sedgwick, 'Fiat in America', *The Veteran and Vintage Magazine*, pp. 40-2. (Taken from xeroxed article supplied by Fiat; date of publication not known.)

5. Lawrence G. Franco, *The European Multinationals* (Harper and Row, London, 1976), p. 11.
6. Wilkins and Hill, *American Business Abroad: Ford on Six Continents*, p. 18.
7. Ibid., p. 50.
8. Ibid., p. 102.

5 THE INTERWAR PERIOD

It is not always realised that the American dominance of the world
motor industry occurred prior to 1914. In the three years before that
date, the US average annual production was 358,000 vehicles, or 78 per
cent of the world total. That superiority was maintained throughout the
interwar years for, although the American share fluctuated fairly widely,
it never fell below 70 per cent. Indeed in 1929 when US output reached
its peak for the period of 5.3 million vehicles, it represented a remarkable 84 per cent of world production. The remainder was divided
between some half-dozen countries of which Britain had the largest
output with an industry hardly one-tenth the size of that of the US.
These were the years when all roads led to Detroit. Paradoxically, they
were also the years when the American companies undertook major
foreign investments.

The Rise of the American MNE

Not surprisingly, the first move outside the home country was to
neighbouring Canada which provided a similar market, a familiar
environment, and less risk than elsewhere overseas. Even before the end
of the first World War, a number of American producers had followed
Ford and set up assembly and manufacturing facilities in Canada, often
by purchasing local firms. The Canadian tariff brought in the American
investment at a time when the incipient Canadian industry was vulnerable. The local firms were generally small, technologically inferior, and
lacking in financial strength, so that they were unable to withstand the
competition of the US subsidiaries. In the end, the American 'takeover'
was well nigh complete, with foreigners controlling 97 per cent of the
capital in Canadian automobile and parts manufacturing.[1]

The growing concentration over the years of the American industry
has left only three survivors in Canada in addition to Ford — American
Motors, Chrysler and General Motors. Strictly speaking, the latter
company became a MNE in November 1918 with the establishment of
General Motors of Canada Ltd. This represented the purchase and merging
of a group of Canadian companies run by the McLaughlin family, which
gave General Motors a significant share of the Canadian market. American

Motors and Chrysler automatically became MNEs on their formation since they both represented mergers of American firms which had manufacturing facilities in Canada. When Chrysler was incorporated in 1925 it assumed the business and assets of the Maxwell Motor Corporation which had a Canadian subsidiary, the Maxwell Chalmers Motor Company of Canada Ltd. Similarly, American Motors acquired Canadian production facilities when it was formed in 1954 with the merger of the Hudson and Nash-Kelvinator Companies.

World-wide assembly

The rapid growth in demand for motor vehicles throughout the world in the 1920s was met predominantly by the American producers. The English, French, German and Italian manufacturers, operating on a small scale in protected domestic markets, were not competitive in third markets, let alone in the United States where the firms were experiencing unheard of economies of scale. Just as the American producers found it economical to establish a regional network of assembly plants throughout North America as demand grew, so too did the two largest firms find that it also paid to set up a world-wide chain of assembly plants as exports increased. In the latter case, the savings in transport costs were more often than not supplemented by gains from the host country's differential tariff which favoured the importation of unassembled vehicles.

The first move was made by Ford and it was to Argentina in 1916 before any tariff advantage was foreseen. Others followed in Europe, South Africa, Australasia, Japan, India and elsewhere in Latin America, so that Ford-US was assembling vehicles in some 20 countries by the end of the decade. As experience was gained of local supply conditions, some use of domestic resources was made for items such as tyres, glass, upholstery, petrol tanks, floorboards and electrical wiring. The rule was to buy locally provided the cost did not exceed that of American materials plus freight, insurance and tariff duties. The latter were often high on certain individual items which were available from domestic suppliers. It was felt too that the use of local materials would help to overcome prejudice against the Ford car as a foreign product. Nevertheless, local content remained small for the most part except in Manchester where, with the exception of the engine blocks which were made in Cork, Ireland, an almost all British car was being made by 1926.

The method of financing this network of wholly-owned subsidiaries is of particular interest. Operations in each location were started in rented properties and, if all went well as it usually did, land was bought and assembly plants built from the retained profits. The rule was that expansion of facilities in any area was to be paid for from profits made in that area. As early as 31 August 1923, the assets of the overseas subsidiaries of Ford, excluding Canada, totalled almost $50 million. Manchester accounted for almost $15 million, Buenos Aires was next with $8.8 million, then Cork with $7.3 million, followed closely by Copenhagen. 'It must be remembered that these assets were almost entirely paid for from overseas profits.'[2]

The branch assembly plant system pioneered by Ford was soon adopted by General Motors, first in the United States and then overseas. Between 1923 and 1928 it established 19 assembly plants in 15 countries. Three more countries were added to the list in the 1930s. As with Ford the company found that tariffs often favoured local assembly, and that there were savings in transport costs. In 1928, for example, General Motors was able to export nine ckd Chevrolets to Europe at about the same shipping cost as two fully-assembled cars.[3] Other benefits were claimed by Frederic Donner after becoming Chairman of the company, benefits which point to wholly-owned assembly facilities rather than to the licensing of local firms to act as agents. Improvements could be made in the world-wide distribution and service system, more dealer sales and service outlets could be franchised, retail financing and other marketing methods which had proved effective in the United States could be introduced. In addition, assembly abroad provided the opportunity to modify certain features of the cars such as interior styling, colour, trim and some accessories, to cater to local tastes.[4]

By comparison with Ford and General Motors, Chrysler's investments overseas were limited. This was partly due to its late arrival on the scene. It was formed in 1925 as a result of the reorganisation by Walter P. Chrysler of the Maxwell Motor Corporation which, in turn, was the outgrowth of a number of mergers in the industry over the years. Nevertheless, the company made an intensive survey of the European market in 1925, and afterwards concentrated the limited resources it had for international operations in Europe. It established its first overseas assembly plant in Berlin in 1927 shortly after Ford and General Motors located there. Chrysler planned to enlarge substantially the Berlin factory in 1929 by doubling its capital to $25 million but its plans were halted by the depression, and in 1932 Chrysler withdrew altogether from the German market. From then on its European operations were concentrated in its Antwerp plant which acted as its assembly and distribution centre for the continent. When it merged with Dodge in 1928, Chrysler acquired an assembly plant in London at Kew which it continued to operate. The factories in Belgium and Britain (plus two in Canada) were the only wholly-owned production facilities Chrysler had outside the United States prior to the second world war. For the most part it relied on franchised foreign distributors to penetrate overseas markets, supplying the distributors with ckd Chrysler vehicles.

Russia – the First Turn-key Operation[5]

> Russia is beginning to build. It makes little difference what theory is back of the real work, for in the long run facts will control. I believe it is my duty to help any people who want to go back to work and become self-supporting. (Henry Ford, 1930)[6]

When the Soviet Union's First Five Year Plan was announced in 1928, the country had no automobile industry. All cars had to be imported as well as most trucks. A single factory, the AMO-Fiat plant in Moscow, produced less than 400 trucks a year. In 1928 the Ford Company was approached by officials of the Amtorg Trading Corporation and the Moscow Automobile Trust with a proposal. They wanted technical assistance in setting up a factory to make Fords, at first using parts shipped from Detroit but gradually shifting to Russian components. A plant making 25,000 cars on one shift or 50,000 on two was suggested. Henry Ford and his advisers rejected this as too small to interest them. Nevertheless, the company signed a contract with the Supreme Council of the National Economy of the USSR and the Amtorg Trading Corporation on 31 May 1929. This granted the Russians an exclusive licence for nine years to manufacture and sell in Russia, the Ford Model A car and Model AA truck. The Company agreed to provide the plans for these models and access to information and patents on equipment, tools and techniques for producing them. It also agreed to supervise the building of plants and to make detailed layouts for their equipment with a capacity of 100,000 units a year. Ford technical personnel would assist in getting production under way, and up to 50 Russians a year were to come to the Rouge plant for technical training in manufacturing and assembly. For their part the Russians contracted to pay the costs incurred by the Ford Company in preparing the drawings and plans, the salaries and expenses of Ford personnel working in the Soviet Union and of Russians at the Ford plant, and also the actual cost of services (labour and overhead) rendered by company engineers. In addition, the Russians agreed to purchase the equivalent of 72,000 Ford cars and trucks (less tyres) within the next four years, and to procure from the Ford Company any imported parts purchased for repair or assembly purposes. The price for the 72,000 units was to be factory cost plus 15 per cent, with payment in cash.

Assembly from imported parts began in 1930 but it was not until the end of January 1932 that the first all-Russian Ford vehicle, a Model AA truck, was built. No Ford official was present at the time and the company never learned what production was at this plant. The depression and the contraction in world trade made it difficult for the Russians to fulfil the terms of the contract. They sought to discuss credit terms but Ford was not interested. In the event, they purchased less than half the 72,000 vehicles they had agreed to buy, plus a quantity of spare parts. Ford's financial data, admittedly poor for this period, indicate a final loss of over $500,000.

Ford's great rival, General Motors, had no objection to selling vehicles to the Soviet Union, but apparently that was as far as they were willing to go in their dealings with the Russians. During a visit by Vauxhall officials to the USSR in 1933 to sell Bedford trucks, the Russians made a serious request to buy the dies and tools of the previous American Buick model, for which they were prepared to pay well and in gold. James D. Mooney, Vice President in charge of General Motors' overseas business at the time, thought that the offer was a fair and good one but the head office response was 'not for sale'.[7]

Japan Shuts the Door

In view of the subsequent importance of Japan in the motor industry, developments there in the interwar years are of particular interest. The immediate stimulus to foreign investment in Japan was supplied by Tokyo's great earthquake in 1923 which destroyed the city's railway and tramcar systems. There was a sudden increase in demand for motor vehicles to meet basic transport needs, a demand which Japan's very small-scale producers, technically backward and undercapitalised, were unable to meet. One thousand buses were hurriedly imported from Ford-US and by the end of 1924 that company had established a wholly-owned assembly plant in Japan.

Scarcely a year after Ford had begun to assemble trucks in Yokohama, General Motors was assembling Chevrolet trucks in its wholly-owned subsidiary in Osaka. The latter's decision to invest arose largely from concern that Ford might otherwise dominate the Asian market through its Japanese subsidiary.[8] The circumstances under which that investment took place are revealing. In 1925, General Motors sent a representative to Japan to investigate the possibility of establishing an assembly plant. That gentleman set up headquarters in the Imperial Hotel and simply waited for officials of the various Japanese cities to approach him. Osaka was chosen, partly because Ford was in Yokohama, and partly because of the offer of a four-year tax exemption and the use of city facilities in the construction of the plant. The contrast between this regal entrance into the Japanese industry in 1925 and the manner and terms of General Motor's re-entry in the 1970s could hardly have been greater.

The two American plants, assembling parts and sub-assemblies shipped from the United States, quickly supplied the vast majority of motor vehicles to the Japanese market despite a 35 per cent tariff. In 1929 their combined output was over 29,000 units, compared to imports of 5,000 built-up vehicles and domestic production of less than 500. Japan's dependence on foreign technology and production facilities for an increasingly essential civilian and military product was almost complete. Yet 10 years later, Japanese firms produced nearly 35,000 vehicles, mostly trucks of which roughly half were for the army, while output at Ford and General Motors' plants was grinding to a halt.

The policies of the Japanese government were, of course, directly responsible for the dramatic change. Strongly influenced by the army, the government tried in various ways in the first half of the 1930s to encourage national production. Nevertheless, domestic production remained low, scarcely more than 5,000 four-wheeled vehicles in 1935. It became apparent to the government that protection from foreign capital as well as from imports was essential if a national industry was to be established. The Japanese manufacturers were handicapped by scale disadvantages, lack of adequate assembly technology, inability to finance car purchases on competitive terms, and the absence of efficient local suppliers of parts and components. They simply could not compete with the local subsidiaries of Ford and General Motors as long as the latter were permitted unlimited production levels.

What the army and the government had failed to achieve by persuasion and pressure was accomplished through legislation with the passage of the Automobile Manufacturing Law of 1936 which effectively excluded foreign companies from manufacturing. However, until the Japanese industry was in a position to meet the country's requirements, the assembly operations of the American subsidiaries were allowed, even encouraged, to continue. But, as time wore on, production ceilings were imposed, tariff rates on imported engines and parts were raised significantly and, after 1938, the government gradually reduced exchange and import permits until foreign production had practically ceased.

The response to all this by the American companies is illuminating. Obviously they had little influence on the policies of the Japanese government. Both foresaw that survival in the Japanese market would depend eventually on manufacturing locally, and both were willing to link up with domestic firms to achieve this. General Motors was apparently the first to become concerned over the attempts by the government to foster a Japanese motor industry. In the early 1930s, 'when the army began pressuring the Zaibatsu to support an automobile trust, G.M. secretly applied to the Ministry of Commerce and Industry to see whether it could participate in the venture'.[9] The government rejected the proposal but this was not the end of the story. The Japanese firm of Nissan became aware of this move by General Motors and sought to exploit the company's fears by suggesting a joint venture and demanding a controlling interest. General Motors finally agreed to Nissan having 51 per cent control in April 1934.[10] Under the agreement Nissan sent two men to Detroit to study the latest production techniques, but the Japanese government was dissatisfied with the arrangement and the joint venture proposal eventually collapsed.

The first move by the Ford company did not come until 1936 when a 91.5 acre site was bought in Yokohama. However, applications for permits to build and operate assembly and manufacturing facilities there were refused by the government. The company then sought a Japanese partner and, for the first time in its history, was willing to accept a minority interest, even as little as one-third. A union was considered with the Furukawa and the Mitsubishi interests. Joint venture proposals were discussed with Toyota, with Nissan, and later between Nissan, General Motors and Ford. The Japanese firms were interested in such ventures as a means of gaining access to advanced technology, but the army successfully opposed all such proposals. Blocked in their efforts to manufacture in Japan, the American companies continued their assembly activities until the government and army decided that they could dispense with their output.

The Move into Manufacturing[11]

The only countries outside America with a motor industry of any significance in 1920 were Britain, France, Germany and Italy. Their combined market was then over 200,000 vehicles or about half the entire market outside North America. Domestic producers in these countries supplied about three-quarters of this market and they were determined to exclude American imports. This they did mainly by high tariffs and tax systems which discriminated against American automobiles. The British Board of Trade calculated in 1919 that the prevailing protection from duties and differential taxes amounted to 88 per cent of the value of imported cars. In Italy the duties on imported cars ranged between 122 per cent and 212 per cent. French tariffs too were high and supplemented by a tax system that discriminated against American vehicles and by a quota on imported cars. In Germany the market was more or less open to imports until 1927 when the tariff was increased on all automobiles and parts and this sounded the death knell for American assembly plants there.

It seems highly likely that without such protection American imports would have flooded the European market and completely undermined the national industries, so great was the disparity in the volume of output, and hence in costs, between the major US producers and their European counterparts. In 1919, when production by Citroen had reached 100 cars daily, a small car cost in the neighbourhood of $1,000. At that time the Ford Model T was selling for less than $500 in the United States. In Germany before the 1927 tariff, the lightest, cheapest cars were roughly twice the price of equivalent imported American automobiles after payment of tax.[12]

Given the determination on the part of the European governments concerned to protect their domestic motor industries from imports, the American manufacturers were faced with the choice of being gradually excluded from sizable markets with a strong growth potential in which they already had a stake, or investing abroad on a much larger scale and manufacturing behind protective barriers. Ford and General Motors chose to move into Europe, aware that at that time their size and technological and marketing ability would enable them to compete successfully against the local producers.

Shortly after the first World War, General Motors' executives began to consider seriously the possibility of manufacturing in Europe. After turning down a half interest in the French firm of Citroen in 1919 and nearly acquiring the Austin company in England, General Motors purchased Vauxhall Motors Ltd in 1925. That company made a relatively high-priced car, roughly comparable in size to the American models. Its output was only some 1,500 cars a year and it was on the verge of bankruptcy. Of this acquisition, Alfred P. Sloan Jr, the General Motors Chairman wrote, 'It was in no sense a substitute for Austin; indeed I looked on it as a kind of experiment in overseas manufacturing. The experiment seemed appealing, however, and the investment required was only $2,575,291.'[13]

Mr Sloan makes it quite plain that, despite these three moves to

secure manufacturing facilities in Europe, the company had no decided
policy concerning manufacturing abroad and that the Executive Committee remained doubtful about the investment. The driving force
behind the Vauxhall acquisition was James D. Mooney, a Vice President
and also head of the Export Company. He feared that the American
economy and the dollar were moving away from the British pound. To
safeguard sizable General Motors' investment throughout the sterling
area, he wanted an English production base as an insurance policy in
case people in the sterling area could not get the dollars to buy
American cars. The take-over of Vauxhall Motors Ltd had been Jim
Mooney's idea. He had carried it out on his own initiative without full
support from his colleagues in the General Motors hierarchy.[14]

The question whether to manufacture a small car in England and
Germany was discussed by the Executive Committee throughout almost
all of 1928. Strong sentiment still existed for sticking to exports of
American products. Consideration was given to the design of a modified
'small-bore' Chevrolet which would escape the horsepower tax in
England and Germany and might make manufacturing abroad unneces-
sary. The decision to acquire the German firm of Adam Opel in 1929
for $33.3 million meant the end of the policy debate. General Motors
had now become an international manufacturer, ready to support its
world-wide markets with manufacturing and assembly facilities
wherever this seemed justified.

Why was an acquisition considered preferable to the addition of
manufacturing facilities to the existing General Motors' assembly plant
in Berlin? On this Mr Sloan writes, 'If the idea was to make a very small
car, much smaller than the Chevrolet – then we might be better off
dealing directly with Opel. I felt that we would get off to a better start
that way than we would by trying to compete on our own in a country
with which we were largely unfamiliar.'[15] A later Chairman, Frederic
Donner, gives two reasons. General Motors wanted to compete effectively in the shortest possible time and for this it needed a product
with an accepted name and a strong marketing organisation. Secondly,
there was a shortage of experienced engineers and management personnel
because of the rapidly expanding US market.[16] Further light on the
'build or buy' decision is given in the General Motors' Study Group
Report on Opel. The terms of purchase included $12 million over and
above the estimated value of the net tangible assets of the business.
'For us to build or equip for manufacturing a new factory in Germany
would require at least two or three years before operations could be put
on an efficient and profitable basis. The amount paid Opel in excess of

net assets would be returned within the time required to start from the ground up.'[17]

Meanwhile the Ford company was greatly increasing its manufacturing and assembly facilities in Europe. The McKenna duties made full manufacture essential in the UK and plans were made to move production from Manchester to Dagenham where the world's largest automobile plant outside the US would be built. In planning for Dagenham, Henry Ford did almost exactly what he had done 25 years earlier in Canada. Detroit would engineer the product but there would be local management and direction, with the public owning a substantial proportion of the shares. Just as Ford-Canada had wholly-owned subsidiaries in its overseas territories, so Ford-UK would own the majority of stock in the Ford companies in the continental countries and provide leadership. In short, there would be three manufacturing centres for the Model A and each would have a group of foreign assembly plants and marketing countries under its control. Output at Dagenham was planned to be 200,000 units per annum, and the new factory would supply cars, trucks and Fordson tractors to the UK, Irish Free State, Europe (except European Russia), Asia Minor, including Palestine, Syria, Arabia (except Aden), Iraq, Persia, Afghanistan, Egypt and certain other parts of Africa. Empire markets would continue to be supplied by Ford-Canada and all other markets by Ford-US. Perry, head of Ford-UK from its establishment, was keen to have the European demand for Ford products filled from Dagenham, partly to justify the size of the plant and partly because he wanted to control assembling and selling on the continent as well. Continental Europe's imports from Ford-US came to about $7 million and most of this business was transferred to Ford-UK.

The years from 1928 to 1932 were difficult ones for Ford-UK. Building the Dagenham plant had been more expensive than expected and it did not become a working reality until 1932. The depression and tariffs greatly reduced sales; to make matters worse, the Model AF was not a success and the Model A was too expensive for the British market. The goal of 200,000 vehicles a year was reduced to the more plausible one of 400 per day (120,000 per annum), although still high in UK terms. Short of cash, Ford-UK increased its capital to £9 million early in 1931 by creating additional shares of £1 per value. It put them on the market at the current rate of £3 a share and Ford-US bought its quota (1,200,000 shares) at this premium. It was its first capital investment in Europe. 'In a defensive mood, Perry repeatedly stated to Henry and Edsel Ford that prior to the 1931 capital increase the American company had never remitted any cash to Britain or the continent. The business there had been developed almost entirely from profits of the several companies, and by receipts from the sale of stock. The American company had steadily furnished credit in the form of goods, but it had just as steadily been paid for these goods. During the three fiscal years ending 30 June 1931, Europe in fact remitted to Detroit almost $5,000,000 in dividends and fees.'[18]

The introduction of a new small car in 1932, the Model Y (rated at 8 hp in the UK) saved the company. Designed in Detroit, it would be made and sold world-wide only by Ford-UK. However, the high hopes for the Dagenham plant were never realised. One of the major reasons for this was the subsequent establishment of manufacturing facilities in Germany and France by Ford-US. This development highlighted the conflict of interest between the continental companies and Ford-UK, which had a controlling interest in them. Not surprisingly the conflict was resolved by decisions made by Ford-US.

German tariffs forced Ford-US to shift assembly from its small Berlin plant to a new factory in Cologne and to manufacture the Model A there incorporating a large number of German-made components. However, Ford-Germany desperately needed a model it could sell in quantity and urged that the Model Y be produced there. Ford-UK pointed out that it would cost $400,000 to convert the Cologne plant to Model Y production and that this was 'out of the question apart from the handicap which Dagenham would suffer from the loss of business.'[19] But it became impossible to sell a foreign car in Germany after the Nazis seized power and this was a blow to Dagenham which had manufactured a considerable portion of the Model Y as sold in Germany. By the end of 1935, Ford-Germany was producing a 4-cylinder car as well as the V-8, all made entirely from German materials. Next came government pressure to export and the granting of export subsidies. (One consequence was that Opels flooded into the UK subsidised by the Nazis.) By 1936 all manufacturers were required to export in order to get the foreign exchange they needed for essential imported raw materials. Ford-US and Ford-UK went to great lengths to enable the German company to meet these requirements. At one point Ford-Germany feared that it would have to close unless it could arrange to buy abroad the rubber needed for the production of its tyre requirements. Ford-US agreed to supply $60,000 worth of rubber monthly in exchange for various exported items from Cologne and this arrangement worked well. Further deals to procure raw materials were made and Ford-Germany exported items such as truck transmissions, axles, speedometers etc., which Ford-US placed in large part in assembly plants in Japan or South America. But Cologne relied chiefly on car exports for foreign exchange as permission for its domestic sales depended on fulfilling export targets. Charles E. Sorenson of Ford-US repeatedly urged Perry to let Ford-Germany sell more in northern Europe. 'This would cut into your market considerably,' he conceded but argued that 'the very life of Cologne was at stake, and England should make the sacrifice.' Perry finally agreed, but warned Sorenson that he would not 'keep off the grass entirely with the Dagenham product, so as to permit Germany to build up a monopoly for Cologne cars of the small type'.[20]

The behaviour of Ford-Germany during the period 1934-8 has been well summarised.

The policy of Cologne during the preceding four years had paved the way to its present status. Despite some brave remarks by Perry and Sorenson in 1933 and 1934, the only road it could take to success after the political revolution of the former year was one of teaming up with the National Socialists. Albert, a former anti-Nazi perceived this, and his English and American associates soon swallowed any qualms they may have had and joined him in a bid for prosperity.

The Nazis made them pay dearly for it. They forced the company to manufacture in Germany of German materials practically all the cars it sold there, they compelled no small degree of standardisation, set up an export policy that required galling accommodation from both Dagenham and Dearborn, blocked remittances of profits earned in Germany, and imposed truck developments that served their military purposes.[21]

Just as in Germany, tariffs and other measures forced the Ford compan˙ to move from assembly to complete manufacture in France. Assembly had been moved from Bordeaux to a new and better plant at Asnières, near Paris, where operations began in 1925. The French Managing Director, Maurice Dollfuss, argued that manufacture in France was essential to be competitive. But Perry held that Dagenham must supply the European companies in order to achieve the volume necessary to make its operations economic. The outcome was a compromise and Ford-France increased its use of locally-made parts but this failed to solve the problem. Ford-US decided in 1934 that its cars would have to be produced in France and that it would put up the money for it. This led to Ford's first joint venture, a 60 per cent share in a new company, Matford SA, in 1934, in partnership with a well-known French producer, E.E.C. Mathis. The move was unsuccessful and ended in bitterness on both sides.

In May 1938 Ford-France approved construction of a plant near Poissy on the Seine for the manufacture of the V-8 and a proposed 4-cylinder car which would be a French version of the latest German Ford. Ford-France was to have a new, modern plant as well as Dagenham and Cologne, and one larger than Ford-Germany. Engineers and designers at Ford-US worked rapidly on the proposed 4-cylinder car, and machinery for it was about to be shipped from America when the war began.

The only other country where the MNEs embarked on manufacturing in the interwar period as opposed to more or less assembly operations was Australia. With a population of only some seven million people, it would seem to be an unlikely place to attract foreign investment to manufacture motor vehicles. But special circumstances in the short run, coupled with long-run optimism concerning the growth in demand in such a vast country, were largely responsible for this development. It all started during the first World War when the Australian Government banned the importation of car bodies to save shipping space. Body-building facilities quickly developed out of necessity and these were protected by a prohibitive tariff after the war.

Prior to 1925, Ford-Canada had a local distributor in each of the five States in Australia, each one of which manufactured the bodies for the vehicles they assembled. These differed widely in design from State to State, and the cost of the bodies largely determined the prices of the finished vehicles. These were 'astonishingly high' compared to the price of a Model T in Canada and this led the Canadian company to establish Ford-Australia in Geelong, Victoria to make the bodies for all the Fords sold in Australia. At the same time Ford-owned assembly units were set up in each State. This dispersion of assembly facilities was necessary because of poor inland transportation. Assembly plants had to be located on the coast so that bodies could be supplied from Geelong by boat while the chassis went directly from Ford-Canada to each factory. The goal was to manufacture 30,000 bodies and to assemble the same number of Model Ts annually.

One of the reasons why that goal was not achieved was increasing competition from General Motors which, in 1926, also established its own assembly plants in each State. Bodies were supplied by Holdens until 1931 when, largely as a consequence of the depression and the freezing of the currency by the Australian government, it was acquired by General Motors. Prior to that, General Motors cars were sold by the assembly plants to dealers and the money transferred to the US. Because of the currency restrictions, General Motors Australia could not remit profits or pay for the chassis imported from the US so that funds were piling up in Australia at a time when there was much uncertainty as to the future value of the Australian pound. Meanwhile Holden's ordinary shares, which were quoted at 57s 6d in April 1930 fell to 7s 6d in the middle of the depression when output had fallen by about 95 per cent. General Motors decided that the best move would be to put its blocked funds into tangible assets and gave their preference shares for the ordinary shares of Holden.

Tariffs imposed on a number of components led to their manufacture in Australia but both Ford and General Motors resisted government attempts to induce them to undertake the local production of chassis and engines. The government sought the complete manufacture of motor vehicles in Australia but the American companies considered this would be uneconomic. They were to change their minds after the war.

European Developments

Just as the first foreign subsidiaries of American companies were established across the border in nearby Canada, so too the initial foreign investments of European firms were made, with one exception, in neighbouring countries. In all cases the motive was the same, namely, to get behind tariff barriers.

The exception, appropriately enough, was Rolls-Royce Ltd which in 1919 acquired an American subsidiary, Rolls-Royce of America Inc, in Springfield, Massachusetts.[22] The terms were reminiscent of the establishment of Ford-Canada. The US company was set up solely with American money, with Rolls-Royce Ltd receiving 75 per cent of the common stock and full control in return for supplying all design, patent and manufacturing information requested by the affiliated concern, together with one set of drawings of all existing and future models. Rolls-Royce Ltd agreed to withdraw completely from the American market except on agreed terms, and the US company agreed not to compete in any way with the British company in England or the rest of the world outside the North American continent.

Initially the policy was to make the American and British products identical and, although the English management in Derby reluctantly accepted some differences as time went on, it never gave up the idea.

This imposed very great cost handicaps as it meant that Springfield could not take advantage of low costs achieved through the mass production of parts and components by local suppliers. E.W. Hives, later to become Managing Director of Rolls-Royce Ltd, was sent to America to investigate these early difficulties and wrote back to the parent company:

> There ought to be some scheme developed whereby the costs of Derby and Springfield are constantly compared, not only raw material costs, but machining costs, fitting costs, testing costs and office costs. I saw enough in the USA to realise that in all departments there is something to be learned from American methods.[23]

His remarks did not increase cost consciousness at Derby and no such comparison was ever made.

Almost from the start the new enterprise suffered from chronic financial problems and, with the American Rolls-Royce selling for $8,000 to $12,000 more than the most expensive models of its US competitors, sales proved disappointing. The British company would not allow the American management to differentiate the product or to do anything else felt to be necessary to succeed in the US market. Moreover, it was not willing to give financial support nor would it sell its shares. It was a recipe for failure. In October 1929 Springfield ceased production with the 2,900th car and tried unsuccessfully to carry on as a sales agency for English Rolls-Royces. Liquidation in 1931 brought to an end the first 'invasion' of the US by a foreign automobile producer. The demise of Rolls-Royce of America Inc created little stir or embarrassment within the parent company, which had never included its shares in its US affiliate among the assets in its balance sheet.

Another English firm, the Austin Motor Company, chose to license production of its popular 'Seven' rather than to invest abroad. Known as the Austin 'Bantam' in America it was a dismal failure, but it enjoyed a moderate success as the 'Rosengart' in France, the 'Dixi' in Germany and the 'Datsun' in Japan.

Austin's main rival Morris made one attempt to manufacture abroad, an amateurish effort which was a complete failure. In December 1924 he bought the factory and assets at Le Mans of the established French motor firm of Leon Bollee. A 4-cylinder, 12 hp car along the lines of the existing Leon Bollee car, with certain improvements, was produced. Little attempt was made to integrate the production of the French and English plants and difficulties were encountered from the start. In two years only half the original production programme of 2,500 cars had been sold despite a reduction in prices which made them considerably cheaper than corresponding French models. By 1928 the company had lost £150,000 leaving little option but to cease production and gradually liquidate stocks of unsold cars and parts. The company was finally wound up and the assets sold in 1931.[24]

The French producers were more successful than the British in establishing themselves abroad. Both Citroen and Renault set up wholly-owned assembly plants in Belgium in the 1920s and in England in the 1930s. The Belgian tariff favoured unassembled vehicles, but the British was the same (33 1/3 per cent) for parts and components as for built-up units after 1925. This led to the use of some British material and parts and even to some local manufacture. The French companies felt also that local assembly enabled them to produce cars more suitable for the British customer. They were also anxious to be able to show them as British vehicles at a time when there was a very serious 'Drive British' campaign in force.

· The Italian firm of Fiat owned no assembly facilities in the UK but it did establish affiliates in two European countries which assembled its vehicles with some local content. A former NSU factory was acquired in Heilbron, Germany in 1930 and Deutsche Fiat produced cars for the German market until 1973. Fiat also held a substantial minority interest in Fiat Francaise, a company formed by a Franco-Italian, Henri Theodor Pigozzi, to make Fiats under licence in 1932. Two years later the name was changed to Societe Industrielle de Mechanique et Carrosserie Automobile (SIMCA), with Fiat still retaining its financial interest until the Chrysler takeover of SIMCA in the 1960s. The Austro-Fiat car continued to be made in Vienna under licence until the mid-1920s with local capital participation, and Fiat vehicles were made under licence in Poland from 1932 to 1939.

The foreign investments that were made were all small-scale, tentative attempts to secure a foothold in neighbouring and jealously-guarded national markets. Ultimately they were all abandoned, except for those in Belgium and when some of the European firms became multinational in the true sense of the word, it was because of investments outside the EEC countries.

Summary and Conclusions

By 1939 there were really only two firms in the motor industry which could be called MNEs — Ford and General Motors. In addition to their numerous subsidiary assembly plants scattered throughout the world, both companies produced complete motor vehicles in the US, Canada, Britain and Germany, and manufactured car bodies and assembled units in Australia. Ford also built complete vehicles in France. Chrysler, outside the US, had only two plants in Canada, a small commercial vehicle factory in England and an assembly plant in Antwerp. Elsewhere it relied on independent agents for local assembly of its products where tariffs made this necessary. It probably lacked the resources to do more to match the overseas moves of its main US rivals. As for the European producers, a few had established small-scale assembly plants in neighbouring countries.

At this early stage in the development of the industry there is little doubt that the American firms with their mass-production methods were technically superior to the rest of the world. This alone gave Ford its head start. But of importance too was the greater organising ability and cost-consciousness of management, coupled with an ability to 'think big', derived from their experience in the home market, in a way which astounded foreign managers. Altogether it was more than enough to offset the cost handicap of manufacturing abroad.

Ford became a MNE without any overseas capital investment. Not until 1931, when the parent company bought its share of the additional stock issue by Ford UK, was any cash remitted abroad. Before that date the expansion outside the US had been financed entirely by profits earned abroad, credit extended by the parent company to subsidiaries for the purchase of vehicles and equipment and the sale of shares in Europe. This was partly a consequence of being first in the field with a successful product, and partly the result of Ford policy. General Motors, on the other hand, achieved MNE status mainly through the acquisition of foreign companies so that its investment 'package' included capital.

The motive for this foreign investment almost invariably was to get behind tariff barriers. It was defensive investment, designed to preserve or to penetrate a market otherwise closed to outside producers. The one significant exception was Ford's 1911 move to England, and that probably would not have taken place at that time had it not been for the initiative of an Englishman, Perry, who took charge of the UK operations. Moreover, the undertaking of complete manufacture in England after the first world war was brought about by the McKenna duties.

The tariffs of course were imposed to protect and develop a domestic motor industry. They sheltered national producers from the competition of imports but not from the competition created by incoming foreign direct investment. The Italian and Japanese manufacturers were protected from both. Japanese policies forced the American assemblers to withdraw from Japan, and Italian policies in effect excluded foreign investors. The government would not grant permission to Ford to construct a new assembly plant at Livorno in 1929 and it also blocked a Ford-Isotta merger. The Duce wanted Ford to make an arrangement with Fiat, and Ford did approach that company but was unable to accept Fiat's terms. Subsequently a gradual evacuation from Italy was decided upon by Ford in 1934. Moreover, the high Italian duties on parts finally drove out even the few European firms, such as Citroen, which had been allowed to establish small assembly operations in Italy. The French government gave a mixed reception to foreign direct investment, opposing General Motors' proposal to take a half interest in Citroen in 1919 and yet not, apparently, objecting to the entrance of Ford. Probably the policy was to preserve a predominantly French-owned industry, with toleration of a limited amount of American investment if it seemed to bring substantial benefits.

One thing is clear. The pattern of foreign investment and the structure of the world motor industry was not the result of the free play of market forces. The direct foreign investment that took place was induced by the policies of host governments, and the kind of motor industry that emerged in each one of the producing countries was the logical outcome of its particular policies on trade and investment. It was these policies that were ultimately responsible for the existence of MNEs in the motor industry before the second world war, not Ford and General Motors.

Having been induced to manufacture abroad, the two MNEs found the new plants useful as suppliers of third markets. Their European factories exported the typical small cars they produced, and Canada was the export base for the large American cars destined for British Commonwealth and Empire markets. But the manufacturing subsidiaries in Europe had little connection with each other. They operated in protected, national markets and behaved similarly to their nationally-owned competitors.

Table 5.1: Unit Overseas Production of Cars and Trucks by Ford and General Motors, 1938 (Thousands)

Country	Ford	General Motors*
Canada	68	56
United Kingdom	77	60
Germany	37	140
France	8	—
Total overseas	190	256
Per cent of total output	23.2	19.6

*Unit sales.
Source: M. Wilkins and F.E. Hill, *American Business Abroad: Ford on Six Continents* (Wayne State University Press, Detroit, 1964), p. 436; Alfred P. Sloan, Jr, *My Years with General Motors* (McFadden Books, New York, 1965), p. 445.

Notes

1. Report of the Task Force on the Structure of Canadian Industry, *Foreign Ownership and the Structure of Canadian Industry* (Queen's Printer, Ottawa, 1968), p. 11.

2. Allen Nevins and F.E. Hill, *Ford, Expansion and Challenge 1914-1933* (Charles Scribner's Sons, New York, 1957), pp. 376-7.

3. Frederic G. Donner, *The World-wide Industrial Enterprise* (McGraw-Hill, New York, 1967), p. 13.

4. Ibid., pp. 13-14.

5. This section based largely on Nevins and Hill, *Ford, Expansion and Challenge 1914-1933*, pp. 677-82.

6. M. Wilkins and F.E. Hill, *American Business Abroad: Ford on Six Continents* (Wayne State University Press, Detroit, 1964), p. 226.

7. Sir Lawrence Hartnett, *Big Wheels and Little Wheels* (Gold Star Publications (Austr) Pty Ltd, 2nd edn, 1973), p. 50.

8. William Chandler Duncan, *US-Japan Automobile Diplomacy* (Ballinger Publishing Company, Cambridge, Mass., 1973), p. 61.

9. Ibid., p. 65.

10. Ibid., p. 65

11. Much of the material pertaining to the Ford company in this section is drawn from Wilkins and Hill, *American Business Abroad: Ford on Six Continents* and Nevins and Hill, *Ford, Expansion and Challenge 1914-1933*.

12. Nevins and Hill, *Ford, Expansion and Challenge 1914-1933*, p. 235.

13. Alfred P. Sloan Jr, *My Years With General Motors* (McFadden Books, New York, 1965), p. 320.

14. Hartnett, *Big Wheels and Little Wheels*, p. 36.

15. Sloan Jr, *My Years With General Motors*, p. 323.

16. Donner, *The World-wide Industrial Enterprise*, p. 18.

17. Sloan Jr, *My Years With General Motors*, p. 326.

18. Nevins and Hill, *Ford, Expansion and Challenge 1914-1933*, p. 548.

19. Wilkins and Hill, *American Business Abroad: Ford on Six Continents*, p. 247.

20. Ibid., pp. 280-1.

21. Ibid., p. 284.

22. The account of Rolls-Royce in America is drawn from Ian Lloyd, *Rolls-Royce The Years of Endeavour* (Macmillan, London, 1978), pp. 23-82.

23. Ibid., p. 38.

24. P.W.S. Andrews and Elizabeth Brunner, *The Life of Lord Nuffield* (Basil Blackwell, Oxford, 1955), pp. 158-60.

25. Gerald Bloomfield, *The World Automobile Industry* (David & Charles, Newton Abbot, 1978), p. 304.

6 WAR AND THE MULTINATIONAL ENTERPRISE

As far as the *first* world war is concerned, the Ford company was the only MNE of any significance. But the existence of its factory in England and its assembly plant in France did raise some interesting questions. What does the subsidiary in a host country involved in war do, when the home country of the parent concern is ostensibly neutral? And when, as in this case, the owner of the parent company holds strong pacifist views? The unmistakable answer was that the subsidiary 'goes to war' with the host country.

By. 18 August 1914 Perry was loyally supporting the British Cabinet and working 'to secure orders from the Government for our chassis for war purposes and for ambulance work'. Henry Ford had not yet begun his pacifist campaign but Perry was aware of his sentiments and as far as he was concerned Ford-UK must be loyal to its government. Early in 1915 he 'undertook a contract [the first of a number] for the manufacture of shell containers for 18 pound guns'. All its stationery was stamped: 'This establishment is controlled by the Munitions of War Act, 1915.'[1]

Henry Ford's 'Peace Ship' and his pacifist views were of course highly unpopular in England. Many British newspapers would not accept advertisements for Ford cars. In defence Perry pointed out, 'Mr. Ford has never at any time taken any action to communicate or impose his political views upon the company', and he indicated that with respect to the war, Ford and the Ford Motor Company (England) Ltd did not see eye to eye and that Ford accepted that fact.[2]

As for Ford-Canada, the company at first apparently regarded the European conflict as remote and advised its officials and dealers to 'go calmly and honestly about your business'. However, in June 1915 it stated, 'Like all British subjects we regret that war was thrust upon us. But now that there is war we are glad we can do our share to mitigate its hardships and sufferings.' McGregor, like Perry, recognised that any British Ford company would have to participate in the war effort.[3]

The Spanish Civil War, which broke out in 1936, posed more serious problems in that the American MNEs, with assembly plants in Barcelona, were inevitably involved with both belligerents. General Motors unquestionably took sides. It closed its Barcelona assembly plant when the civil war started.[4] Presumably the Republican forces took the factory over and made what use they could of it. On the other hand, Opel cars continued to be sold to dealers in Nationalist-held territory and General Motors gave Franco war supplies on credit.[5]

The Ford company was neutral in the sense that it supplied both sides throughout most of the war. It was Ford-UK rather than Ford-US that appears to have made the decisions. Perry instructed Juan Ubach, the assistant manager in Barcelona, not to take any part in politics, not to try to resist the Republican government, and to submit to coercion by the authorities. At the same time, the Ford company in Portugal was shipping products into Nationalist-controlled areas to dealers against payment in dollars and pounds. Perry even asked Ford-Germany to assist Ford-Portugal in supplying Franco's forces. When the latter's troops captured Barcelona, Ubach was thrown into jail, but was later released in response to British efforts. Ford-Spain then did its best to placate Franco, who disliked the company because it did not give him his war supplies on credit, but the ill-feeling lasted for many years.[6]

In the second World War, the subsidiaries again 'went to war' along with their respective host countries before the home country and parent company became directly involved. But this time the subsidiaries were located in both camps.

It was a weird situation with Ford production in Europe serving the two opposing camps. The British were fiercely active with Ford output rapidly rising. Cologne, with greatly inferior resources, was working for Hitler, but its vehicle production of from 14,000 to 16,000 a year was not more than a quarter of Dagenham's. Indeed, while the Germans commanded Ford establishments in France, Belgium, Holland, Denmark, Finland, Italy and Hungary and would soon have another, for in November 1940 Roumania was drawn into the axis, the great English plant contributed more to its cause than all these and Cologne combined did to Hitler's.[7]

The situation was, of course, just as weird for General Motors. Its Opel properties were seized by the German government soon after the war began and, in this case, Hitler acquired a plant with more than twice the capacity of Vauxhall in England. (The latter, however, had the all-important commercial vehicle side and its Bedford 3 and 5 tonner was a standard army truck.) Not long afterwards Nazi commissars would be operating General Motors' facilities in Belgium, Denmark and France.

However, in far-off Australia, the English General Manager of General Motors lost no time in supporting the Allied cause.

Immediately war was declared, I put the whole of the GM-Holden's organisation to work for the war effort. Our primary objective as a company, I announced, would be to make the maximum contribution. This was an odd situation. GM-H was an American-owned company, and the US was a neutral power. I was responsible for GM's investment in a country at war, and had put American-owned resources to work for a belligerent nation.[8]

Similarly in Canada, which declared war one week after France and England in September 1939, the General Motors and Ford subsidiaries promptly devoted their facilities as needed to military uses. Ford-Canada, for example, began adapting trucks for the use of the Canadian land forces, supplying them to the first two divisions as soon as required. Late in 1939 the company joined with the Department of National Defence in the development and engineering of a series of vehicles for the military. It had to set up an engineering department of its own to do this as it had always been dependent on Dearborn for its designs, and the parent company, being neutral, could not do the development work required. In May 1940 it received its first contract for the universal carrier, a large armoured vehicle. Its Managing Director, Campbell, was very 'war minded'.[9]

The Ford enterprises in Europe were profitable during the war. Dagenham paid over $8 million in dividends for the period 1939-45 inclusive. Surprisingly,

The European companies operated at a handsome profit in all years except 1943, when they showed a loss of $1,780,000 chiefly due to the impending collapse of Germany. Germany also showed a loss for 1944, but it was not sufficient to create a deficit for total European operations. Their blocked dividends did not come to Dagenham or to Ford-US, or to the Ford family who had a share in them, until after the war. The net paper profit for the war years was $10,978,000.[10]

After the war the continental Ford companies made a speedy recovery. On 4 May 1945 a team of Dagenham executives visited Cologne and concluded that production could be resumed at once. Supplies, especially of steel, were a problem, but by the end of the year 2,443 trucks had been built — almost half the German total output. The company built a variety of vehicles for the armies of occupation, and also reconditioned engines. After severe losses in 1944 and 1945, an all-time peak of profits was reached in 1946 due, it is said, to a reduction in

overhead and operating costs and to the fair prices set by the control
authorities.[11] By July 1946 every West European Ford assembly plant
had started producing trucks, and all but the Spanish and German
companies had begun to assemble pre-war passenger cars. However, the
Berlin factory in the Russian zone never resumed output after the war
and the assembly facilities in Romania and Hungary were nationalised.
The former had been established in 1935 by Ford-UK with the purchase
of land in Bucharest. It commenced operations in May 1936 and
assembled some 2,500 cars annually. It proved modestly profitable and
was financed entirely from its own earnings. The Hungarian plant had
been owned by Ford-Werke, incorporated in 1938 and began assembly
operations in 1941.

General Motors was less fortunate in Germany as far as resuming
production was concerned. Its plants were extensively damaged and
many pre-war tools, dies and fixtures had been either removed or
destroyed, and the remaining Opel facilities were under the jurisdiction
of the Allied occupation forces. However, under a ruling which the US
Treasury Department had made concerning assets in enemy hands, the
company was allowed to write off the investment in Opel, which in
1942 amounted to $35 million, against current taxable income.[12]

Executive opinion was divided on the question of resuming control
of Opel after the war. As late as April 1948 the Financial Policy
Committee turned down the recommendation of the study group set up
to consider the matter. However, a month later the Committee recon-
sidered the question and recommended that General Motors resume
control of Opel on the understanding that the parent company would
supply no funds or in any way guarantee additional funds to Opel, and
that the Federal income tax position of General Motors would not be
adversely affected. One of the participants in that decision, who later
became Chairman, subsequently wrote that they were influenced by
three factors:

(1) Despite the heavy destruction of plant the facilities needed to
resume production were available. If the German monetary system
were reformed, sufficient funds for the reconstruction of the plant
could be generated by the Opel enterprise itself. This was important
because General Motors' own corporate resources were already
stretched thin in the US.
(2) They were confident that the market in West Germany and Western
Europe would grow with stabilisation and recovery.
(3) The General Motors' network of overseas assembly plants required

the support of a full-scale manufacturing operation strategically located on the European continent.[13]

General Motors resumed management control of Opel on 1 November 1948 and the following year output was 40,000 vehicles.

Notes

1. Allan Nevins and F.E. Hill, *Ford Expansion and Challenge 1914-1933*, (Charles Scribner's Sons, New York, 1957), pp. 60-2.

2. Ibid., p. 64.

3. M. Wilkins and F.E. Hill, *American Business Abroad: Ford on Six Continents* (Wayne State University Press, Detroit, 1964), p. 226.

4. Myra Wilkins, *The Maturing of Multinational Enterprise: American Business Abroad from 1914-1970* (Harvard University Press, Cambridge, Mass., 1974), p. 185.

5. Nevins and Hill, *Ford, Expansion and Challenge 1914-1933*, p. 103.

6. Ibid., pp. 102-3.

7. Wilkins and Hill, *American Business Abroad: Ford on Six Continents*, p. 320.

8. Sir Lawrence Hartnett, *Big Wheels and Little Wheels* (Gold Star Publications (Austr) Pty Ltd, 2nd edn, 1973), p. 119.

9. Wilkins and Hill, *American Business Abroad: Ford on Six Continents*, p. 322.

10. Ibid., pp. 334-5.

11. Ibid., p. 346.

12. Alfred P. Sloan Jr, *My Years with General Motors* (McFadden Books, New York, 1965), p. 331.

13. Frederic G. Donner, *The World-wide Industrial Enterprise* (McGraw-Hill, New York, 1967), p. 13.

7 THE GREAT POSTWAR BOOM 1946-1973

We believe that at some time during the 20-year period following this war, the overseas markets for cars and trucks will at least equal the market in the United States and Canada. We feel that the need for motor transportation of goods and people will be so compelling that the world *will be motorized* — regardless of all problems and obstacles.

(General Motors Overseas Policy Group, July 1944).[1]

The motor industry has been one of the main industries responsible for the spectacular growth in the number, size and importance of MNEs in general since 1945. This period saw the appearance of a number of European MNEs, a major bid by Chrysler to match the overseas expansion of its big American rivals and, toward the end of the period, foreign direct investment by some of the Japanese producers. Altogether some 15 firms established significant overseas production facilities and joined Ford and General Motors in a competitive struggle for shares in the world market for motor vehicles.

Two factors were primarily responsible for the increase in the number of automobile MNEs. First, steadily rising world incomes resulted in a rapidly-growing demand for motor vehicles which led to a ten-fold increase in production by 1973, and the emergence of one or more large-scale manufacturers with sizable financial and managerial resources in each of the major producing countries. Accompanying this expansion in output was an even more dramatic increase in exports from Europe and Japan of smaller, less expensive, and more economical-to-run automobiles than those produced in North America. Secondly, the drive to industrialise in many developing countries often called for the creation of domestic motor industries and, beginning in the late 1950s, governments offered various inducements to foreign firms to invest in production facilities. One of the inducements was a local market protected from the competition of imports. Rather than lose profitable export markets built up since the war, and perhaps also the opportunity to share in a potentially sizable market in the future, firms invested abroad and hence new MNEs were born.

Chrysler, a late-comer to the American motor industry, had additional reasons for becoming a major MNE. It did well financially in the early 1960s in the US but, unlike Ford and General Motors, it had no significant subsidiaries in the large and rapidly-growing European

market. Total sales in the United States reached a peak in 1955 of
slightly over 8 million units, a figure which was not surpassed for seven
years. During that time, new registrations in Western Europe more than
doubled to roughly six million vehicles. Not only did its American rivals
participate from the start in that expansion, but their European plants
served as bases to supply smaller cars and trucks to third markets, and
even to the United States itself as a counter to the exports of European-
and Japanese-owned firms to America.

The increase in the number of MNEs, coupled with the reduction in
tariffs and, eventually, almost free-trade in most of Western Europe and
North America, resulted in fiercely-competitive conditions in the world
motor industry. This took the form of competitive investments in the
nascent industries of developing countries, the penetration of each
other's home markets by means of exports or direct investment (with
the exception of Japan which protected its domestic industry from
imports and blocked foreign investment in Japan until the 1970s), the
licensing of production in certain countries particularly in Eastern
Europe, and intense rivalry in exports to remaining world markets.

The structure of the world motor industry changed profoundly
during this period. Within each of the major producing countries output
became concentrated in the hands of a few producers, partly as a result
of competitive elimination, but mainly as a consequence of mergers.
This brought the number of major manufacturers down to less than 20
and, with few exceptions, the survivors were MNEs. The governments
of the European countries and Japan played an important role in the
restructuring of their respective industries. At the same time a half-
dozen developing countries began manufacturing motor vehicles under
the guiding hand of their respective governments, largely with the aid of
foreign investment. By 1973, sweeping changes had taken place in the
share of world production. The United States, which had accounted
for some 80 per cent of the total before the war, saw its share fall to
about one-third as Western European output rose to equal that of
America, and Japan became the world's second largest producer. Meanwhile, behind the scenes so to speak, the USSR and the East European
countries tardily developed their own motor industries helped by
Western MNEs.

Home Countries and the MNE

United States

America emerged from the war as the home of the MNEs. Six years of destruction had crippled the Continental European producers, closed down their small assembly plants in neighbouring countries so that neither they nor their British rivals were even nominally MNEs. The vast surge in world demand for motor vehicles after the war had the effect of greatly increasing the multinationality of the American manufacturers.

Although new registrations in America grew from their 1930s peak of 4.1m in 1937 to 14.4m in 1973, a 3.5-fold increase, the expansion of demand in the rest of the world was proportionately and absolutely much greater. Comparable figures for new registrations outside the US show a rise from 2.3m to 24.8m or nearly an 11-fold increase. Obviously the American producers would seek a share in this huge growth of sales in overseas markets, either through exports from the US or by means of investment in production facilities abroad. In the event there was no real alternative to a major increase in foreign investment.

Two developments were largely responsible for the decisions made by the American firms to expand productive capacity overseas. The first took place in the fast-growing European market where tariffs were primarily responsible for blocking American exports just as they had done in the interwar years. However, this time the inducement to invest behind tariff barriers to ensure a share in an important national market was strengthened by the formation of the EEC and the EFTA, and the opportunities presented by their plans for free trade in motor vehicles between the member countries of each group. Up to the formation of the EEC the six member countries had separate external tariffs ranging from 17 per cent in Germany to 45 per cent in Italy. The higher rates were gradually reduced, and when the first common external rates became effective in July 1968 they were 22 per cent for assembled cars and 14 per cent for components imported for assembly. After the 'Kennedy Round' in 1972 these were lowered to 11 per cent and 7 per cent respectively, with the duty on commercial vehicles remaining at 22 per cent. Starting in 1956 the British duty of 33 1/3 per cent was gradually reduced until it was in line with EEC rates from 1968 onwards. Tariffs were, of course, not the only obstacle facing American exports to Europe in this period. The dollar shortage after the war meant restrictions on dollar imports which lasted for more than a decade. Higher labour costs in the US plus an overvalued dollar as time went on led to non-competitive prices. Finally, the large size and heavy petrol consumption of American cars greatly limited their appeal to European buyers. Indeed, so great was the difference between

American and European (or Japanese) cars that the non-US producers
were in effect insulated from direct competition from the much larger
American firms.

The second post-war development responsible for much American
foreign investment originated in the industrialisation plans of a number of developing countries in which the creation of a domestic motor
industry represented a key element. Typically, such a plan included
regulations calling for the more or less gradual increase in the local
content of motor vehicles sold in a particular developing country by the
substitution of indigenous production for imported built-up vehicles,
parts and components. It inevitably meant the loss of the export market so that the only choice left to the US manufacturer was to comply
with the regulations which involved additional foreign investment, or
withdrawing. The decision depended on whether the market in question had a growth potential and presented a profit opportunity which
justified the investment. More often than not the decision was to
invest, but there were withdrawals, notably by Ford and General
Motors from India in 1954.

The great expansion and spread throughout the world of production
facilities owned by American motor manufacturers is discussed in
subsequent sections of this chapter. The overall increase in the relative
importance of their foreign subsidiaries and affiliates can be roughly
indicated here by comparing overseas unit sales (including Canada) of
cars and trucks with total unit sales before the war and at the end of
the period under consideration. Taking General Motors, for example,
such sales for 1936 and 1937 averaged about 12 per cent of the total,
while the average for the years 1971 to 1973 was roughly 25 per cent.
Similar figures for Ford were 15 per cent and 36 per cent respectively.
For Chrysler, which had no manufacturing capacity abroad before the
war, the average for the latter period was about 43 per cent. The
average dollar value of sales of foreign-produced vehicles for the years
1971 to 1973, as a percentage of total dollar sales was: General
Motors 14 per cent, Ford 25 per cent and Chrysler 26 per cent.[2]

Although it might be argued that each member of the Big Three
reacted independently to what was seen as profitable opportunities in
Europe and in certain developing countries, it seems more likely that
oligopolistic rivalry played a part in these foreign investment decisions.
Certainly the competitive struggle between the three companies at home
was reproduced abroad in market after market. Not to match each
other's investment moves would allow rivals to pre-empt markets of
potential importance, would lead to a falling share in the world market,

and perhaps in the longer run to a decline in competitiveness. Chrysler's massive overseas investment, estimated at $350 million during this period, seems to have been motivated to an important extent by the need, imagined or real, to counter the overseas moves of Ford and General Motors. As its Chairman, Lynn Townsend put it in 1965, 'Our competition is Ford and General Motors. Wherever we go, our entire worldwide effort is in competing with those two companies.'[3]

Throughout this period in which the multinationality of the American firms was increasing very significantly, there was no counter-investment by foreign MNEs in the US home market. There was, however, one fascinating 'might-have-been'. During the mid-1950s the sales of Volkswagen cars in America had begun to gather momentum. In the autumn of 1955, the year in which the company's US sales reached nearly 29,000, Heinrich Nordheim, who completely dominated the Volkswagen organisation, paid a lightning visit to America and purchased an assembly plant from the Studebaker company in Brunswick, New Jersey, for $3 million. He planned to assemble cars partly from US components and partly from German components. However, the initial estimates from the American suppliers turned out to be too low. When they discovered that the Volkswagen components would require separate tooling, the suppliers raised their prices with the result that Volkswagen abandoned the idea and sold the plant the following year.[4] Underlying the decision must have been the much lower German wage costs, the relatively low US tariff of 8.5 per cent on imports of built-up cars, and the dollar-mark exchange rate which greatly favoured German exports over direct investment. The decision to rely on exports can hardly be called the wrong one since it led to more than $10 billion in sales proceeds over the next 20 years. On the other hand, had Nordheim gone through with his original plan, Volkswagen today might own a huge manufacturing subsidiary in America with assets worth several billion dollars and which supplied 10 per cent or more of the US market. Or it might not.

But if the American producers remained safe from competition from foreign-owned plants established in their home market, they had to face a major threat from abroad in the form of exports to America by European, and later Japanese, MNEs. Their response to that threat reveals much concerning oligopolistic competition[5] and MNE behaviour in the home country.

Immediately after the second world war there seemed to be a general feeling in America that the low-priced cars of the Big Three were larger, better outfitted, and more expensive than needed, and that a lighter, cheaper car was required. Responding to this apparent demand, Ford and General Motors separately announced in May 1945 that they intended to build light-weight cars. A year later Chrysler indicated that, if the market existed and if its rivals produced low-priced cars, it would be ready with something competitive. Intensive work continued on the small car until September 1946 when Ford and General Motors announced the cancellation of their projects. The main reason seems to have been that postwar car sales did not reflect the view that what America needed was a small car. People were trying to buy more Chevrolets, Fords and Plymouths than could be produced.

The episode revealed one of the advantages of multinationality. For a national car firm the research and development expenditure on these models probably would have been a total loss. However, General Motors, which was reported to have spent $17 million on its light car, was able to use it in Australia where it appeared in the autumn of 1948 as the Holden. The Ford light car appeared in France at the same time as the Vedette.

Subsequently four of the so-called Independents rushed in where the Big Three did not choose to tread. Between 1950 and 1954, Nash, Kaiser, Willys and Hudson offered compact cars to the public. Lacking the resources needed to risk a low-price, high-volume strategy, they were forced to charge about as much for their compacts as their bigger rivals were asking for their large cars. Faced with the choice between a small car and a large car with the same price tag, not many buyers chose the small one. By 1955 only the American Motors' Rambler and the smaller Metropolitan which it imported from England survived in the small car field.

Then came the first wave of imports and proof that there was an appreciable demand for small cars that were cheaper than the products of the Big Three which were gradually becoming even larger and more expensive. From a mere 58,000 units in 1955, import sales rose to 207,000 in 1957 and 379,000 in 1958. Sales of the Rambler whose prices were now under those of the low priced Big Three models (unlike the early 1950s) rose to 91,000 units in 1957 and to 186,000 in 1958. The combined sales of imports and Ramblers represented over 12 per cent of the 1958 car market. Studebaker-Packard, the only remaining Independent then brought out a successful compact, the Lark, and its sales plus those of the Rambler and imports totalled 18.4 per cent of the market in 1959.

The response of the Big Three to these developments was delayed and reluctant. They expressed doubts about the possibility of producing an acceptable small car at a price sufficiently below that of their cheapest existing models. There were fears that sales of their own small cars would be mainly at the expense of their larger, higher-priced, and more profitable models. Moreover, they preferred to wait until the small car market was large enough for all three firms to enter since each one expected its move would be met by similar moves by the other two. Hence the statement in October 1957 by Mr Edward N. Cole, then head of the Chevrolet Division, that the small car market would have to reach a size of 500,000 units before General Motors would be interested in entering. This implied a 'room-for-all' proposition.[6] Correctly judging that that figure would be exceeded in 1958, the Big Three, early in that year, placed the necessary tooling orders to enable them to bring out compact cars in the autumn of 1959. These new compacts were very successful and served to reduce import sales from a high of 609,000 units or 10.1 per cent of the market in 1959 to 339,000 units or 4.9 per cent of the market in 1962.

The use made by the MNEs during this period of so-called 'captive imports', that is, imports from their own subsidiaries abroad, is of interest. Such imports were of little significance until 1958 when, as a stopgap measure until the American compacts appeared, 33,000 English Fords, 17,000 Vauxhalls (GM), 16,000 Opels (GM) and 17,000 Simcas (Chrysler) were sold through distribution channels of the Big Three. The combined total increased from 83,000 in 1958 to 140,000 in 1959, declining thereafter to almost nothing by 1962. In other words, when the American compacts appeared the door was closed to captive imports. Moreover, this action in itself was responsible for half the decline in imports between 1959 and 1962.

The respite was shortlived, however, as a second wave of imports began in 1963. The response of the Big Three was almost identical to that following the earlier inflow. Small car sales were disparaged, captive imports were resumed, until finally and reluctantly all three producers announced plans in late 1968 to manufacture small, European-type cars referred to as 'sub-compacts'. But the same response did not produce the same results. Imports increased year after year, exceeding one million cars in 1969 and reaching a peak in 1973 of 1.7 million or 15.2 per cent of total retail sales.

So great was the shift in demand to small cars that the sale of American-produced sub-compacts failed to halt the rising trend of imports. The fact that Chrysler simply could not afford to bring out a sub-compact at this time left a gap to be filled by imports. It was a gap that Chrysler hoped to fill with captive-imports – Mitsubishi Colts from Japan and Plymouth Crickets from England. This strategy proved singularly unsuccessful for not only was Chrysler's share of the sub-compact market insignificant, but even its captive import sales were considerably below those of Ford and General Motors.

Captive imports clearly reflect managerial decisions at the highest level in parent companies. That the combined total of such imports by the Big Three never exceeded 224,000 or only 13 per cent of import sales suggests that the American companies never intended to rely on their foreign subsidiaries to meet the US demand for small cars. This conclusion is supported by the limited use made of their extensive distribution networks for the sale of their captive imports. In 1968 Chrysler had 6,500 dealers in the US and of these only 389 handled Simcas and 98 Rootes. Ford had 7,400 dealers of which 802 sold Cortinas; General Motors had 14,500 dealers of which 1,500 sold Opels.[7] That both companies chose German subsidiaries rather than English ones to supply the limited, but still sizable, captive imports, reflected another top level decision, one with important economic consequences for the subsidiaries and countries concerned. The Vauxhall Viva was exported to America until about 1960 but there-after responsibility for the American small car market was given to Opel by General Motors although Vauxhall still retained the Canadian market. Similarly Ford replaced the reasonably successful English Cortina in 1970 with the German Capri. For the MNE, such decisions are inescapable.

Once the decision had been taken to build sub-compacts in America, the companies still had the option to obtain the major mechanical components from their European subsidiaries. Back in the early 1960s when Ford first made preparations to build a sub-compact provisionally called the Cardinal, the transmission and engine were to be made in Germany while the rest of the car was to be produced in America and assembled in Ford's Louisville assembly plant. The project was aband-oned but the Cardinal eventually appeared in Germany as the Ford Taunus 12M. This time the engines for the new Pinto were to be sup-plied by both Ford-Germany and Ford-UK, and an £18 million expansion of engine-making capacity was put in hand at Dagenham. How-ever, because of technical and labour problems, more engines were supplied initially from Germany, and Ford later announced that Euro-pean-built Pinto engines would be phased out by 1973 in favour of a new engine plant in Lima, Ohio.

General Motors built a completely new plant in Lordstown, Ohio to make its sub-compact, the Vega, using specially designed materials,

parts and processes to make it competitive. The car was entirely
American except for the manual transmissions which were supplied by
Opel. As demand grew for the Vega the decision had to be made
whether to increase capacity in Germany to supply the domestic
German market and the US, or to produce the American requirements
at home. As the volume was considered adequate for US production
on a competitive basis, it was decided that the American transmission
needs would be met by production in a General Motors plant in
Muncie, Indiana.

Although the Vega plant had an assembly capacity of 400,000 units
a year and was highly automated, using robots for assembly, it is difficult to explain these decisions to produce small cars in America on the
basis of costs alone. In February 1973, hourly labour costs including
supplementary benefits in General Motor's German subsidiary were 35
per cent below those in its US plants, and in the English subsidiary, 63
per cent below.[8] The European companies were already reaping considerable economies of scale in the production of small cars. Expanding
European output to meet US needs would give economies denied sub-
compact production in America. There must have been factors other
than costs which entered into the decisions. As Raymond Vernon,
Harvard University's specialist on MNEs gingerly put it, 'The US automobile companies' decision to produce the new 1970 compact car lines
in the United States was probably induced by a set of calculations that
was not entirely confined to comparisons of cost in rival locations;
questions of relations with the US government and US labour were
surely involved.'[9]

Western Europe

Against the background of a rapidly-increasing European and world-
wide demand for motor vehicles throughout this period, there emerged
a number of domestic producers who successfully met the threat of the
American firms to dominate the European market through their subsidiaries, who captured a sizable share of the American market by means
of exports, and who challenged the US firms in most third country
markets. In the process, some became MNEs, notably, British Leyland,
Citroen, Daimler-Benz, Fiat, Peugeot, Renault, Volkswagen and Volvo.
Their foreign direct investments in manufacturing in Spain and outside
Europe are discussed in the following section. The motive behind such
investment was almost invariably to prevent the loss of export markets
threatened by tariffs and the desire of more and more countries to develop their own motor industries. Where there were no significant barriers

to exports, as was true of the American market, exports were preferred to investment.

Within Western Europe, which was moving towards free trade, there was the same preference to invest at home and export. No firm invested in new manufacturing capacity outside the home country and, with the sole exception of Belgium, the investment in foreign assembly plants that did take place was induced by tariffs. There were, however, some attempts made to create a strong European MNE by means of acquisition or merger, but these were largely blocked by national jealousies. Noteworthy was Fiat's short-lived move to link up with Citroen which began with the purchase of a 15 per cent stake in the French company in 1968. In December 1970 the two firms merged with the establishment of a holding company with Michelin, which had a majority of the stock in Citroen, in which Fiat's share was 49 per cent and Michelin 51 per cent. The French government had opposed the purchase of over 50 per cent by Fiat. Citroen, which had lost $80m in 1970 badly needed financial help, while Fiat's motive for the merger was the goal of complete integration of the two companies and the creation of a giant European firm capable of holding its own against the American companies. Financial recovery in 1971 and 1972 gave Citroen back its independence and, aided by the French government, it blocked Fiat's proposals for closer integration. In 1973 a disillusioned Fiat sold its share back to Citroen for $50m which just about covered its investment in the holding company.[10] Fiat did, however, end the period owning one manufacturing facility in Europe outside Italy. It had had a financial interest in Simca dating back to before the war and this was sold to Chrysler in 1967. In exchange it gained Simca Industries which included UNIC, a French company manufacturing commercial vehicles and tractors. In 1973, Fiat-France SA-UNIC produced some 7,000 trucks and 3,000 tractors and was closely integrated with the Fiat organisation.

The only other transnational automotive acquisition during these years was British Leyland's purchase of Innocenti Autoveicoli for £3m in 1972. The Italian company had started importing British Minis in 1966 and subsequently assembled them, combining the mechanical components from British Leyland with locally-made bodies. The new subsidiary sold 60,000 Minis in Italy in 1973 to capture 4.5 per cent of the market, and the English parent company hoped to increase production and to supply other European markets from their Italian base.

As mentioned earlier, the European firms did not invest in foreign assembly plants (other than in Belgium) unless induced to do so by tariffs. In Portugal, for example, built-up imports were restricted and duties on ckd imports decreased the greater the Portuguese content of the final product. Assembly began in 1963 and ten years later nearly 96,000 vehicles were being assembled by 18 firms. The European firms with affiliates and their percentage stake in them were as follows: British Leyland (20), Citroen (100), Fiat (50+) and Renault (95). Ford and General Motors were also represented with wholly-owned subsidiaries and Chrysler had a 50 per cent share in a local firm. Noteworthy was the presence of Toyota, which had a 27 per cent interest in a joint venture in 1968 with Salvador Caetano Industries Metalurgicos e Vehiculares de Transport. This was the first foreign direct investment by a Japanese company in automotive production facilities in Europe.

In the Republic of Ireland, where the tariff structure also discriminated heavily against imports of built-up vehicles, local assembly was brought into being. Fiat had a majority interest in its assembler set up in 1952, and Ford and Chrysler had wholly-owned subsidiaries. There were also a number of independent distributors assembling vehicles under licence for various foreign manufacturers, including three Japanese companies. Total assemblies in 1973 amounted to 62,000 units.

Tariffs were also primarily responsible for the establishment of subsidiary plants in Belgium and in the Netherlands by the Swedish producers Volvo and Saab-Scania. Volvo officials have said that they probably would not have constructed a car assembly plant in Belgium in 1964 had it not been for the 22 per cent common tariff wall being created around the EEC for cars as against half that for unassembled vehicles. Saab-Scania set up a subsidiary truck assembly plant in the Netherlands in 1964 and entered a joint venture with IMI in Belgium in 1973 for the assembly of Saab cars, each partner having a 50 per cent interest. British Leyland's car assembly plant at Seneffe in Belgium dates back to 1965 when the Belgian distributor of BMC (later merged with British Leyland) built a factory at his own expense to assemble Minis and 1100s within the EEC tariff walls.

In contrast, assembly plants were closed where tariffs no longer applied. Citroen shut down its assembly plant in the Netherlands, and Fiat ceased assembling Deutsche Fiats in its German factory in 1973 leaving all of the European market except Ireland to be supplied with built-up vehicles from Italy. The American companies also closed assembly plants for the same reason. When Chrysler acquired Simca in France it abandoned its factory in Rotterdam. Ford and General Motors closed down their assembly plants in Sweden, and Ford also ceased assembling in Denmark.

But tariffs were not always the decisive factor in the closure of plants as the ending of assembly operations in Britain by the two French companies, Renault and Citroen demonstrates. The UK tariff remained above 30 per cent until 1962 and was the same for pa:ts and components as for built-up vehicles, so that local assembly only resulted in savings on import duties to the extent that British labour and materials were used instead of imports. Renault resumed assembly operations in its London plant after the war, but ceased production in 1950. By that time the huge increase in output in the French parent company made it cheaper, despite the tariff, to import cars built-up rather than to assemble them on a relatively small scale in England with some local content. Presumably the same considerations were responsible for the closing down of the Citroen plant.

And of course the large amount of foreign investment in assembly facilities in Belgium during this period was not induced by tariffs as far as the French, German and American producers were concerned. Over one million vehicles were assembled in that country in 1973 and no less than nine foreign firms owned plants there. Clearly they were influenced by Belgium's strategic location in the EEC, its excellent port facilities and good road connections to the rest of Continental Europe, the availability of labour at a time of shortages elsewhere, and its relatively low wage rates. For General Motors, in particular, it provided a means of further integrating its European, and even world-wide, operations. In large part, however, Belgium's success in attracting foreign investment reflected a deliberate government policy to exploit the country's geographical position and to replace its traditional industries with more modern technological ones, as well as to provide employment, especially in the depressed areas. Tax and other incentives were offered and an attractive climate for investment, domestic or foreign, was created. General Motors, for example, after shopping around for a site for a $100m assembly plant, decided on Antwerp. It obtained a long lease on 370 acres of previously unreclaimed land in the port area, local property taxes were waived for three years, and there were financial incentives.[11] The latter included a 5-10 year loan carrying an interest rate subsidy of 2-2½ per cent. The loan was to be paid back out of earnings and secured by the assets of General Motors' European subsidiaries. The whole of the Antwerp investment was financed by credit raised in Europe.[12]

This plant, established in 1967 with a capacity of 300,000 units a year, assembled cars and commercial vehicles from General Motors'

factories in Germany, Britain, US and Canada, although German Opels
represented the bulk of its output for sale in Europe and abroad,
especially in the US. The Ford assembly plant at Genk in Belgium, also
with an annual capacity of 300,000 units, was established in 1964 when
Ford-Germany had outgrown its premises in Cologne. Belgium was
selected 'because of labour availability, help from the Belgium government, and better access to parts of Germany than its Cologne plants
could give it'.[13] The two operations were closely integrated from the
start, with trains leaving Genk every evening loaded with assembled
vehicles for Cologne and returning the following morning with engines
and other mechanical components to be used in the Belgian plant the
following day. Other exports from Genk were sent primarily to the
Netherlands and France.

Of the continental European producers, Volkswagen was the only
one to set up a new assembly plant in another EEC country. Its Belgian
plant opened in 1972 and about 85 per cent of its output was exported in 1973, mostly to the Netherlands and Britain. The three major
French producers — Citroen, Peugeot and Renault — inherited assembly
plants from the interwar years, and these facilities were maintained and
expanded after the war.

The concentration of assembly operations in Belgium ran counter to
the world-wide trend towards the establishment of national motor
industries. The formation of the EEC made this development possible.
Without European free trade, Belgium would not have attracted foreign
assembly plants on anything like this scale, nor could it have hoped to
create a national industry because of its small domestic market. With
European free trade, Belgium may achieve the status of vehicle manufacturer as well as assembler. By 1973, a number of the vehicles assembled there did have considerable local content — tyres, tubes, radiators,
springs, wheels, exhaust systems, fuel tanks, shock-absorbers, seats,
trim, paint and electrical equipment. It is customary to regard a vehicle
as being manufactured in a particular country if the local content is
more than 50 per cent by value. Authorities have differed over the
classification of the vehicles assembled in the Belgian Ford plant (a
subsidiary of Ford-Germany) which represent about one-quarter of
the total assemblies for Belgium.[14] If these are considered to have
more than 50 per cent local content it would make Belgium, statistic-
ally at any rate, a manufacturing country.

The American 'Invasion'. If the American producers were to participate
in the booming European market, it would have to be through foreign

direct investment since exporting was almost entirely ruled out by tariffs, the dollar shortage, high labour costs and the large size of American cars. In addition, to the sizable assembly capacity acquired in Belgium, both Ford and General Motors invested heavily in the large-scale expansion of their prewar facilities in Germany and the UK, and also in automatic transmission plants in France. Offsetting this to some extent in the case of Ford, was the decision, after 20 years, to abandon vehicle production in France with the sale of its subsidiary there to Simca in 1954.

The entry of Chrysler into production in Europe (and other overseas markets) was predictable. As a very large firm, but nevertheless the smallest of the American Big Three and basically still a national concern, it was highly likely that it would try to counter the direct foreign investment of Ford and General Motors. However, entry into Europe was bound to be difficult and costly, and at this late stage Chrysler had no alternative but to acquire existing firms. To have constructed its own production capacity, developed new models, built up a distribution and service network, and captured a viable market share in the face of the intense competition in Europe, would have taxed the resources of a firm far stronger financially than Chrysler. Various European firms were approached and by 1973 the American company had acquired 100 per cent ownership of Simca, Barrerios and Rootes. With its French, Spanish and British subsidiaries, Chrysler then accounted for 7.3 per cent of the output of Western Europe. But the entry fee had been some $325m and its European operations as a whole were running at losses the company could ill afford.

One other American manufacturer gained a foothold in Europe by means of a partial acquisition in 1972. International Harvester, producer of heavy trucks and agricultural machinery, obtained a one-third interest in the commercial vehicle activities of the small Dutch firm DAF for an exchange of know-how, sales outlets and research findings. DAF emerged as a vehicle manufacturing concern in the postwar period due to the enterprise and ingenuity of the Van Dorne brothers. Producers of trailers before the war, they added commercial vehicles in 1950, with engines originally based on Leyland licences, and in 1959 began the mass production of one of the earliest European cars fitted with automatic transmission. The Dutch company's output of 94,000 cars and 12,000 trucks in 1973 placed the Netherlands amongst the world's manufacturing countries.

The American invasion was met by the European firms with heavy investment to expand capacity at home to meet both the dramatic rise in domestic demand and in export markets for European-type cars, particularly in the United States. No attempt was made to establish the European counterpart of Ford-Germany or Opel in America. On both fronts the strategy was reasonably successful. The share of Ford in total European production in 1973 was slightly less than before the war. General Motors, although its operations in Germany were successful and profitable, saw its dominant prewar position in that country eroded and this largely contributed to a 45 per cent fall in its share of European production as a whole. Even when Chrysler's European output is included, the combined share of the American companies was actually somewhat less than before the war. In the event, fears of an American takeover of the European motor industry proved groundless although, admittedly, the three major American companies were established in the UK and accounted for roughly half the country's output in 1973.

Table 7.1: Western European Vehicle Production by US Firms, 1938 and 1973 (in Units and Per Cent Share of Total Production)

	1938		1973*	
	Units	Share	Units	Share
France				
Chrysler	—	—	588,139	16.4
Ford	7,555	3.3	—	—
Germany				
Ford	36,582	10.7	456,022	11.5
General Motors	139,631	41.0	874,355	22.1
Spain				
Chrysler	—	—	93,691	11.4
United Kingdom				
Chrysler	—	—	291,513	13.5
Ford	76,705	17.2	590,665	27.3
General Motors	60,111	13.5	245,610	11.4
Total Europe				
Chrysler	—	—	973,343	7.5
Ford	120,842	11.0	1,046,687	8.0
General Motors	199,742	18.3	1,119,965	8.6
Total	320,584	29.3	3,139,995	24.1

*SMMT.
Source: M. Wilkins and F.E. Hill, *American Business Abroad: Ford on Six Continents* (Wayne State University Press, Detroit, 1964), p. 436; Alfred P Sloan Jr, *My Years With General Motors* (McFadden Books, New York, 1965), p. 445.

Japan

> The US Government never gets tough enough . . . If they (the
> Japanese) go far enough and start importing still more into this
> country, you'll see a lot of action in Congress. (Henry Ford II, 1968)[15]

At the end of the second World War the Japanese economy was
shattered and the motor industry largely destroyed. Less than 7,000
vehicles were manufactured in 1945, all military trucks. Fifteen years
later, 760,000 vehicles were produced — 165,000 cars, 317,000 trucks
and buses, and 278,000 three-wheeled vehicles — and Japan was
designing and building her own passenger cars as well as trucks. The
government, largely through the Ministry of International Trade and
Investment (MITI) played a critical role in this transformation.

In essence the government restricted both imports and foreign direct
investment so that the rapidly expanding domestic market was supplied
almost entirely by Japanese-owned and controlled firms. At the same
time the MITI encouraged the importation of superior foreign technology in the passenger car field. The country's emphasis had always
been on trucks and three-wheeled vehicles so that when production
controls were abolished in the early 1950s the Japanese car producers
were faced with a market opportunity which they were technologically
incapable of exploiting. They turned out little more than 4,000 cars in
1951 and these were uncompetitive in price and in quality with imports.
In 1952, for example, a new four-door 8-cylinder Ford in Japan after
payment of transportation and import taxes sold for only $167 more
than the little 'Toyopet' and the Austin A40 sold for the same price as
the 'Datsun'.[16]

The MITI was convinced of the necessity of importing foreign technology and most of the Japanese manufacturers agreed. In October
1952 it issued the 'Basic Policy for the Technological Licencing and
Assembly Agreements in the Passenger Car Industry'. Foreign exchange
would be made available to cover payments in connection with individual technical and licensing agreements between Japanese and foreign
firms. Potential licensers were offered the opportunity to export substantial parts and sub-assemblies to Japan and remittance of royalties
was guaranteed. However, the Basic Policy stipulated that if the licence
covered complete knock-down assembly of passenger cars in Japan, 90
per cent of the licenced parts had to be produced in Japan within five
years for the guarantee of remittance to be continued. This served
notice that such imports would be permitted for only a limited period
of time and gave domestic manufacturers an additional incentive to

develop the capability to make their licenser's parts.

Within a year four firms had negotiated knocked-down assembly of foreign cars in Japan — Nissan with Austin, UK (Austin A-50), Isuzu with Rootes, UK (Hillman Minx), Hino with Renault, France (Dauphine) and Mitsubishi with Willys, USA (Jeep). In each case the design was gradually modified to meet local needs. Hino, for example, evolved a heavier, more rugged Dauphine to suit Japan's rough roads. Within five years Japanese firms were designing and producing their own passenger cars and the country had achieved nearly complete autonomy in the production of parts and passenger car design.[17] The policies of the MITI had enabled Japan to get foreign technology without foreign investment. More fundamentally, the Japanese educational system provided scientists, engineers and technologists who were familiar with the long-established basic principles of automotive technology and manufacture. The existence of this body of professionally-trained people made it possible for Toyota and Prince, two of the three largest producers of the period, to rely on domestic know-how exclusively, just as it enabled the other four manufacturers to absorb and adapt foreign technology and then to become independent of it in such a short space of time. Toyota did, however, make two attempts at a joint venture with Ford. In June 1950 the company sent the President of Toyota Motor Sales to the US with a proposal to establish a tie-up with Ford. 'Ford executives had another opportunity to join with Toyota in a joint venture in Japan but again they ignored the proposal.'[18]

Modern technology, the experience and the economies of scale made possible in producing for a rapidly-expanding and protected home market combined to make Japanese producers highly competitive, and ready for a major expansion of exports commencing in the middle of the 1960s. Their major target was the world's largest and richest market, the United States. It was also the home of the world's largest automotive MNEs.

The American companies saw Japan become the world's second largest producer in 1967 with an output of over three million vehicles and exports of a third of a million, half of which went to the United States. They were to see US imports of Japanese vehicles rise steeply to over 800,000 vehicles by 1971. At the same time they were denied access to the home market of their Japanese competitors. Not only were they excluded from exporting to Japan, but also they were barred from investing and producing there as well. Not surprisingly, automobiles became a major issue between the two countries in 1967, the year of Japan's first round of capital liberalisation. There followed four years of intensive pressure by the US government and the American firms to get the Japanese to reduce automotive import and capital barriers.

As the negotiations proceeded it became clear that what the American firms really wanted was the opportunity to invest in the Japanese industry and that this was what the Japanese government was determined to prevent, or at least to delay as long as possible. It was prepared to make slow, step-by-step liberalisation of trade by removing quotas and reducing tariffs, but for over two years it held out against American direct investment. During this time the MITI urgently tried to organise the Japanese industry into two groups behind Toyota and Nissan so that if and when capital liberalisation finally came there would be no weak firms for the Americans to acquire, and control of the industry would remain entirely in Japanese hands.

The MITI strategy of consolidation was unsuccessful and the remaining independent producers were left to search for alternative strategies for survival. Mitsubishi Heavy Industries made the first move in May 1969 and announced that it intended to affiliate with Chrysler by hiving off its automotive division and selling 35 per cent of the stock in it to the American company. If this deal were to go through, it would be the first in which a major Japanese firm had given a substantial equity to foreign capital. In doing this Mitsubishi was openly defying the MITI, undermining the latter's strategy of forming two groups, and encouraging the smaller independent firms to look abroad to strengthen their position.

On 31 October 1970 Isuzu and General Motors announced that a basic agreement had been reached between them involving technical co-operation in safety and pollution research, co-operation in selling the small Isuzu truck through the GM sales network, the establishment of a joint venture for the production of gas turbines and automatic transmissions and GM capital participation in Isuzu.[19] Scarcely one week later, Toyo Kogyo reported to the MITI that an agreement with Ford had been reached giving Ford 20 per cent control, with both firms sharing the costs of technological development.[20] And so by the end of 1970 the three major American firms had announced tentative joint ventures with existing Japanese producers of motor vehicles. In addition, Ford had reached an agreement on a joint venture to manufacture automatic transmissions. It was to have 50 per cent of the equity. Toyo Kogyo 25 per cent and Nissan 25 per cent in a new firm, Japan Automatic Transmissions.

Negotiations on a contract between Ford and Toyo Kogyo continued

into 1971 but no proposal was submitted for MITI approval. Henry
Ford II visited Japan in March for talks with Japanese leaders, including
Prime Minister Sato and executives of Toyo Kogyo. He had already
agreed to limit the Ford share to 20 per cent and to forego voting rights
for the time being. The chief stumbling block appears to have been
Toyo Kogyo's desire to prevent Ford from increasing that share in
future. Negotiations were finally suspended in the autumn allegedly
over a difference as to the price at which the Japanese company would
offer for shares to Ford.[21] However, Ford's joint venture with Toyo
Kogyo and Nissan-Japan Automatic Transmissions received government
approval.

The final outcome by the end of 1973 of all the diplomacy, negotiations and proposals represented a very modest success for the Americans in the motor manufacturing sector. Chrysler had a 15 per cent
share in Mitsubishi, but because of its own financial difficulties had
announced indefinite postponement of further investment in the
Japanese company. General Motors owned a 34.2 per cent share in
Isuzu, a firm producing little more than 3 per cent of the industry output, although of some importance as a commercial vehicle manufacturer. Ford had no ownership links with a Japanese vehicle producer.
Both Ford and General Motors had entered into joint ventures with
Japanese partners to manufacture automatic transmissions, Ford with
a 50 per cent share in one, and General Motors with a minority interest
in the other. Still it was a foothold in the world's second largest motor
industry and no European MNE had been able to secure that.

On the trade front, the Japanese tariff had been reduced by stages
from 40 per cent to 6.4 per cent and other barriers to trade liberalised.
Nevertheless, total Japanese imports in 1973 amounted to only 38,000
vehicles. Of these, 12,600 were from America as against Japanese
exports of 823,000 cars and trucks to the US. Japan had opened the
door only when it was considered perfectly safe to do so.

But if direct investment in Japan by foreign vehicle manufacturers
was very limited up to 1973 so too was Japanese overseas investment
in manufacturing and assembly. Indeed so small was the proportion of
overseas production and assets to that of the parent company that, on
some definitions of the MNE, even the largest Japanese companies
would not have qualified. Moreover, each of the foreign plants manufactured or assembled solely for its local market, so that no Japanese
company had the semblance of a multinational network or system. On
the other hand, Nissan and Toyota were very large companies by world
standards and each had investments in half-a-dozen or so countries. The

largest of these was in Nissan's manufacturing facilities in Mexico (85 per cent owned) which in 1973 turned out some 25,000 vehicles. Toyota had a small, wholly-owned subsidiary in Brazil producing utility vehicles and light trucks, with an annual capacity of 1,200 units. For the rest, Japanese firms as a whole had a financial interest in some 15 assembly plants, all joint ventures with local concerns and mostly in south-east Asia. Tariffs and local content requirements meant that some investment by the Japanese firms was needed in each case to preserve access to these markets. That approval by the Japanese government for these investments was obtained is another indication that they were 'necessary', since the policy throughout this period was one of strongly encouraging exports and restricting overseas manufacturing investment.

World-wide Spread of Assembly and Production

Rapid economic growth and the drive to industrialise in developing countries made the further spread of the automotive industry inevitable. Economic development cannot take place without improvements in transport. The modernisation of agriculture calls for the movement of fertiliser and other new inputs to the farms and the delivery of surpluses to the towns. Industrialisation is synonymous with an increased flow of materials and products, while the growth of cities creates new needs for passenger transport, and rising real incomes swells the demand. Initially these requirements are met by imports but the growing burden on the balance of payments tends to become insupportable.

There is an additional and strong reason why so many countries have chosen to foster a domestic motor industry. The manufacture of motor vehicles requires large amounts of materials — iron, steel, glass, plastics, textiles, rubber, chemicals — and a host of specialised parts and components not normally produced by vehicle manufacturers themselves. The presence of the latter, however, serves to generate the growth of numerous suppliers to the motor industry and to industry in general. And there are forward linkages as well, with distributors, garages and service stations. In the process, the general level of technology is raised and the prospects for continuing industrial development enhanced.

The New Manufacturing Countries

For a developing country the transition from importer to manufacturer of complete motor vehicles is a gradual one. Starting with the local

Table 7.2: Production of Motor Vehicles in the New Manufacturing Countries and Share of MNEs, 1973

	Argentina	Australia	Brazil	India	Mexico	Netherlands	Spain	Total	Per Cent Share
British Leyland	—	36,500	—	5,639	—	—	—	85,987	3.1
Chrysler	27,671	50,000	36,826	—	47,864	—	93,691	256,052	9.3
Citroen	17,489	—	—	—	—	—	72,935	90,424	3.3
Daimler-Benz	7,689	—	32,564	—	—	—	—	40,253	1.5
Fiat	66,648	—	—	—	—	—	361,153	427,801	15.6
Ford	62,374	114,000	147,986	—	44,512	—	—	368,872	13.4
General Motors	29,681	176,000	140,567	—	37,170	—	—	383,418	14.0
Nissan	—	—	—	—	24,635	—	—	24,635	0.9
Peugeot	29,102	—	—	—	—	—	—	29,102	1.0
Renault	46,128	—	—	—	21,322	—	181,674	249,124	9.0
Toyota	—	28,085	585	—	—	—	—	28,670	1.0
Volkswagen	—	—	365,472	—	89,624	—	—	455,096	16.6
Others	6,960	6,536	5,076	92,278	20,441	108,254	68,719	308,264	11.2
Total	293,742	411,121	729,076	97,917	285,568	108,254	822,020	2,747,698	99.9

Source: SMMT; *World Motor Vehicle Data* (for Australia).

assembly of cars and trucks formerly imported, it then proceeds to incorporate locally-manufactured parts for which there is also a significant replacement market, such as, batteries, tyres and exhausts. Following this stage is a period during which the local content is gradually increased by adding other parts easily manufactured within the country. The final stage involves the major decision to go ahead with the manufacture of the more complex items, that is, engines, transmissions and body panels.

Throughout this fairly lengthy process, the developing country, lacking the resources needed to create an indigenous motor industry, is dependent on the design and technical resources of foreign MNEs. Moreover, that dependence continues even after the final stage of complete manufacture is reached, for it is rare for the local industry to undertake significant initiatives in design and development. The extent of that dependence is shown in Table 7.2 which also indicates the shares of the MNEs in the output of the seven countries which became manufacturers in the postwar period. The MNEs were directly responsible for roughly 90 per cent of the vehicles produced in these countries. While it is true that not all of the local affiliates were wholly-owned by the MNE, and in a few cases the foreign ownership was a minority one, nevertheless, effective control lay in the hands of the MNE. Indeed the table underestimates their influence since a number of the local firms included in 'others' had a significant foreign holding and most produced under licence from the MNEs.

Noteworthy is the fact that the European MNEs accounted for half of the total, with three of them — Volkswagen, Fiat and Renault — capturing a total of 40 per cent, or somewhat more than the three American producers put together. Significant too is the tiny share of the two giant Japanese firms. A more detailed look at the role played by the MNEs in the development of the motor industry in each of these countries follows.

Australia.

> It's ironic when you consider the vast profits GM-H now make each year out of the Holden car, to realise that the General Motors Corporation did not want to manufacture in Australia. (Lawrence Hartnett, Managing Director, General Motors-Holden 1934-47)[22]

The first country to join the ranks of the motor vehicle producers after the war was Australia. As indicated earlier, local manufacture of bodies and many parts and components had been firmly established by 1939.

In fact two years prior to this the Tariff Board had estimated that, excluding the minority of cars imported more or less complete, the percentage of Australian labour and materials in the factory cost of cars ranged from 43 per cent to 50.5 per cent. As part of a drive to develop a diversified industrial economy and to provide jobs for the large influx of immigrants planned for after the war, the government was determined to create a domestic industry capable of producing all-Australian vehicles. After an unsuccessful attempt to induce an Australian-owned company to enter the industry with the help of the Motor Engine Bounty Bill of 1939, it apparently had decided that it had no option but to rely on the direct investment of foreign firms and in 1944 invited them to submit proposals.

Within three months General Motors had submitted its project. Frederic Donner, subsequently Chairman, has since stated the reasons behind this decision. First, if General Motors did not accept the challenge other manufacturers would and the company would lose all or most of the market in that part of the world. Secondly, the project was economically sound — satisfactory supporting industries were already in existence, the potential market was large enough to support a manufacturing facility, and a car could be produced locally at the demand level anticipated at a lower cost than a comparable import at the prevailing customs tariff rate. Thirdly, General Motors had the technical resources needed to develop 'a distinctive Australian car'. In Mr Donner's words, 'There were a number of good reasons for our entering the Australian market. They were so persuasive that we moved ahead with a manufacturing program.'[23]

Nevertheless, General Motors Finance Committee was only prepared to approve the project if the money to finance it could be found in Australia. The Australian government promptly arranged for the Commonwealth Bank to lend £2.5 million to General Motors' local subsidiary, and the Bank of Adelaide added another £500,000.[24] The 'distinctive Australian car' turned out to be a small car designed and developed by General Motors after the war for the American market, but which had been put on the shelf in September 1946. In largely unchanged form, it rolled off the assembly lines in Australia two years later as the Holden.[25] It was a tremendous success.

Predictably, Ford and Chrysler (which had set up an Australian subsidiary in 1951 when it acquired the local firm which had been assembling and distributing its vehicles under licence) also submitted plans to manufacture and these were accepted by the government. They were joined by another American company, International Harvester, which had been long-established in Australia as a manufacturer of farm machinery and tractors and planned to move into the production of trucks in 1949.

Although not mentioned by Mr Donner, Australia's foreign exchange difficulties after the war must have been a factor in the decision of the American companies to initiate the local manufacture of engines and related mechanical components when they did. Before the war the car companies had resisted government pressure to do this on the grounds that it would be too costly at such low volumes and would mean still higher prices for Australian models. No doubt also they were reluctant to create new capacity in Australia when there was much spare capacity at home for the production of the same engines. But Australia's post-war dollar shortage and the likelihood of severe restrictions on dollar imports for some time to come, threatened the loss of the bulk of the market to United Kingdom producers. In 1949 the latter took 80 per cent of the Australian market compared to roughly 40 per cent before the war. The only means of preventing this loss lay in local manufacture, for the government was prepared to assist companies with approved manufacturing programmes by making additional exchange available for the importation of components during the period when the local content was being increased, and by making tariff concessions on such imports.

In view of the relatively small size of the Australian market, it was fortunate for the country that the European producers were in no position to undertake foreign investment so soon after the war. Moreover, the British producers were the only ones with a sufficient stake in Australia which might have led to defensive investment to retain market shares. That such investment did not occur until much later is due partly to the weakness of the British economy and the desperate need to increase exports, partly to the relatively rapid expansion of output at home which absorbed the available resources of the individual firms, and partly to the belief that direct investment was not necessary in this case. A number of British firms established subsidiary assembly plants in Australia for the first time after the war primarily because tariffs discriminated against built-up imports. With local assembly, no restrictions on sterling imports, plus the drastic devaluation of sterling, British manufacturers probably considered that they could compete effectively against the small-scale local production of the American firms.

But models designed for the United Kingdom home market were not what most Australians wanted; there were delays and difficulties in getting spare parts for them, and two sterling exchange crises occurred

in the 1950s leading to temporary restrictions on sterling imports. All
this finally induced the British Motor Corporation to invest in local
manufacture. Underlying the decision must have been a growing realisation that in the long-run there was no future in the mass market for the
importer-assembler in a country where the government was determined
to develop a domestic manufacturing industry. The British Motor
Corporation later became part of Leyland Motors and in 1973 the latter
company brought out a new large car model, the PL76, the first British
car to be designed in Australia, and it incorporated 85 per cent local
content.

Volkswagen, encouraged by the market penetration achieved with
imported Beetles, decided to invest in manufacturing in Australia,
aiming at 95 per cent local content. Production of body panels began
in 1960 but Volkswagen sales never reached a high enough volume to
make almost complete local manufacture pay. By the end of 1967 the
company resolved to cut its losses and to revert to the smaller-volume
government plan which required only 50 per cent local content but
which limited sales of each permitted type to 7,500 units and meant
that total Volkswagen sales of cars could not exceed 22,000 cars plus
some commercial vehicles. A major reorganisation took place in 1968
when Volkswagen Australasia ceased to exist and a new company was
formed, Motor Producers Ltd (MPL), wholly-owned by Volkswagen
whose sole function was to assemble and supply vehicles to an
Australian-owned distributing and service organisation. By 1973 in
moves to make full use of its capacity, MPL was also assembling Nissan
vehicles, Volvo cars and Mercedes-Benz trucks.

MPL and three other firms dominated the assembly sector of the
industry which accounted for about 20 per cent of Australian production. Leyland Motors, wholly-owned subsidiary of British Leyland, and
as an amalgam of a number of separate British companies, inherited
several dispersed plants and assembled about 30,000 vehicles in
addition to its national production. Australian Motor Industries (AMI)
(50 per cent Toyota and 10 per cent American Motors) assembled
'Toyotas' and a few hundred 'Ramblers'. Renault Australia, wholly-
owned subsidiary established in 1966 was the smallest and assembled
a few 'Peugeots' in addition to 'Renaults'. There were also four,
foreign-owned assemblers of commercial vehicles, Volvo (Sweden),
White (US), MAN (Germany) and Magirus (Germany).

With four firms committed to more or less complete local manufacture of motor vehicles, plus a parts and component sector supplying
them and the replacement market, Australia had succeeded in creating

a national motor industry capable of meeting the bulk of its requirements. Three features stand out. First, the Australian motor industry
was largely owned by foreigners. The car and truck producers were
wholly-owned subsidiaries, and two-thirds of the more important
components manufacturers were effectively controlled by foreign
firms.[26] Secondly, these foreign firms would not have established
production facilities in Australia, had they not been induced to do so
by government policies. Thirdly, there were too many manufacturers
for the size of the Australian market so that none could hope to achieve
an internationally-competitive level of production. The presence of a
number of assemblers further aggravated the situation.

Latin America. Until the mid-1950s, all motor vehicles were imported
either completely built-up or more or less ckd and assembled locally.
By 1973, Brazil, Argentina and Mexico had become car manufacturers.
As in Australia this was accomplished through a combination of government policies and the resources of the MNEs. The policies varied to
some extent but basically provided protection from imports, required a
gradual increase in the local content of vehicles, and extended liberal
treatment to foreign investors which included tax concessions. Without
such policies, the foreign investment would not have taken place. And,
given the internal economic, social and political conditions in these
countries, without the technology, know-how and resources of the
MNEs, there would have been no 'national' motor industries.

Unlike Australia, however, where the process took place over a
period of some 30 years, it was compressed in the three Latin American
countries into five or ten years. Moreover, the development occurred
later at a time when the major European and Japanese firms were much
larger, competitively stronger, and had successfully penetrated export
markets in Latin America. They, as well as their American rivals, chose
foreign investment rather than lose these markets. Unfortunately for
the Latin American countries concerned, this oligopolistic competitive
process resulted in too many manufacturers and models for the size of
each national market so that large-scale, efficient production was not
possible for any of them up to the end of 1973.

There is some evidence that the American firms were reluctant to
invest in manufacturing in Latin America. Ford, which had built a new
assembly plant in Brazil in 1952, did not want to manufacture there.[27]
Initially both Ford and General Motors submitted plans for truck manufacturing only, under the government's programme. Later, when they
realised that they would lose the entire Brazilian market for cars unless

they produced them locally, the government was not keen to admit more manufacturers in that sector, but it eventually did so.[28]

An account of General Motors' decision to invest in manufacturing in Argentina is given by a former Chairman, Frederic Donner.[29] The company's Overseas Policy Group in its review of overseas operations made during the second world war had decided against producing in Argentina on the grounds that the country's general industrial expansion 'would be limited by a lack of strong supporting industries and a shortage of essential raw materials and natural resources such as iron, coal, lumber and waterpower'. Continual reliance on local assembly of imported parts and components was considered preferable for Argentina. However, developments in 1958 and 1959 forced General Motors to reconsider its position. Prohibitive import restrictions passed in January 1959 meant that 'a standard Chevrolet passenger car selling under $2,500 in the United States would have cost over $20,000, including duty and surcharges'. Obviously further importation and assembly would be impossible. With this stick the Argentina government held out the carrots of 'duty free entry of new machinery, tools and equipment; protection against imported products through surcharge schedules favourable to local manufacturers; and official permission to transfer the annual net profits earned on investment through the free exchange market'. General Motors wanted to retain its share of the Argentine market and, given these inducements, investment in manufacturing seemed to be a reasonable risk from a profit point of view. But Mr Donner makes it quite clear that local manufacture would mean reduced efficiency and higher prices to the Argentine customers for some time to come.

But willingly or unwillingly, most of the world's major firms felt it essential to invest in production in Latin America in response to the industrialisation plans of Brazil, Argentina and Mexico. By 1973 the MNEs almost completely controlled the motor industries of these countries.

In Brazil, the motor industry was dominated from the start (1958) by foreign-owned firms, presumably because local companies could not meet the requirements of the government's programme. Of the 17 concerns which applied to become manufacturers, 11 were accepted and 15 years later there were nine firms in existence — Chrysler, Ford, General Motors, Volkswagen, Mercedes (Daimler-Benz), Toyota, Saab-Scania, Alfa Romeo (which had taken over the state-owned truck producer, FNM) and a small Brazilian sports car maker, Puma. There had been a few casualties during the period but none involving a MNE car producer.

In Argentina, 21 companies began production in 1960 under the manufacturing programme, the government having accepted the proposals of all the companies meeting the legal requirements. Of these only four had majority or 100 per cent foreign ownership — Daimler-Benz, Fiat, Ford and General Motors. The rest were Argentine firms, with at least majority local ownership, producing under licence. Some were forced out of business by competitive pressures while others were taken over by the foreign partner of joint ventures or by the licenser, as happened to the local associates of Chrysler, Citroen, Peugeot and Renault. Even Siam di Tella, one of Argentina's leading firms, was forced to sell its motor interest to IKA in 1965 after incurring heavy losses. By 1973 only the state-owned truck producer, IME, remained under local control.

In Mexico, which required only 60 per cent local content, the extent of concentration and of foreign ownership was limited somewhat by the government's quota system. The arrangement gave some protection to the smaller companies since the larger ones were not able to increase their market shares at the expense of the smaller, Mexican-owned companies. Nevertheless, foreign ownership at the assembly/manufacturer section of the industry increased over the period. Of the eight companies which received government approval to produce passenger cars under the local content decree of 1962 only Ford, General Motors, Nissan and Volkswagen were wholly-owned. Fabricas Automex (Chrysler licensee) and Vehiculos Automoves Mexicanos (VAM-American Motors Licensee) were joint ventures with majority Mexican ownership, while two — Diesel Nacional (DINA-Renault licensee) and Fabrica Nacional de Automoviles (FANASA) — were 100 per cent Mexican.

The latter company was an interesting attempt to set up a national company independent of foreign licences. In effect it represented an endeavour to resurrect the bankrupt German firm of Borgward in the new world under new management. A technical assistance contract was signed with a Spanish firm to establish and operate the plant. About 50 engineers and foremen from the former Borgward works in Bremen were hired for periods ranging from nine months to three years, and a great part of the installations was bought at an alleged price of £8 million and shipped to Mexico to a new factory in Monterrey. The aim was to build the former Borgward cars, 'Grosser Borgward' and 'Isabella', at a rate of 15,000 to 20,000 a year.[30] Despite official government encouragement, the company never succeeded in producing more than a few hundred cars a year and closed in 1970. DINA, on the other hand, which was a state-owned concern, managed to survive although it never captured more than 10 per cent of the market. In 1973 it entered into a joint venture with Renault to produce cars (DINA-Renault), with the French company holding 40 per cent of the shares and the government the remainder.

Of the original joint ventures, Automex, the most important, was taken over by Chrysler in 1971 when it increased its share from 45 to 91 per cent. Automex had built a large, new factory in 1968 with an assembly capacity of 126,000 units a year which it operated well below capacity as its market share fell from a peak of 29 per cent in 1965 to 17 per cent in 1971. Heavy losses were incurred in 1970 and 1971 and the company had become increasingly in debt to Chrysler before the takeover.[31] Unlike Automex, VAM survived as a joint venture, partly because the government was the majority stockholder and partly because it had chosen to remain a small-scale producer, thus avoiding heavy expenditure on a larger plant and the massive instalment financing needed to expand sales. American Motors held 38 per cent of the shares.

One of the casualties in Latin America calls for special comment. Kaiser-Fraser had attempted to enter the US market immediately after the second World War but had fared badly with the return to normal market conditions in 1953. In that year it merged with Willys-Overland, a profitable producer of jeeps and small trucks that had re-entered the car market in 1952 with a not very successfull small car. Kaiser-Willys ended US passenger car production in 1955 and provided the plant and equipment for Industrias Kaiser Argentina (IKA), which was shipped in its entirety from the US the following year. In return, Kaiser-Willys received a significant minority share in IKA, with local private interests and the government holding the majority. The same strategy was used in establishing Willys-Overland do Brasil.[32]

The subsequent fate of these companies is a revealing example of the weakness of local concerns in competition with MNEs. IKA was a firm which, along with its sister plant in Brazil (Willys-Overland), represented, in effect, a MNE without a home base. Kaiser-Willys had sought to do overseas what it had failed to do in the US, that is, to establish itself as a new entrant into the motor industry. Without the resources made available with a successful home-based operation, in particular without the research and development capacity to develop its own models, IKA was in a similar position to that of any indigenous firm, and its American know-how, machinery and equipment, plus the advantages of sizable local ownership (including that of the Argentine government), were not enough to save it. The company manufactured Renault and American Motors vehicles under licence and, when it ran into financial difficulties in 1967, Renault assumed control and introduced a necessary programme of investment to modernise and rationalise the firm's productive capacity. The name was changed to IKA-Renault with the French company owning 40 per cent of the shares and American Motors 8 per cent. Also in 1967, the Willys-Overland plant in Brazil was taken over by Ford, thus ending the postwar attempt by the Kaiser group to enter the motor industry.

Table 7.3 reflects the dominance the MNEs had gained in the three manufacturing countries at the end of 1973, and shows the inroads the non-American MNEs were strong enough to make in what was formerly the preserve of the US companies. Control rested overwhelmingly in the hands of the MNEs, whose advantages in terms of superior knowledge and size were so great compared to that of local competitors that the latter were almost all eliminated. This is what the theory of foreign direct investment leads one to expect. With the disappearance of the purely national firms, the growing concentration ceased leaving a relatively large number of MNE affiliates which were far below the optimum size for the industry. This failure of competition to lead to the survival of only low-cost, efficient firms can be explained by an oligopoly model applied to a protected industry with differentiated products and affected by economies of scale which are significant relative to the size of the national market.[33]

In this case, the industry price becomes the world (external) price plus the tariff. This and the initial high level of demand enables a number of firms, domestic and foreign, to enter and make a satisfactory profit at small, inefficient levels of output. After the elimination of the national firms, the survivors are more or less equally matched. Price competition does not pay, partly because each faces a steeply sloping demand curve and partly because of the financial support available from the parent company. Hence no subsidiary or affiliate is able to expand to an efficient size and too many producers are left for the size of the market. To make matters worse, non-price competition leads to the proliferation of models further fragmenting the market and dissipating potential economies of scale. The result is a high-cost, inefficient industry, completely dependent for its existence on a high level of protection from imports and, of course, utterly unable to export without large subsidies.

And pressure to export was growing as time went on. One of the

main motives for seeking to create national motor industries was to ease
the foreign exchange burden imposed by the growing need to import
motor vehicles, but this has proved to be very difficult to achieve in
absolute terms (although an improvement on what the situation would
be with no local production). The Argentine government hoped to
expand production, for example, from about 32,000 vehicles in 1959
(largely assembly) to about 200,000 in 1965 without increasing foreign
exchange payments for imports. The production target was very nearly
reached but, despite the increase in local content, the automotive
import bill rose from $42m to $126m.[34]

Table 7.3: Number and Unit Output of MNEs in Latin America, 1973

	Number	Output	Per Cent of Total Output	Average MNE Output	Per Cent Share American MNE
Argentina	8	286,782	97.6	35,848	41.7
Brazil	5*	723,415	99.2	144,683	45.0
Mexico	6	265,127	92.8	44,188	48.9

*Excludes Toyota as untypically small.
Source: SMMT.

Nor did the capital flows associated with the foreign investment
provide more than a very temporary support to the balance of payments. This is partly because there tended to be very little capital in
the form of foreign exchange in the MNE investment package. In the
case of Argentina, the General Motor's Chairman comments, 'It was our
expectation that the investment in expanded plant facilities could be
accomplished without any considerable dollar outflow from the United
States relying, in part, upon earnings generated within Argentina, and
in part, upon the shipment of machinery and equipment from our
United States operations in return for capital stock in the Argentine
subsidiary.'[35] When Ford and General Motors decided to invest in
truck manufacturing in Brazil, the initial 'going in' amounts were said
to be $21m for Ford and $20m for General Motors. Whether these
funds were transferred from the US or not, 'The required speed for
using locally-produced components turned out to be slow enough to
enable the investing American companies to recover the investment by
profits on the continuing, if declining quantities of components they
exported.'[36]

There are difficulties in obtaining data on the outflow of funds in profits, royalties and technology payments but available estimates suggest that foreign firms were able to recoup their investments in a very short period. Indeed the conclusion drawn from Argentine studies is that 'during the late 1960s and early 1970s, the annual payments of both dividends and royalties were at least as great as the total amount of new foreign capital authorized in the automotive industry during the six years from 1965 to 1970'.[37] Two Mexican studies of capital flows in the transport equipment sector (of which the terminal automotive industry is an important part) indicate that the inflow of foreign capital in the early days of an industry's development soon falls sharply or is financed by retained profits while the remission of profits and other payments abroad increases, resulting in a deficit on capital account. The first study found that in 1967 incoming investment in the transport equipment sector was almost $25m while payments abroad were $8.3m. Only three years later new foreign investment was $4.3m and remissions were $20.9m. The other study halved the remissions figure for 1970 but pointed to the same conclusion.[38]

The need to compensate for the outflow of foreign exchange incurred by the industry led all three countries in the early 1970s to introduce measures designed to improve productivity and to promote automotive exports. Argentina heavily subsidised the export of finished cars and trucks. Brazil reduced the local content requirements for cars from 99 per cent to 80 per cent and for commercial vehicles from 98 per cent to 82 per cent in order to reduce costs by facilitating the interchange of parts between foreign subsidiaries as long as the extra imports were compensated for by increased exports. Mexico, with its relatively low local content requirements (60 per cent), insisted that an increasing proportion of imports be offset by exports, and that 40 per cent of the rising quota of exports were to come from the parts and components sector where firms were required to have 60 per cent Mexican ownership. In addition, fiscal incentives were given to exporters and, if finished vehicles were exported, the local content could be as low as 40 per cent. The measures were quite successful in increasing exports in all three countries and served to open up, to some extent, closed national industries and markets to international influences. In effect it meant the closer integration of these domestic industries with the world-wide operations of the MNEs. Some saw this as the only way of making high-cost, protected industries efficient, internationally competitive and capable of further growth. Others saw it as the further tightening of the screw of foreign exploitation of poor developing countries.

Spain. As part of its plan to industrialise and modernise the Spanish economy after the war, the government was determined to create a national motor industry. It apparently felt that the country lacked the financial and technical resources to develop such an industry on its own and so deliberately created the conditions which would induce multinational firms to make direct investments. Basically this meant tariffs high enough to insulate domestic producers from imports despite the cost penalties of rapidly rising local content requirements. Low wages, the prohibition of strikes and government encouragement served as additional inducements. Through the Instituto Nacional de Industria (INI) established in 1946 to encourage industrialisation, the government has played an active role in negotiating agreements with interested MNEs and holds a majority interest in the largest producer, Sociedad Espanola de Automovils de Turismo (SEAT).

By 1973 eight MNEs had invested in the Spanish motor industry. In general the pattern was one of joint ventures to start, with the local partner producing foreign models under licence, and then the MNE increasing its share in the partnership over time as the local content and output increased. Fiat, with a 36 per cent holding in SEAT began production of Fiat models in 1953. In this case the state through the INI provided the funds to meet the local share in the increased investment requirements. Renault also commenced operations in 1953, with a 15 per cent stake in a local company, Fasa, and this was increased to 49.8 per cent in 1965 when the concern became Fasa-Renault. The Bank Iberia and the Spanish public each owned half the remaining shares. Chrysler appeared on the scene in 1963 when it purchased a 40 per cent share in Barrerios. Majority control was gained in 1967 and by 1972 Chrysler owned 98 per cent of Chrysler Espania. The fourth largest producer, Citroen, began production in 1958 with a 45 per cent share in Citroen-Hispania. In 1973 British Leyland had a financial stake in two Spanish companies. The largest, Authi had commenced production of the Mini in 1967 under licence from the British Motor Corporation which had a 50 per cent share in the Spanish company. British Leyland, after its acquisition of BMC, increased this to 98.5 per cent for a purchase price said to be a little over £4m. As part of the deal it sold its 25.1 per cent holding in the government-controlled commercial vehicle firm ENASA which produced a number of heavy duty engines under licence from British Leyland. The other Spanish company in which it had an interest was Metalurgica Santa Ana, manufacturers of Land Rovers under licence. The British Leyland share was 25.1 per cent. Mercedes-Benz and Volkswagen each had a 26.8 per cent share in

MENOSA a firm producing their commercial vehicles under licence. Finally Massey-Ferguson had a 36.5 per cent stake in Motor Iberica, a company created from the old Ford assets which produced 'Ebro' trucks, a British Ford vehicle also made under licence. Motor Iberica acquired Fabrica Diesel SA (FADISA) in 1967.

Together these MNEs and their local partners accounted for 96 per cent of Spain's output of 820,000 vehicles in 1973. The remainder, all commercial vehicles, was produced by three Spanish companies, two of them, ENASA and AISA, controlled by the government through the INI. The third company, VIASA made jeeps under licence from American Motors. Government policies had successfully created a Spanish motor industry from scratch with the aid of the know-how and capital of MNEs. Within the space of 20 years Spain had become the world's ninth largest producer, fifth largest in all of Europe not counting the USSR. Exports had expanded rapidly in the early 1970s to reach nearly 20 per cent of the total vehicle output in 1973. However, the domestic market was still heavily protected and too fragmented for most of the producers to withstand the competition that would result should Spain become a full-fledged member of the EEC. With this in mind, in December 1972, the government liberalised the local content rules from 70 per cent to 50 per cent if exports were increased. Expansion was encouraged with tax concessions and access to official sources of credit, particularly in the case of export-orientated concerns. These policies contributed to the decision made later by Ford to establish a major subsidiary in Spain, with far-reaching consequences for the European industry.

India. The Indian motor industry, although privately owned, was very much the creation of the government, which reserved the home market for domestic producers. That government was wary of foreign investment, preferred technical collaboration with foreign firms, screening agreements to ensure reasonable terms and favouring those where Indian technology was clearly deficient or where there were good export prospects. And the planners gave a low priority to private passenger car production.

In the early postwar years, Ford and General Motors opened the assembly plants they had established there before the war. Other assembly plants were subsequently set up with Indian capital and supplied with ckd packs and technical assistance from overseas. To foster manufacturing the government decided in 1953 to limit production to those companies with approved programmes to make engines, transmissions, axles and other components. Ford and General Motors were unwilling to accept the government's conditions and closed down their factories in the following year. Three Indian assemblers whose manufacturing programmes were accepted, together with their domestic suppliers, succeeded in raising the local content of Indian vehicles to 95 per cent or more, using foreign designs and aided by financial and technical agreements with foreign firms. Another Indian concern produced Jeeps under licence from American Motors. But there was no foreign direct investment in the final stage of manufacture and assembly in the passenger car sector, nor were there any new technical collaboration agreements concluded with overseas producers. One consequence was that twenty years later the Indian motor industry was still turning out the models of the 1950s – the Morris Oxford, the Fiat 1100 and the Triumph Herald.

Some foreign investment took place in the commercial vehicle sector. British Leyland had a 52 per cent interest in Ashok Leyland and Daimler-Benz an 11.5 per cent holding in Tata Engineering (Telco) as well as a 26 per cent share in Baja-Tempo. There were also some joint ventures involving foreign firms and domestic suppliers of components as well as a larger number of purely technical agreements. The government considered a foreign equity holding of more than 40 per cent as undesirable and was very critical of attempts to restrict markets and the use of know-how. The terms it allowed under technical agreements were not generous, for royalty payments did not usually exceed five per cent and even then were subject to taxation at the rate of 50 per cent. In the early 1970s, most new agreements were for five years and were not usually renewable. Doubts were expressed by observers as to the profitability for foreign companies in such agreements and there was said to be a danger that they would only be willing to offer technology already obsolete.[39]

Still, the government had succeeded in bringing an Indian-owned and controlled motor industry into existence and had avoided costly foreign collaboration in the manufacture of private cars, which it regarded as luxury items. On the other hand the growth of the industry as a whole remained slow despite the vast potential for motor vehicles. The Indian producers appeared unable to design and develop new products or create their own technology. Old-fashioned models and a stagnating technology largely ruled out exports and, although the home market was reserved for local manufacturers, only a tiny proportion of India's huge population could afford car ownership at half the prices demanded by the small-scale, high cost producers.

Assembly

There were 81 countries assembling motor vehicles from ckd or semi-knocked-down imports in 1973, usually with some degree of local content. MNEs had subsidiaries or affiliates in almost half of them. The remainder of the assembly operations were carried out by local agents under licence from the overseas manufacturer. All the investment in assembly facilities, domestic as well as foreign, was induced by tariffs or other measures discriminating against built-up vehicle imports.

As would be expected, the foreign direct investment tended to take place in the larger markets, especially where governments had the establishment of a national motor industry in view, as in South Africa, Venezuela or Portugal. The American firms were well represented except for Africa where the European companies predominated, partly because of former colonial ties. Noteworthy was the sparsity of foreign investment in assembly facilities by the Japanese firms, even in the Asia-Pacific area. Two of the assembly countries call for further comment.

South Africa, where the government introduced measures to encourage local manufacturing, provided a good example of oligopolistic competition. Most of the world's major producers crowded into a market barely large enough to support one medium-sized firm at a reasonably efficient level of output. They competed with 40 models which were committed to the goal of 66 per cent local content. Only 14 of these models had an annual output of more than 5,000 units.[40] South Africa also highlights the difficulty the MNE faces when it attempts to be a 'good citizen' in every country in which it operates. To abide by the laws, rules and social customs of that country is in effect to accept apartheid, and at the same time to be in dramatic conflict with the values and beliefs of most people in the home countries of the MNEs, as witnessed by the pressures on them in some nations to disinvest in South Africa.

Chile, with the election of President Allende in 1970, provided an interesting example of what a Latin American socialist government's policies might be regarding a national motor industry, and how the MNEs might react. It was never a question of 'going it alone' but of how the industry was to be organised and the terms under which foreign participation could be obtained. The plan envisaged foreign firms forming joint enterprises with the state corporation, CORFO, with the latter holding a majority share. The maximum rate of repatriation allowed would be 12 per cent of capital and resources. Production was to be standardised and restricted to three models — a small car, medium

car, and a truck and bus chassis. Six MNEs participated in the bidding
– British Leyland, Citroen, Fiat, Peugeot, Renault, Volvo – as well as
Pegaso from Spain and the Yugoslav firm of Fap-Famos. The French
companies and Pegaso were successful, but the military coup of September 1973 put an end to the developments initiated by the Allende
regime.

Summary and Conclusions

Just as in the interwar period, the pattern of foreign investment in the
motor industry up to the end of 1973 reflected the policies of national
governments on trade and investment. When there was free trade,
foreign markets were supplied by exports. Within the EEC there was
some tendency for intra-European takeovers to occur as part of the
concentration taking place in the industry, but these were discouraged
by governments seeking to preserve nationally-owned firms. Where
there were barriers to trade, foreign investment to retain markets considered important by the manufacturers tended to take place, unless
blocked as was the case in India and Japan. Ironically it was the state,
that most national of institutions, that fostered the growth of that
uniquely international organisation, the MNE.

The new manufacturing countries sought foreign investment to save
foreign exchange, increase employment and stimulate economic
growth. In varying degrees their governments tried to ensure that at
least part of the industry would be nationally-owned and controlled,
but the MNEs ended up dominating the industries of which they were
a part. This was as predicted in the theory of foreign direct investment.
But it did not necessarily mean 100 per cent ownership. Unlike Ford
and General Motors who, as a matter of policy normally insisted on
having wholly-owned subsidiaries, the new MNEs were quite willing to
enter joint ventures with local partners, even at times in a minority
capacity. However, as these enterprises grew in size and in capital
requirements, there was a strong tendency for the share of the foreign
partner to increase.

But if the superior knowledge and resources of the MNEs resulted in
the competitive elimination of indigenous firms, the survivors were left
with no major advantages over each other and plenty of staying power.
They shared a protected national market which was too small for any
one of them to achieve the economies of scale essential for efficiency
and international competitiveness. Oligopolistic competition between

the relatively few survivors, with its proliferation of models and emphasis on advertising and selling expenditure, further aggravated the situation in these high-cost industries.

Within each major national market, the MNE subsidiary remained
more or less self-sufficient. Nevertheless, some integration of MNE networks was beginning to take place under various pressures. With the
heightened competition in free-trade EEC, the American companies,
particularly Ford, started to reorganise and link up their European
manufacturing operations. Under the export incentives and requirements latterly adopted by developing countries, MNEs sought sales
outlets elsewhere within their individual networks. This trend towards
integration was greatly heightened by the oil crisis of 1974 and the
first serious fall in production the world industry had suffered since
the second world war. It was a development which spelt the end of
purely national motor industries for most countries if not all.

Notes

1. Frederic G. Donner, *The World-wide Industrial Enterprise* (McGraw-Hill,
New York, 1967), p. 27.

2. Figures in this paragraph taken from H.K. Heider, *International Operations
and Growth of the Firm: A Study of the Experience of General Motors, Ford
and Chrysler*, unpublished doctoral dissertation (Cornell University, 1975).

3. *Fortune*, November 1965, p. 105.

4. Lawrence J. White, *The Automobile Industry Since 1945* (Harvard
University Press, Cambridge, Mass., 1971), pp. 62-4.

5. Lawrence J. White, 'The American Automobile Industry and the Small
Car 1945-1970', *Journal of Industrial Economics* (April 1972), pp. 179-92.

6. Ibid., p. 186.

7. Heider, *International Operations and Growth of the Firm*, p. 51.

8. Thomas A. Murphy, Vice Chairman, General Motors Corporation, *The
Economic Impact of the Multinational Corporation*, Statement presented to the
Senate Committee on Finance, Washington, DC (27 February 1973), chart 7, p. 8.

9. Raymond Vernon, 'Future of the Multinational Enterprise' in Charles P.
Kindleberger (ed.), *The International Corporation*, (MIT Press, Cambridge, Mass.
and London, 1970), p. 382.

10. *Business Week*, 'Why Fiat-Citroen Called It Quits' (30 June 1973), p. 20.

11. *Business Week*, 'GM Shakes Europe's Auto Makers' (30 January 1965),
p. 130.

12. Y.S. Hu, *The Impact of US Investment in Europe. A Case Study of the
Automotive and Computer Industries* (Praeger, New York, 1973), p. 173.

13. J. Wilner Sundelson, 'US Automotive Investments Abroad' in Kindleberger
(ed.), *The International Corporation*, p. 260.

14. Until 1980 the SMMT classified these vehicles under assembly, in contrast
to the US Motor Vehicle Manufacturers Association which listed the Ford
vehicles as being manufactured in Belgium in *World Motor Vehicles Data*.

15. William Chandler Duncan, *US-Japan Automobile Diplomacy* (Ballinger
Publishing Co, Cambridge, Mass., 1973), p. 32.

16. Ibid., p. 72.

17. US Department of Commerce, Bureau of International Commerce, 'The Rationalisation of the Japanese Motor Vehicle Industry' in *Japan: The Government Business Relationship* (US Government Printing Office, Washington DC, 1972), p. 115.

18. Duncan, *US-Japan Automobile Diplomacy*, p. 73.

19. Ibid., pp. 48-9.

20. Ibid., p. 48.

21. Ibid., p. 50.

22. Sir Lawrence Hartnett, *Big Wheels and Little Wheels* (Gold Star Publications (Austr) Pty Ltd, 2nd edn, 1973), p. 183.

23. Donner, *The World-wide Industrial Enterprise*, p. 54.

24. Hartnett, *Big Wheels and Little Wheels*, p. 192.

25. White, *The Automobile Industry Since 1945*, p. 179.

26. Peter Stubbs, *The Australian Motor Industry* (published by Cheshire Publishing Pty Ltd, Melbourne for the Institute of Applied Economic and Social Research, University of Melbourne, 1972), p. 76.

27. M. Wilkins and F.E. Hill, *American Business Abroad: Ford on Six Continents* (Wayne State University Press, Detroit, 1964), p. 414.

28. Ibid., p. 417.

29. Donner, *The World-wide Industrial Enterprise*, pp. 64-7.

30. *The Economist* (20 July 1963), p. 288.

31. Rhys Owen Jenkins, *Dependent Industrialisation in Latin America, The Automotive Industry in Argentina, Chile, and Mexico* (Praeger, New York, 1977), pp. 167-8.

32. Ibid., p. 50.

33. Richard E. Caves, 'International Corporations: The Industrial Economics of Foreign Investment', *Economica* (February 1971), pp. 15-16.

34. Jack Baranson, *Automotive Industries in Developing Countries*, World Bank Staff Occasional Papers Number Eight (1969), p. 35.

35. Donner, *World-wide Industrial Enterprise*, p. 66.

36. J.W. Sundelson, 'U.S. Automotive Investments Abroad' in Kindleberger (ed.), *The International Corporation*, p. 245.

37. Jenkins, *Dependent Industrialisation in Latin America*, pp. 179-80.

38. Ibid., p. 181.

39. Economist Intelligence Unit, *Motor Business*, no. 82 (Summer 1975), p. 44.

40. Ibid., no. 73, p. 37.

8 RECESSION AND RECOVERY

Following the oil crisis in the second half of 1973 and the subsequent steep rise in oil prices, the world motor industry suffered its first real setback since the war. By 1975 total output had declined 15 per cent from the peak level of 37.9m vehicles in 1973 and several major companies found themselves in serious financial difficulties. But recovery for the industry as a whole came more rapidly than many observers anticipated. Most of the ground lost was recouped in 1976 and output continued to rise to reach a new peak of 41.4m units in 1978, some nine per cent higher than the 1973 level.

In the meantime, the US government reached decisions on fuel economy which were to have a profound effect on future developments. By 1980 the cars produced annually by each American manufacturer were required to have an average fuel consumption of at least 20 miles per gallon, and by 1985 at least 27.5 mpg (33 per Imperial gallon). Only by making the bulk of American cars very like most European and Japanese models could this requirement be met. The stage was set for the appearance of 'world cars'.

The necessity in America of developing and tooling up for the production of much smaller cars, the recovery in demand and the expectation of continued, if moderate, growth in demand, led to renewed investment, particularly toward the end of the 1970s. The location of that investment is of interest.

The Pattern of Investment

Two-way Traffic

The three largest American car companies now have major investments in Japan. Why are there no similar Japanese investments in the US? (Henry Ford II, 1979)[1]

If they (the Japanese) are going to be as big a factor in the market as they have been, then I think that it is high time they did build plants and bring some employment opportunities here. (Thomas Murphy, Chairman, General Motors, 1980)[2]

As discussed in the previous chapter, American investment in the

Japanese motor industry took place in the early 1970s after much dip-lomatic pressure on the Japanese government to permit it. It was then that Chrysler secured a 15 per cent stake in Mitsubishi Motors, and General Motors a 34 per cent share in Isuzu. Talks on a joint venture between Ford and Toyo Kogyo in 1972 broke down because of 'un-acceptable' demands by Ford for effective control, according to the Japanese company. However, the two firms co-operated together in various ways with Ford marketing the Toyo Kogyo Courier pick-up truck in the US. In July 1979 an agreement was concluded which gave Ford a 25 per cent share in Toyo Kogyo.

Having had such difficulty in getting a relatively small ownership stake in the Japanese industry, it is somewhat surprising to find the American producers not only welcoming Japanese investment but even pleading with the Japanese companies to manufacture in America. In this the US firms were joined by Mr Douglas Fraser of the United Auto Workers Union who threatened to seek protectionist controls against imports if such investment was not forthcoming. Faced with a choice between a very high and perhaps still rising level of Japanese imports or Japanese investment, American management and workers clearly preferred the latter.

From 1974 onwards, imports as a proportion of US car sales aver-aged some 15 per cent a year until 1979 when they soared to almost 22 per cent of the market. The Japanese companies supplied 70 per cent of those imports at a cost to the American economy of almost $8bn, which represented one-third of the US trade deficit with all countries. And it represented the loss of tens of thousands of jobs in the American motor industry. If protection was ruled out then the only solution to the excessive drain of dollars and jobs seemed to be the establishment of Japanese plants in the US producing cars with a high local content.

The Japanese firms resisted the mounting pressure on them to produce in America and, from a purely economic standpoint, their reluctance to invest in the US is understandable. They had demon-strated that it is possible, given free trade, to capture and retain an appreciable share in the world's largest car market, relying solely on exports. Clearly the greater flexibility argument for local manufacture did not impress them, nor did they feel that they had to produce in a major market in order to be better able to adapt their products to local tastes and conditions. And they certainly did not need to see the Industry Study for the US general Accounting Office, made in the summer of 1979 when $1 =¥ 217, to know that they could land a typical small car (sub-compact) in the US for $500 per unit less than Ford or General Motors could sell an equivalent car to dealers.[3] The subsequent fall in the value of the yen against the dollar increased the advantage by another 10 to 15 per cent. Why throw away the cost advantage, spend some $500m to start producing in an alien environment at a time when the American companies would be turning out a new generation of small cars, and on a massive scale?

Nevertheless, following intense US government pressure on Tokyo to cut car exports and undertake instead direct investment in the American car industry, Honda announced in January 1980 its decision to build a car assembly plant on a site next to its motor cycle factory near Columbus, Ohio. Honda, a late entrant into the car industry and much smaller than Toyota and Nissan, was relying mainly on exports for expansion. As almost all of its exports went to the US, it would be the hardest hit if the American government were to impose import restrictions. Even so, it was a bold decision, reflecting the aggressive strategy of a company striving to become a major producer by world standards. The plant was to cost an estimated $200m and was due for completion in 1982. Its planned capacity, 10,000 cars per month, seemed small. Both Toyota and Nissan had concluded that American sales of a single model would have to reach 20,000 units a month before local assembly would be economic. This was in line with a study made by Renault which indicated 200,000 units a year as the break-even point for assembly in the US. And 200,000 units per annum was the initial capacity of Volkswagen's American plant, again all one model.

A fortnight after the Honda announcement, Nissan officials confirmed plans to go ahead with an assembly plant in America for small trucks. Capacity 10,000 units a month and operations would start on a ckd basis, with a gradual increase in locally-made parts as suppliers are found. This coincided with moves by the US Treasury to close a tariff loophole dating back to the so-called 'chicken war' between the US and the Common Market in the 1960s. America retaliated with a 25 per cent duty on truck imports which effectively put a stop to such imports from Europe, mainly Volkswagens. However the Japanese manufacturers found that by shipping their small trucks with the cab and truck back as separate parts that they could bring in the vehicles under the 4 per cent duty on parts, and could quickly and easily re-assemble them in the US. This enabled them to take over virtually all the American pick-up truck import market and a substantial share of the entire US market for these vehicles. Nissan's share was apparently large enough to justify production in the US. Light trucks, which are comparatively simple to make, could then serve as a base for eventually moving into car production if conditions warranted it. Toyota, also with an established US market for pick-up trucks, seems likely to adopt the same cautious approach to manufacturing in America, especially since this tariff loophole has recently been closed.

Unlike the Japanese firms, Volkswagen needed no encouragement or prodding from America to induce it to invest in the US – the purely economic pressures were compelling enough. By 1976, when the decision to establish an American assembly plant was taken, the gap between the wages of German and American car workers had closed and the dollar had fallen from DM3.60 in 1970 to DM2.50. The Rabbit (Golf) cost $500 more than the Ford Pinto, and total Volkswagen sales in the US had fallen by more than 50 per cent from the 1970 peak of 583,000, raising the possibility of a break-up of the distribution network with dealers deserting to Japanese firms. It was clear to the German trade unions and politicians who had opposed Volkswagen production in America that the US market could no longer be retained with exports from high-cost Germany. It was the classic case of defensive investment to prevent the loss of a major export market and, it was hoped, would ensure a continued demand for German mechanical components for the Rabbit for some time ahead and also stimulate sales of other, more expensive, imported Volkswagen models.

The company considered, and rejected, some kind of joint venture with either Chrysler or the American Motor Corporation, using their facilities. It wanted to have complete control over production and quality standards. A plant in Pennsylvania was chosen, one which was originally intended for Chrysler but never completed. The planned output of cars, all one model, was 200,000 per annum and the total cost of the investment was reported to be $300m. Volkswagen raised more than $200m itself through European bond issues but also took about $40m at extremely low rates of interest from two local Pennsylvanian pension funds. The first Rabbit rolled off the US assembly line in April 1978, incorporating 25 per cent American content, including stamping, tubing and lights, plus of course painting and final assembly. It was said that this reduced the cost of the car by about $200 and, as the dollar continued to fall against the mark, the local content rose to 75 per cent by the end of 1979. With the success of the American-produced Rabbit, manufacture in the US of the engines and transmissions was felt to be inevitable within a few years.

The only other European car producer to invest in the American industry was Renault.[4] Unsuccessful in capturing a significant share of the US import market, it sought an American partner with an established dealer network and idle capacity. Protracted negotiations led to an agreement with the relatively small and financially weak American Motor Corporation (AMC). Under its terms Renault was to pay $100m for an eventual equity stake of 22.5 per cent and to provide another $50m as working capital. The Renault 5 and 18 models were to be distributed through the American company's 2,400 dealer network, and the AMC Jeep through the Renault network. Much more significant was the decision to assemble a wholly new Renault model in 1982 in the AMC plant at Kenosha, Wisconsin. Most of the main mechanical parts would come from France but the bodywork would be from American sources and somewhat different from the European version to suit tastes in the US. The French company clearly hoped that a manufacturing presence in America would stimulate sales to something above the 200,000 units a year its 1978 study concluded it would need to justify production in the US.

Unlike Volkswagen, the French decision to produce cars in America does not seem to have been prompted by relative costs or adverse changes in exchange rates. Renault's acquisition of a 20 per cent stake in Mack, an American producer of heavy trucks, indicates that built-up trucks could be shipped from France and be competitive in the US market. Under the arrangement Mack agreed to distribute Renault's 9 to 15 ton trucks through its North American outlets under the 'Mack' badge. Presumably, if future currency changes created problems, the way would be open to assemble the trucks in America with appreciable local content. Commenting on the deal the Chairman of Renault Vehicules Industriels (RVI) said that it meant the output of medium-weight trucks would double 'and that will keep our prices competitive. We won't make a profit at first on the trucks sold in the US but we shall fill the French plant, and the profit on European sales will rise.'[5]

Certainly the German producers of trucks had no choice if they wanted to compete in America. Daimler-Benz, through its subsidiary Mercedes-Benz of North America, began construction in 1979 of an assembly plant in Virginia costing $6.6m. It was to have an initial capacity of 6,000 medium-duty Mercedes trucks, with the major components being supplied by the company's Brazilian subsidiary, by US firms and by its German plants. According to Daimler-Benz, the project would contribute to the capacity utilisation of its domestic plants in the future, and the planned use of US parts would facilitate adapting the trucks to the requirements of the American market and would offer advantages with regard to service and parts stocking. Prior to this development, Daimler-Benz had acquired Euclid Inc. at Cleveland, Ohio in 1977 from the White Motor Corporation, the weakest of the American heavy-truck-producing companies. Euclid, which manufactures special, extra-heavy-duty vehicles, had sales of US $212m in 1978.

Volkswagen plans to extend the capacity of its US plant from 800 a day to 1,200 a day by 1981. It has recently decided on a second assembly plant in America with an initial output of 800 cars a day and there is talk of establishing an engine plant in the US to supply it. But even if, as seems likely, other foreign companies invest in productive capacity in America, that investment will be far outweighed by the investment of US firms in Europe.

Ford, for example, spent over $800m mainly in Spain, and to a lesser extent in West Germany and the UK, on the Fiesta project in the mid-1970s. In 1979 General Motors announced plans to spend $2bn to expand its car capacity in Europe by 300,000 units. The Ford company had earlier, in 1978, decided on a £400m capital investment programme in the UK as part of a new light car project, the Erica, now named the Escort. This included a new £180m engine factory near Cardiff with an annual output of 500,000 units. Nor was high-cost Germany left out. General Motors' Opel announced it would spend £1,230m over the period 1977 to 1982 and Ford-Werke £735m for the same six years.

Chrysler, of course, was busy disinvesting in Europe towards the end of the 1970s, but one other American vehicle producer moved across the Atlantic to establish a manufacturing presence – International Harvester, maker of agricultural equipment, tractors and heavy trucks. Already holding a one-third share in DAF trucks in the Netherlands, in 1974 it purchased the British firm of Seddon-Atkinson, also a producer of heavy trucks. Early in 1980 International Harvester concluded an agreement with the Spanish government which gave it a 35 per cent interest in ENASA, the Spanish-owned and controlled truck company. The remaining 65 per cent will be held by INI, the state holding company. The American company is to provide management, technical services and technology immediately as well as to link ENASA with its distribution network. More importantly, International Harvester has agreed to build a $100m engine plant in Madrid through a new company in which it will own 65 per cent and INI 35 per cent of the shares. The plant will have a capacity of 100,000 units and roughly 80 per cent of this production will be geared to export. The move confirms International Harvester's intention to become a major contender in the European commercial vehicle market in the 1980s. It now seems likely that another American truck producer, the Pacific Car and Foundry Company (PACCAR), maker of heavy vehicles, will establish itself in Europe by buying the English firm of Foden, now in receivership.

Summing up, for the first time in the history of the motor industry, the completely asymmetrical pattern of investment between America and the rest of the world was effectively broken. The flows are still heavily weighted in favour of the foreign investment of the US multi-nationals, but several European and Japanese producers now have an ownership stake in the American industry and the foreign equity is likely to grow in future. Renault has invested a further $200m in American Motors, increasing its share to 46 per cent. Of particular interest are the discussions now going on between Toyota and Ford (initiated by Toyota) regarding a joint venture to produce cars in the US.

Other Foreign Investment

There has been no two-way traffic between Europe and Japan, on the contrary, foreign direct investment between these areas has been practically non-existent. The European manufacturers have shown no interest in investing in the Japanese industry on the one hand, and on the other they have opposed direct investment in Europe by Japanese producers. Mitsubishi Motors, for example, was unable to secure government approval to set up a truck assembly plant in the UK. After two years of negotiations with the Department of Industry it abandoned its plans at the end of 1978. It was said that no agreement could be reached on the extent of the locally manufactured content or on the proportion of output to be exported. Relevant also was the existence of an agreement between the British and Japanese governments that no commercial vehicles above 3½ tonnes would be imported into the UK, so that this was not a case of foreign investment replacing imports.

In any event, until recently, Toyota's 27 per cent holding in a small firm in Portugal represented the sole inter-area investment. There are now strong indications, however, that Japanese firms intend to establish themselves in Europe. In January 1980 Nissan purchased Massey-Ferguson's 36 per cent share of Motor Iberica, Spain's largest agricultural machinery manufacturer and also a maker of light industrial vehicles. The deal provided Nissan with the opportunity to produce its own trucks for the European market after Spain joins the EEC. Eventually it could serve as a base for producing passenger cars, in which case Nissan would in all likelihood seek a majority interest. Nissan has also entered a joint venture with Alfa Romeo to produce cars in Italy. It appears highly likely that Toyota will link with SEAT in Spain and eventually replace Fiat as the foreign partner.

Outside the main producing areas of North America, Europe and Japan, almost all the foreign direct investment went toward the expansion and modernisation of capacity in countries with already existing manufacturing or assembly facilities. With the exception of South Korea (discussed in Chapter 12), no new national motor industries were established in the 1970s. Of major importance was Fiat's $650m investment in a car factory and foundry in Brazil which came into operation at the end of 1976. The Italian company had previously left the Brazilian market alone under the terms of a 1953 agreement with Volkswagen which allocated Argentina to Fiat and Brazil to Volkswagen. (The German firm subsequently established itself in Argentina in 1979 with the purchase of Chrysler-Argentina.) The Brazilian state of Minas Gerais has a 42 per cent equity interest in the Fiat operation and it provided a package of incentives that included low-cost land and a 25.6 per cent rebate on the state sales tax for up to five years. By 1978 Fiat had captured 11 per cent of the Brazilian car market.

Another newcomer to Brazil was Volvo, who established a $40m plant with an annual capacity of 6,000 trucks and buses which commenced production in 1979. Volvo had assembled trucks locally with some success in the 1950s but had to withdraw when the government insisted that 95 per cent of the components be manufactured in Brazil. That ceiling has now been reduced to 72 per cent provided that 25 per cent of production is exported. This has enabled Volvo to gain the support of its unions for the investment.

Sizable foreign investments are now being made in Mexico, partly because of booming domestic sales and partly as a consequence of the 1977 government decree which requires car producers to balance imports with exports by 1982. Investment plans to increase capacity include $400m by General Motors, $132m by Volkswagen, $44m by Ford and an undisclosed amount by Renault.

Even Argentina, after years of political instability and economic stagnation, has begun to attract new investment in its motor industry despite General Motors decision to liquidate its plants at the end of 1978 after 53 years of car production there. In 1979 Ford revealed plans to consolidate its dominance of the car and truck market in Argentina by spending $76m over the following two years in retooling and expanding production. Daimler-Benz in the same year embarked on a $50m, four-year programme to modernise and expand its truck facilities. Volkswagen is to put $50m into improving the plants it acquired with the purchase of Chrysler Fevre Argentina.

The complete withdrawal of Chrysler from South America in 1979 was, of course, a major event in the competitive struggle of the MNEs in that part of the world. Volkswagen's position was appreciably strengthened by its acquisition of Chrysler's 48 per cent interest in its Argentina subsidiary for $50m and Chrysler's 67 per cent holding in Chrysler-Brazil. No price was officially stated for the latter but $50m was being widely quoted in Brazil. It was expected that Volkswagen would eventually gain full control of Chrysler-Argentina since the other shareholders were mainly dealers and suppliers of the subsidiary who have indicated that they would be willing to sell. General Motors' purchase of Chrysler's wholly-owned subsidiary in Venezuela and the company's 77.4 per cent interest in Chrysler-Colombia, at an undisclosed price, will provide it with much-needed capacity in Venezuela and a significant market share in Colombia where it was not represented before. On balance, the majority share of the European producers in Latin America has been further increased since 1973.

Across the Pacific in Australia, the major development was the move into local manufacture of the major Japanese companies. Having captured 40 per cent of the market with exports, despite import duties of 45 per cent, they subsequently found themselves faced with import quotas designed by the government to preserve roughly 80 per cent of the Australian market for local producers. Nissan and Toyota decided to register under the government's manufacturing programme which required each to achieve by 1980 an average of 85 per cent local content in the vehicles they sold in Australia. Given government approval, both built engine plants and other manufacturing facilities. Mitsubishi Motors, whose cars were selling well through Chrysler-Australia's dealer network, bought a 30 per cent share in the Chrysler subsidiary. Subsequently the American interest was bought out and the name changed to Mitsubishi Motors Australia Ltd. Of major importance too was General Motors' decision in 1979 to go ahead with its proposal to build a 'world class' plant for the production of 4-cylinder engines. The factory was to cost $210m and produce some 240,000 engines a year, two-thirds of which would be exported. Lastly, after operating at a loss in Australia for a number of years, British Leyland withdrew as a manufacturer in 1974.

Just as there have been no new national automotive manufacturing industries established since 1973, other than in South Korea, so too there have been few additions to the world MNE assembly plant 'map' since that date. Of these the most important is Nigeria. Assembly is merely the first phase in the government's programme to establish a domestic vehicle manufacturing industry through joint ventures with foreign MNEs. The aim is to take the content of Nigerian components as close as possible to 100 per cent by 1990. Negotiations with over 20 interested MNEs ended in the selection by the government of three firms to assemble cars and four to assemble trucks. The plants were to be dispersed throughout the country so as to spread employment and industrialisation as widely as possible. Peugeot-Citroen and Volkswagen now operate car assembly plants each producing about 24,000 units a year from imported kits. Nissan, given approval for a plant at Llorin right in the centre of the country has not proceeded with the project as yet. The four truck companies selected were Leyland Vehicles (BL's truck and bus divisions), Daimler-Benz, Fiat and Steyr-Daimler-Puch. In addition, a Unilever affiliate, UAC, established in 1959 with a 60 per cent Nigerian interest, assembles Bedford trucks from Vauxhall in England.

Each of the foreign MNEs who established companies in Nigeria under the government's scheme was limited to a 40 per cent share, with the government taking 35 per cent and other Nigerian interests the remainder. Aside from the promise of tariff protection, no other inducements to encourage foreign investment were publicised. It may be that a large, oil-rich developing country, with a population unofficially estimated at 80 million to 100 million people was inducement enough, even on a joint venture basis.

In the Far East the main development was further investment by some MNEs in existing subsidiaries to provide manufacturing facilities for producing engines and other components primarily for export. The most spectacular was the new car body stamping plant built by Ford in the Philippines which commenced production in 1976. Costing $33.4m the plant has a capacity of 70,000 bodies a year. Using sheet metal imported from Japan, body parts were made for the Cortina model and about 70 per cent exported in order of quantity to Ford plants in Australia, England, New Zealand, Taiwan and Singapore. Related to this venture was the expansion of engine capacity in Ford-Lio Ho in Taiwan from 35,000 units to 70,000 units annually, a substantial proportion for export to Australia and the Philippines. A transmission plant in New Zealand formed another link in what the Ford company termed 'complementation'. There were signs that General Motors was moving in the same direction. Its engine plant in South Korea had a capacity twice that of its assembly facilities which catered solely to the domestic market.

This brief survey of MNE investment in host countries is, of course, far from complete. There was more investment by the firms mentioned and it is in the nature of MNE competition that investment in any particular market tends to be matched sooner or later in that market by rivals. After recovery from the oil crisis and its aftermath, it seems likely that the level of foreign investment by MNEs was comparable with the average for the period up to 1973. But how did it compare with investment by MNEs in their own home countries?

Home vs Foreign Investment

A few automotive MNEs show the allocation of capital expenditure between domestic and foreign members of the group in their annual reports. Ford is unique in providing a breakdown by geographic areas.

Table 8.1: Ford Motor Company Capital Expenditure by
Geographical Regions, 1977-1978 ($ Million)

	1978	1977
US	1,135	784
Canada	71	86
Europe	269	152
Latin America*	58	41
Asia-Pacific	39	27
Total	1,572	1,090

* Includes Mexico.
Source: Ford Motor Company, *Annual Report*, 1978.

Somewhat over 70 per cent of capital expenditure was made in the US in both years. The total for North America was 76 per cent in 1978 and 80 per cent in 1977. Since the early 1970s, Ford operations outside North America have accounted for about 25 per cent to 30 per cent of the company's total revenues and about the same share of capital expenditures. Looking to the future, it seems highly probable that capital expenditures at home will rise in relation to those made abroad as a result of the massive investments required to meet the stringent US government fuel economy, emissions and safety regulations. 'For Ford North American products, the investment for tools, facilities, engineering and launch is estimated at $20 billion for the years 1978 through 1985, compared with $6 billion in the prior eight years. Inflation accounts for more than $6 billion of this increase and $8 billion reflects spending primarily related to new government regulations.'

It seems fair to say that had there been no new regulations to meet, much of these heavy capital expenditures would have had to be made anyway in order to compete effectively against the growing tide of imports of smaller, cheaper-to-run Japanese and European cars. What is interesting is that in a mature industry, at a time when standardised 'world cars' could be produced almost anywhere, Ford chose to supply the American market from US plants where labour costs were still relatively high compared to many possible alternative locations. Such a decision is not easy to reconcile with the product cycle theory.

The same conclusion applies even more so to General Motors. That company's world-wide capital expenditures in 1978 amounted to $2,737.8 million an increase of 46 per cent over 1977. This provided for capacity expansion, modernisation, plant replacements and new-model programmes. Of these expenditures, approximately 86 per cent were made in the US, three per cent in Canada and 11 per cent overseas. General Motors expected in 1978 that annual capital expenditures would be in excess of $5 billion (including special tools) in 1979 and beyond. There seems little doubt that the great bulk of this will be spent in the US.

Of the European companies, Vokswagen has made the largest overseas investments. In 1978, capital expenditures at home represented 68.6 per cent of the total, with over half the foreign investment going to Volkswagen-US. But the domestic share has varied considerably over the past eight years from a high of 79.4 per cent in 1971 to a low of 57.1 per cent in 1977, with no real trend in evidence. The annual average is 65.2 per cent which makes Volkswagen more multinational (in this respect) than Ford. Nevertheless, with almost two-thirds of capital expenditure being made at home, it is clear that high-labour-cost German plants will continue to be responsible for the European market and an appreciable level of exports as well. Volkswagen's German rival, Daimler-Benz, spent DM1.5 billion world-wide in 1978 on plant and equipment, 80 per cent at home. The proportion for Fiat's automotive activities is probably around that figure, while for the remaining MNEs in Europe and elsewhere it would be considerably more.

Regional Integration and International Sourcing

The automobile industry will become a continental industry. South

America is independent, and Africa and Asia will become independent entities. There will be some links in know-how and technology for some time. But each area will be more or less self-sufficient. (Umberto Agnelli, Vice-President, Fiat, 1978)[6]

The multinational sourcing of some parts and components will become standard operating procedure for any automobile producer that elects to manufacture on a global scale. (Donald Petersen, Executive Vice-President, Ford-US, 1979)[7]

Regional Integration

The United States-Canada Automotive Agreement of 1965 (referred to in the previous chapter) represented the first major move to integrate national motor vehicle industries on a regional basis. The subsequent rationalisation of production between the two countries and the massive increase in trade in automotive products across the border has meant, in effect, that the US motor industry and the Canadian motor industry have become the North American motor industry.

In Western Europe, the gradual freeing of trade in manufactures within the EEC, which by 1973 included Britain and seemed likely to admit Spain and Portugal by the mid-1980s, not only made integration possible but also inevitable as competition intensified in the formerly protected national markets of the producing countries. For the American MNEs, with manufacturing subsidiaries already established in two or more European countries, integration would enable them to standardise the model range and allocate vehicle and component production between affiliates to give them economies of scale comparable to their major European competitors.

Ford-US, with the setting up of Ford of Europe in 1967, was the first MNE to move toward the co-ordination of development, production and marketing on a European basis. The Ford Escort, built to a common design in Britain and West Germany, marked the start of product rationalisation which has now been extended throughout the entire model range. Product and production rationalisation was carried to its logical conclusion with the first Ford front-wheel drive 'mini' — the Fiesta. It was conceived, designed and engineered by joint teams seconded from Ford's UK and German companies. Production of major components was centralised on one spot in Ford plants in four countries, for example, engine blocks in the UK at Dagenham, carburettors in Northern Ireland, while the machining of the engines was to be done at the new Spanish factory. Final assembly was to be carried out in

Spain, Germany and the UK. Only a European car and integrated production could hope to achieve the planned output of 500,000 units a
year needed to cover the estimated £400m cost of the project and
return a profit. Truck development and manufacturing continues to be
concentrated in the UK, although heavy trucks are also assembled in
Amsterdam, largely from British-made components.

General Motors continued to make separate car models in its European subsidiaries in Germany (Opel) and in the UK (Vauxhall) for
longer than Ford but integration, when it came, was even more drastic.
In 1979 Opel was made responsible for car development and Vauxhall,
which produced only 75,000 cars the preceding year, would in future
import German models, some built-up and some for assembly in Britain
with varying degrees of locally-manufactured content. All will be
sold under the Vauxhall badge but the export of cars from the UK to
the eleven main Continental countries will cease in 1981. At the same
time Bedford, Vauxhall's subsidiary, was given responsibility for truck
development so that Britain remains the manufacturing base for
General Motors' commercial vehicle production in Europe. Like Ford,
General Motors has established a major components factory in France.
General Motors, Strasbourg, manufactures automatic transmissions,
torque converters and carburettors for other General Motors' companies. It also has three other plants in France making automotive
components, batteries and radiator heater components. And, of course,
the proposed Spanish assembly and components plants as well as the
engine plants in Austria will be integrated into the company's European
network.

Chrysler's integration of its French, British and Spanish subsidiaries
was very limited. Some product rationalisation came with the Chrysler
180, designed in the UK but produced in the other affiliates as well.
Chrysler-UK also designed the Alpine which was introduced in France
and subsequently assembled in Britain. With the takeover of Chrysler's
European operations, in 1978 Peugeot-Citroen faced the monumental
task of doing what Chrysler-US admitted it never could afford to do.
Very much at stake is the role Chrysler-UK will play in an integrated
French MNE.

The European producers were handicapped in their response to these
moves by the American companies. Having no manufacturing facilities
outside their home countries, the only road to further European integration in the 1970s lay in transnational mergers. But these proved
difficult to arrange, largely because of opposition from governments
anxious to preserve 'national' motor industries. A few such mergers

occurred but for the most part the need to integrate, felt most strongly by the smaller manufacturers, was met by pooling resources in various kinds of co-operation agreements.

Fiat, the most international-minded of the European manufacturers which had failed in its attempt to integrate Citroen into its Italian operations, was determined to establish itself as a major force in the European commercial vehicle industry. In 1975 it formed a holding company, Industrial Vehicles Corporation (IVECO) which brought together its commercial vehicle interests in Italy and France (UNIC) with the truck subsidiary of the West German firm of Klockmer-Humbolt-Deutz (KHD). The latter held 20 per cent of the equity and Fiat 80 per cent. Subsequently, it was announced that Fiat would assume complete control but it has recently refused to take 100 per cent of IVECO.

Volvo's attempt to integrate with the Dutch car manufacturer DAF ran into financial difficulties in the second half of the 1970s (discussed in Chapter 11). Volvo was also concerned in the only other equity link between European manufacturers in this period. The Volvo Car Corporation was formed in January 1980 as a separate operating company from Volvo's truck and other activities and a deal made with Renault in which the French company was eventually to acquire a 20 per cent share in Volvo Car for around £36m. The intention is to combine and share the production of as many components as possible for Renault and Volvo models in the same market sector.

One method which avoided transnational mergers, but which offered some of the benefits of integration, was joint participation in a new company set up for a particular purpose. Among them was the Société Franco-Swedoise formed by Peugeot, Volvo and Renault in 1974 to share the output of a new 2.7 litre engine to be manufactured at Douvin in northern France by the Société Française de Mecanique (a jointly-owned subsidiary of Peugeot-Citroen and Renault). Each of the three companies was expected to take between 30,000 and 50,000 engines a year for its own use. None could have contemplated an individual plant for such small numbers. In 1978 Daimler-Benz and Steyr-Daimler-Puch established a joint subsidiary in Graz, Austria to make an up-market cross-country vehicle with an initial capacity of 25,000 units, probably rising to 50,000. The following year Fiat and Peugeot-Citroen became equal partners in an Italian state-aided scheme to build a new light van plant in southern Italy to cost £153m. The new company, Société Europeene des Vehicules Legers, will use component parts from the parent companies, arranged to secure a satisfactory balance. Also in 1979 the Société Franco-Italienne des Moteurs was formed to make diesel engines in another plant in southern Italy in which Fiat had a 52.5 per cent share, Renault 35 per cent and Alfa Romeo 14.5 per cent.

Of particular interest was the announcement in February 1980 that Fiat and Peugeot-Citroen have signed a protocol agreement to merge their car operations in Argentina. In 1979 Peugeot-Citroen produced 26,000 cars there and Fiat 42,000 and their combined output was 35 per cent of the market. The plan is to set up an equally-owned joint company to embrace their manufacturing and sales operations in Argentina. Production will be rationalised, especially for components, and sales activities unified, although their respective marques will be kept separate. The arrangement could be the forerunner of similar deals between European companies in Latin America and perhaps elsewhere overseas.

The latest joint-venture deal, recently approved by the Italian government, does not reflect the integration of European production facilities but is highly significant as being the first link of its kind between a European and a Japanese manufacturer, the partners being Alfa Romeo and Nissan. The state-owned Italian company, with an annual output of some 220,000 cars, had been actively seeking a partner for a year or more. 'This reflected' said its Chairman, 'the company's need to increase the group's production volumes' to meet the challenge of rival car manufacturers.[8] The deal had the approval of the main Italian engineering unions and the Communist Party but was bitterly opposed by Fiat. It involves the establishment of a joint company with Alfa Romeo and Nissan controlling an equal share in its capital. The new company, entirely under the management of Alfa Romeo, is expected to build a plant for the production of a new car which will also be assembled at the Alfasud complex near Naples. Nissan is to supply the body parts and the Italian company the engine and mechanical components. Initial production is expected to be 60,000 cars a year based on the Nissan-Datsun 'Cherry' model.

A number of other co-operative agreements between producers have not involved equity links. Saab, for example, has been co-operating with Fiat's subsidiary Lancia since 1976. The Lancia Delta, introduced early in 1980, will be called the Saab-Lancia 600 in Nordic countries. In 1979 the two companies signed a contract for the future development of a range of cars for the mid-1980s. They will split development and construction costs but the end product will be two entirely different cars — one for Saab and one for Lancia — although they may have some common components. The main advantage of the agreement was said to

be sharing the massive burden of new car development estimated at
$357m to $476m.

Like Alfa Romeo, BL Cars was actively seeking a partner, or partners, during 1979. According to Mr Roy Horrocks, Managing Director,
the investment required to develop new cars and components was so
vast that more comprehensive co-operation and collaboration would
be inevitable for smaller manufacturers such as BL. As with Alfa
Romeo, the partner turned out to be a Japanese company. However,
the agreement did not include any financial links. Starting in the
summer of 1981, BL is to produce under licence a new car designed by
Honda. The main mechanical components and the body dies will be
supplied by Honda, the body pressings and other parts by BL. The car
can only be sold in the present EEC countries under the BL badge while
Honda will market its version everywhere else. BL will pay the Japanese
company a royalty of £250 for each car so that if sales reach the
80,000 units a year forecasted, it would mean annual royalties of £20m.

More European integration is clearly on the way as the motor industries of Spain and Portugal prepare for the expected entry of these
countries into the EEC in the mid-1980s. Without the economies of
scale that can be achieved by linking their Spanish production with
their other European operations, Fiat, Renault and Peugeot-Citroen
cannot hope to compete with Ford (and later General Motors) in an un-
protected Spanish market. For the French companies this will be relatively easy since it is simply a question of rationalising operations over
which they have majority control. For Fiat with a 36 per cent holding
in SEAT, a company looked upon as a 'national' producer, the situation
was more complicated.

The Spanish company had been set up in the 1950s with minority
participation by Fiat to produce a comprehensive range of cars for the
domestic market. When its competitors appeared in the 1960s and concentrated on specific sections of the market, SEAT's share fell drastically from 60 per cent to 33 per cent in 1978, and this led to excess
capacity and heavy losses. Moreover, exports had been restricted by the
Fiat-SEAT agreement of 1967, an unhappy compromise which allowed
the Spanish firm to use the Fiat overseas sales network but in effect
left it with the less attractive markets. While it would have been
possible for INI the state holding company to buy Fiat's share in SEAT,
since the latter was technologically dependent on the Italian group and
had no international sales network of its own, a 'national' solution was
rejected. The INI concluded that only a major reorganisation and
investment programme, coupled with full integration with Fiat, would

enable SEAT to survive. But of course, this would not have been acceptable to the Italian company without majority control. This was agreed with the understanding that Fiat's share would eventually increase to about 80 per cent. There was also agreement on a major reconstruction of SEAT involving an investment of $770m by 1982 and the concentration of production on two or three new Fiat models with a minimum daily output of 500 units.

Unexpectedly in June 1980, Fiat refused to take over the Spanish company. INI resumed the management of SEAT and faced a host of complicated problems. It subscribed to Fiat's defaulted share in the expansion so that the equity base became INI 48.3 per cent, Fiat 32.3 per cent, Spanish private banks 13.9 per cent and other Spanish share holders 5.5 per cent. The company is to continue to produce existing Fiat models during their life, including the new Panda. It exports at present roughly one-third of its production and one of the immediate problems is to work out an agreement on exports with Fiat. A separate technology and licencing agreement remains in force for another five years and under it Fiat currently earns $212m a year in royalties.

Significantly, the Spanish authorities see no future for SEAT as a Spanish-controlled company and want it to be fully integrated with another MNE. The field of potential buyers of Fiat's stake has narrowed to Toyota with whom negotiations are now taking place. After some 30 years with a minority interest in SEAT, the break leaves a sizable gap in Fiat's plans for European integration and will eventually reduce the world-wide production of the Italian company by some 400,000 units.

Portugal, which signed a free trade agreement with the EEC in 1972, has asked for a five year extension of restrictive quotas on imported vehicles and parts due to be abolished in January 1980, to guarantee the survival of its weak and very uncompetitive vehicle assembly industry. This was accepted by the EEC Council of Ministers in Luxembourg in November 1979 and has been referred to the EEC Commission for final approval. By 1985 the Portuguese government envisages that at least a dozen of its 20 vehicle assembly plants will close down and that output will be concentrated in technologically-advanced assembly and component units firmly integrated into the European production structure. Its final agreement with Renault, signed early in 1980, represented a most significant initial move in this direction. Under its terms Renault will have a 70 per cent stake in a £275m expansion programme, the largest foreign investment ever made in Portugal. Renault will increase its assembly of cars from 10,000 units to 80,000 units a year in a reconverted plant near Lisbon. Production of engines for the Renault 5 will be stepped up to include the manufacture of 220,000 units by 1987, mainly for export at another reconverted factory near Oporto which will also produce gearboxes and rear axles. A new foundry will be built and Renault's assembly plant at Granada altered to implement the manufacture of engines and components. Local content in the assembly plant will be increased from 20 per cent to 60 per cent, and to 80 per cent in engine production. Renault will be entitled to tax deductions available under existing legislation for priority investments and the agreement includes a number of generous incentives through which Renault is expected to increase its share of the Portuguese market from 10 per cent to more than 30 per cent. Other MNEs with subsidiaries in Portugal will have to negotiate similar agreements with the government if they wish to remain as serious contenders for the domestic market.

Another country on the fringe of Europe with a vehicle assembly industry which will be profoundly affected by free trade is the Irish Republic. When the latter joined the EEC the Commission found that the 1967 agreement with Britain limiting the number of built-up vehicles entering Ireland was against the principles of free trade and ruled that the restrictions had to end by 1985. Without a Portuguese-type plan for the industry, which would hardly be feasible with Ireland's relatively small population and geographical location, the country faces an almost certain phasing out of most if not all of its assembly operations by the late 1980s. Even with some savings on transport cost and lower labour costs, assembly on such a small scale is not economic. Of the MNEs concerned only Ford, which has been in Ireland since 1917 and is the largest producer, is specific in its intention to carry on.

Latin America. Unlike the formation of the EEC which resulted in free trade in manufactured products within the area and in the increasing integration of the European motor industry, the creation of the Latin American Free Trade Area has had little or no effect on the regional industry structure. The economic case for a regional motor industry with optimum-sized plants located in different countries serving the entire market was strong when contrasted with the alternative of a dozen or more fragmented, small-scale, high-cost 'national' industries, each producing for a limited domestic market. Moreover, the MNEs in general were firm supporters of trade liberalisation which would have enabled them to rationalise production and reduce the mounting investment costs of meeting rising local content requirements in each country. Against these arguments were the political objections to trade liberalisation and the latter proved to have far more influence over policy.

The formation of a common market or free trade area composed of a group of developed countries may well result in a rationalisation of industry on a regional basis which benefits all the members. But the adoption of free trade by a group of developing nations in various stages of industrialisation benefits the larger and relatively more advanced at the expense of the rest whose infant industries cannot meet the competition. For the Latin American automotive industry, free trade also raised the problem of disposing of the excess capacity brought into being by systems of national protection and said to be ten times what would be economically viable in the late 1960s.[9] To make matters more difficult, the parts and components section of the industry consisted, in proportions varying from country to country, of assemblers that had integrated vertically backwards, foreign parts and components firms and large numbers of indigenous companies, for the most part small and reliant on a low level of technology. The last group was opposed to integration and their governments supported them. All in all it is not surprising to read, 'In the automotive industry during the seven-year period 1961-1968, not a single automotive item has been added to the national list for tariff concessions.'[10]

Nevertheless, integration offered the only escape at that time from the fragmented, high costs of production in each isolated motor industry and attempts were made to negotiate so-called complementation agreements whereby two countries agreed to exchange certain components or specialise in particular classes of product. Even these have been few in number, limited in nature and, in some cases, actually increased costs. MNEs with affiliates in several Latin American countries welcomed such agreements but political approval was seldom forthcoming. Argentina and Brazil, for example, rejected a proposal whereby one MNE made a 4-cylinder engine in one country and a 6-cylinder engine in the other, despite a bilateral balance in the proposed exchange. Nor would they allow another MNE to produce left-hand side panels for trucks in Argentina and right-hand side panels in Brazil and swap, although the Brazilian plant was turning out one month's sales in two days of production. A few agreements were concluded but the position was summed up in the early 1970s as follows, 'The prospect for use of complementation agreements to integrate the key industries of petrochemicals and automobiles is bleak.'[11]

There are now signs that the situation is changing, at least as far as the smaller South American countries are concerned. After many years of fruitless negotiations, the five Andean Pact countries of Peru, Bolivia, Ecuador, Colombia and Venezuela have agreed to develop a regional motor industry. This objective is being pursued under the Andean Automotive Industry Development programme which aims to have 70 per cent of all vehicle components produced within the region by 1985. The regional market is currently around 300,000 vehicles a year and the objective is to get economies of scale by limiting the number of assembly plants and model types in each country, and by the specialisation and exchange of automotive parts and components. The Pact members are now in the process of selecting the companies to assemble the model types assigned to them under the programme.

Argentina, with car sales in 1979 of about 190,000 units, appears also to be taking renewed interest in trade liberalisation and integration with its neighbours, especially Brazil. The number of reciprocal arrangements in automotive components has been increasing. Scania, for example, exports gear boxes from its Argentinian plant to Brazil in exchange for engine components from its factory in Brazil. It seems highly likely that Chile, with a much smaller market than Argentina, will be forced to seek similar arrangements if it carries through with a plan currently under consideration to reduce appreciably the import duties on cars.

In short, the integration of the motor industry in Latin America is far less advanced than it is in Europe. But the political opposition to it is growing weaker under the economic pressures, and the one-time goal of most of the Latin American countries of establishing a more or less self-sufficient industry has been abandoned except for Brazil and perhaps Mexico.

Asia-Pacific. Integration here is in its early stages, with Ford-US taking the initiative as it had done earlier in Europe. In 1971 Henry Ford II had talks with government leaders in nine countries in the region, pushing the idea of complementary production of the principal automotive parts, with final assembly in each country. If political agreement on duties could be achieved, the participating countries could bypass the evolutionary import-assemble-manufacture stages of production, with its costly local content requirements and inefficient small-scale production for limited domestic markets. The Philippine government has been most active in supporting the scheme, viewing its Progressive Car Manufacturing Programme (PCMP) as part of a regional integration proposal for the Association of Southeast Asian National (ASEAN) – Indonesia, Malaysia, the Philippines, Singapore and Thailand.

Prior to the introduction of the PCMP in 1972 there were eleven assemblers and the Philippine industry was stagnating. Five were chosen to continue under the Programme on various criteria, which were weighted to favour exports and exports to ASEAN in particular. Those participating were Ford, General Motors, Chrysler-Mitsubishi, Delta (associated with Toyota) and DMG (associated with Volkswagen).

The Ford proposal under the PCMP was based on the building of the body stamping plant in the Bataan Export Processing Zone and was considered a major step towards integration in the Asia-Pacific region. General Motors proposed the manufacture and export of transmissions to Australia and ASEAN, Chrysler-Mitsubishi transmissions destined for Japan and ASEAN, Delta engine blocks to Japan, and DMG various components to Germany. The latter was unusual in that Volkswagen offered to train local manufacturers of components, give them technical assistance and loans and purchase components for export. In other words, Volkswagen would not directly control component manufacturing in the Philippines but would act only as an intermediary or co-ordinator.

What is of particular interest is that these economic decisions preceded political moves to liberalise trade in the area and hence appeared to involve considerable risk. However, the MNEs concerned had links outside ASEAN and, as long as the intra-firm trade culminated in an end product that could be sold profitably somewhere, integration could be introduced without securing commitments from other governments. Should the abolition of duties follow later, so much the better.

Africa. Aside from South Africa, the continent is still very much in the assembly stage with no scope for integration. Links between South Africa and the other African countries seem highly unlikely and it may be that Nigeria will attempt to 'go it alone' and become the Brazil of Africa.

International Sourcing

The same competitive pressures leading MNEs to integrate their operations on a regional basis could be expected to push them to seek worldwide for low-cost sources of supply for materials, parts, components and even final products for profitable use anywhere in their international networks. For a mature industry such as the motor industry,

with well-established techniques of production and more or less standardised products, this is what is predicted by the Product Cycle Theory.
In effect this implies foreign investment in low-wage developing countries by the MNEs themselves, since sub-contracting to technically
backward and uncontrolled foreign firms in these countries is not
considered feasible. Unlike the earlier investment induced by government policies in developing countries, which resulted in isolated industries and inefficient production solely for the domestic market, this
kind of investment would be internationally competitive and supplant
production elsewhere in the MNE network. There is a growing body of
evidence suggesting that this is what is now taking place in the motor
industry.

Scattered examples of sourcing in low-wage developing countries
that have come to light point to Brazil and Mexico as being by far the
most important supplying countries, exporting both to parent companies and to subsidiaries elsewhere in MNE networks. Chrysler, Ford
and General Motors have imported items such as engines, engine blocks
and specialised tooling and dies from their Brazilian and Mexican subsidiaries. In 1976 Ford's new engine plant in Brazil supplied engines for
the small Pinto model assembled in Canada. Out of the first 500,000
engines produced, the Brazil plant shipped 308,433 units to Canada,
36,719 to West Germany and 18,912 to Japan. Ford-Brazil has shipped
cams and chassis parts to Ford-Australia and dies and production fixtures have been sent to Ford's European factories from both Ford-
Brazil and Ford-Mexico. The latter has also supplied engines to Ford-
Venezuela. Of particular interest is General Motors' decision to convert
its present diesel engine plant in Brazil to the production of multi-fuel
engines for its 'world cars' to be launched in 1982. The production rate
for the new engines is expected to be 330,000 units a year, with
between 230,000 and 250,000 being exported, primarily to the European subsidiaries Opel and Vauxhall. Part of the European market was
deliberately left for Brazil when the operation was planned.

Of the European MNEs, Volkswagen, Fiat and Daimler-Benz have
made appreciable use of subsidiaries in Latin America as low-cost
suppliers. In 1978 Volkswagen-Brazil shipped to the parent company
daily almost 600 engines and 400 gearboxes. The Brazilian subsidiary
is also the source of ckd kits shipped to Nigeria and other developing
countries and supplies Volkswagen-South Africa with large numbers of
components. Volkswagen-Mexico is used as a source for rear axles,
radiators and other selected parts for Volkswagen of America. The
cross-country car Safari is exclusively built in the Mexican subsidiary

and exported mainly to Germany and the US. Volkswagen-Brazil exported 64,370 vehicles in 1978, a considerable portion of which consisted of Passat deliveries to Algeria. Both subsidiaries are now the only source for the famous Beetle and 15,958 were shipped from Mexico to Europe in 1978.

Fiat obtains engines from its Brazilian subsidiary, 133,000 units were shipped to Italy in 1977 for the 127 car. Starting in 1980, Fiat-Brazil is to export 20,000 of the world's smallest, diesel-engined cars to Europe. According to the company, shipping costs of about $300 per car will be offset by the lower production costs in Brazil. The same engine will also be used in the Fiat Ritmo diesel which will be assembled in Italy.

Daimler-Benz used Brazilian-sourced trucks to get into the American medium truck market and its Brazilian subsidiary now supplies components for the new Daimler-Benz assembly plant in Virginia, which also utilises some components from American suppliers and from the parent company itself. Brazilian components, including engines, have been imported at times by the German concern.

Aside from Latin America, there is not much evidence of sourcing in low-wage developing countries. In the Asia-Pacific area there is no sign of exports in any significant amounts from subsidiaries to parent companies for use in home markets. However, trade between subsidiaries of American MNEs located in the area seems to be supplanting some exports to the region from Europe and the US. Ford's Asian subsidiaries can now get body pressings from the Philippines and engines from Taiwan where output is well in excess of local needs. The same is true for General Motors' Asian subsidiaries in the case of transmissions from the Philippines and engines from South Korea.

What do these examples (and there must be many more) add up to? Table 8.2 gives some idea of the quantitative importance of the sourcing of parts and components in low-wage countries for use in final products sold in the home countries of the MNEs. The inability in general of independent concerns in developing countries to produce high quality inputs tailored to meet the needs of a particular manufacturer, plus the reluctance of MNEs to rely on indigenous suppliers in such countries, ensures that the bulk of the trade indicated in the table represents intra-company transactions.

International trade statistics are not always entirely reliable but those in Table 8.2 are in accord with figures showing the intra-firm transactions of two of the American MNEs in Table 8.3. What is perhaps surprising about the two tables is not that MNEs are spending millions of dollars on parts and components from developing countries and that the amounts are increasing fairly rapidly in real terms, but that sourcing in low-wage countries is so insignificant compared to parent company sales.

Table 8.2: Imports of Certain Automotive Products from Developing Countries, 1973 and 1977 ($ Millions)

	EEC		USA		Japan	
	\multicolumn{6}{c}{SITC 711.5*}					
	1973	1977	1973	1977	1973	1977
From developing countries	14.7	115.3	37.0	123.7	.8	21.0
In America	8.0	82.3	35.7	115.3	.0	17.7
	\multicolumn{6}{c}{SITC 732.8**}					
From developing countries	36.4	86.5	39.1	194.4	2.1	9.2
In America	13.8	40.3	36.7	183.5	1.7	3.6

* Internal combustion engines other than aircraft.
** Bodies, chassis, frames and other parts of motor vehicles other than for motor cycles (not including rubber tyres, engines, chassis with engines mounted, electrical parts).
Source: OECD Trade by Commodities, Series B.

Table 8.3: Intra-MNE Sales Among Geographic Regions, *Ford and General Motors, 1978 ($ Millions)

	Ford	General Motors
From Latin American subsidiaries	203	94
From Asia-Pacific subsidiaries	17	5
Total	220	99
Total as per cent of parent company sales	.008	.002

*US, Canada, Europe, Latin America, Asia-Pacific.
Source: Company Annual Reports, 1978.

The conclusion must be that international sourcing in low-wage developing countries for use by parent companies in their home markets is insignificant. Table 8.3 indicates that such countries are also unimportant as suppliers of subsidiaries in third regions, at least as far as the American MNEs are concerned.[12]

A good deal of the sourcing that does take place in developing countries may owe as much to the generous export incentives provided by these countries as to the low wages. Certainly international sourcing is not confined to low-wage countries. Almost all captive imports of vehicles come from developed countries. As for parts and components, Ford-US imports the greater part of the automatic gearboxes made in the Ford plant at Bordeaux, France. Its associate in Japan, Toyo Kogyo, is to supply 300,000 manual front-wheel drive transaxles a year for the 1980/1 small Ford. General Motors' French automatic transmission plant at Strasbourg was designed to export part of its output back to the US. Of the company's four new plants to be located outside America to produce engines for a 1982 model, only one is to be in a developing country – the one in Brazil previously mentioned. The others will be in Japan, Austria and Australia. The latter plant, located in a high-wage economy remote from Europe, is to export two-thirds of its output to the General Motors' facilities there.

Clearly low wages can only be one of a number of influences on international sourcing, perhaps only a minor one at that. Low wages do not necessarily mean low wage costs and economies of scale must be one of the factors. It is significant that such economies are found in Brazil and to a lesser extent in Mexico, the only developing countries of importance as supply sources. Other major influences are balance of payments considerations and host country characteristics and incentives.

When the competitive pressures leading to regional integration and international sourcing are combined with the huge costs of research, development and design associated with meeting the fuel, safety and pollution standards of the 1980s, the result is a largely standardised product, what is popularly referred to as 'world cars'.

World Cars

When the full impact of the financial and technical challenge here at home began to sink in, we had one more good reason to look seriously at reducing product duplication on a truly world-wide basis, at the international sourcing of components as a way of reducing capital demands and for a more fluid exchange of technology between North America and overseas. (Elliot M. Estes, President, General Motors, 1979)[13]

(The world car is) a vehicle which shares the same basic design and as many common or interchangeable parts as possible and which will compete successfully in the world's major automotive markets,

modified and tuned to their particular requirements. (Alex
Cunningham, Vice President, General Motors, 1979)[14]

In 1979 Detroit estimates of the cost of designing, engineering and
tooling up for the production of cars that would comply with the US
government standards for 1985 ranged from $50 billion to $70 billion.
They included the cost of developing new techniques, new materials
and practically re-inventing the American car. At the end of it the US
companies would have a range of new cars virtually identical in size
and performance with those built in Europe and Japan. No need to
duplicate costly design and engineering expenditures in overseas subsidiaries and affiliates for what will be multimarket models. But where
to build these standardised cars?

Theoretically, in a completely free trade world the purely economic
answer would be where production costs were lowest. Conceivably this
could be in one country, perhaps in the US where the new cars were
developed, and the world supplied by expanding capacity with very
capital-intensive, optimum-sized plants scattered throughout the nation.
But given a world of competing sovereign states with national, often
conflicting goals, and an environment made up of trade barriers, investment inducements, balance of payments difficulties, fluctuating
exchange rates, unemployment problems and various economic, social
and political pressures, Ford and General Motors appear to have decided
that the best long-run policy is widespread international company
production. Large-scale manufacture in the world's major markets (in
facilities already established anyway) and the sourcing of parts and
components in optimum-sized plants in as many countries as is profitably possible where the companies' vehicles are assembled and/or sold.
And because world cars will be standardised and produced on a massive
scale, more than one supplier of a particular major component will be
needed, and since these will be located in different countries the
existence of such alternative sources will provide some flexibility in a
very complex logistical operation.

In 1977 General Motors launched its first international 'project
centre' at Warren, Michigan with the aim of co-ordinating future car
design between its five US divisions and two of its foreign car divisions.
The concept is now used in the development of specific models,
bringing together experts in design, manufacturing, assembly, marketing
and customer service. The centre is disbanded when the project is
completed. In 1979 the company set up a new project centre to develop
world-wide truck programmes, adapting the world car concept to find

common components which could be used in trucks around the world. Ford, already producing a common model range throughout its European plants, has installed computer links between its design and engineering teams in the US and Europe. Its 1980 Escort was developed jointly by engineers in West Germany, the US and Japan. The Ford goal, as expressed by Donald E. Petersen, Executive Vice President of the company's international automotive operations — 'We are looking to a future where we work with common engineering, even if we do the tooling locally.'[15]

The European producers, already making a range of cars smaller and more fuel efficient than the US manufacturers, have not had to face such a mammoth research, design and engineering task. But they have become more international in design which, along with research and development, has always been concentrated in the hands of the parent companies. According to Claudio Ferrari, president of Fiat Motors of North America Inc, 'Fifteen years ago we designed cars for the Italian market. Ten years ago we began designing "European" cars. Now we develop them for the country with the biggest market — the US — and scale them down for the others.'[16] Similarly Renault, following its agreement with the American Motors Corporation, is to assemble a wholly new Renault model at the AMC plant in Wisconsin in 1982. It will be designed for the US market but will be similar to a car to be launched about the same time in Europe. Volkswagen too must have had the American market very much in mind in designing the Golf/Rabbit model as the replacement for the Beetle which had dominated the US import market for so many years before being eclipsed by Japanese cars.

Of the European manufacturers, Fiat and Volkswagen are the most multinational in structure and policy. The latter, with its firmly-established assembly plant in America and appreciable manufacturing capacity in Brazil, Mexico and now Argentina, has become a major producer on three continents with scope to allocate component production within the organisation to gain the greatest economies of scale. Fiat too is strong in Latin America and, with its latest models now to be produced in Argentina, Brazil, Poland and Spain at the same time as in Italy, is very multinational in outlook. That, together with the long-established link with Yugoslavia, has made an international rationalisation programme for component production possible.

Peugeot-Citroen, since its acquisition of Chrysler-Europe, has been preoccupied with rationalising production on a European basis in Spain, England and France. As the largest European producer it will no doubt seek to become multinational in a wider sense. Renault, leading car producer in Spain and probably the future leader in a reorganised Portuguese motor industry, linked with Volvo and its small-car subsidiary in the Netherlands, has much scope for component rationalisation on a European basis. Its deal with American Motors and expansion plans for Renault de Mexico are indications of its long-run strategy to be one of the major contenders for the world car market.

The big gap in the European MNE networks is the Asia-Pacific region. Unlike the American companies, not one of the European firms has formed a financial link with a Japanese producer or has established a manufacturing presence in the area. This may be a costly omission in the long run. However, when Africa enters the manufacturing stage, the European MNEs are poised to play a dominant role.

Given that overseas production and world-wide sourcing of components represents the basic trend of the motor industry, Japan is clearly the odd man out. Nissan, Toyota and others will of course produce 'world cars' — their heavy and growing dependence on the US and European markets ensures that. But with no multinational networks to speak of, the cars will be manufactured entirely in Japan. The success of such a policy will not depend primarily on costs for the large size of the Japanese industry itself will enable the cars and their components to be made in optimum-sized plants. What will be crucial is continued access to US and European markets, supplemented by the opportunity to send ckd shipments to Third World countries for assembly by local firms.

Summary and Conclusion

The oil crisis in the latter half of 1973 and the soaring prices of petrol were responsible for the first serious setback in the world motor industry since 1945. Two major MNEs were forced to abandon for the most part their overseas production and to seek government help to avoid bankruptcy. Although world output returned to its former level within three years, the crisis had a lasting and profound effect on the industry structure through the US government's fuel economy requirements for automobiles. In effect they meant that by 1985 the bulk of the cars produced in America would be very like those produced in Europe and Japan. To avoid duplication of very heavy research and development expenditure, the same models, with minor modifications, would be made in the overseas manufacturing subsidiaries. In particular, the European subsidiaries of Ford and General Motors which formerly produced 'European' cars would now be producing basically the same 'world cars' as their parent companies. This, of course, is what the overseas manufacturing subsidiaries of the European MNEs had always done.

At the same time the industry began to integrate on a regional basis. The Canadian industry, controlled by the American MNEs, became a part of the North American motor industry. An integrated West European industry is coming into being with the freeing of trade as the MNEs link their production on a Continental basis so as to reduce unit research and development costs and maximise economies of scale. National industries have become European industries just as national models have become European models. In the developing countries there has been a growing realisation that heavily-protected, small-scale motor industries are extremely costly, and an increasing willingness to participate in regional schemes which, through special-isation and exchange, enable each country to produce on an efficient scale and earn enough foreign exchange to finance the imports needed to make final assembly possible. Such schemes, if successful, suggest that there is likely to be a Latin American motor industry, an Asia-Pacific motor industry and, eventually, one for Africa. In this the MNEs have a key role to play.

Looking ahead, the typical MNE of the future will have a world-wide network of subsidiaries and affiliates made up of an integrated group of firms in each of the major regions — North America, Europe, Latin America, Asia-Pacific and Africa — with each regional bloc being more or less self-sufficient. But there will be production as well as techno-logical links between firms in different regions because of world-wide sourcing of components and built-up models in short supply or missing from the range of an individual subsidiary. This may stem from host country pressure to export or financial incentives to do so, from the wish to use a low-cost source of supply or to make use of idle capacity, or simply to exploit a profitable opportunity.

Such a policy reflects the view that if you want to sell motor cars world-wide you must manufacture world-wide. It attaches much weight to balance of payments considerations and seems to fit the pattern of investment in the industry since 1973. On the other hand this con-clusion conflicts with the Theory of Investment and the Product Cycle Theory. The former maintains that foreign direct investment cannot take place unless the investing firm has superior knowledge or other advantages over domestic producers in the host country. But at this late stage in the development of the industry is any MNE technologically superior to any of the others? And if it were would not this advantage be quickly matched by rivals? Moreover, how can Volkswagen's American subsidiary be 'superior' to the US firms in America and at the same time subsidiaries of the latter in Germany be 'superior' to Volkswagen? As for the Product Cycle Theory, that predicts that in a mature, oligopolistic industry, competition will force firms making more or less standardised products to shift production to low-wage developing countries. How to reconcile this with the fact that most of the investment since 1973 has taken place in high-wage developed countries? Indeed, how can any cost-orientated theory explain cross investment?

If world-wide MNE production represents the shape of things to come, the future of the major Japanese producers as global competitors is bleak unless they move quickly to invest in multinational networks of their own. Their present policy of supplying world markets almost entirely from Japan must be based on the assumption of more or less continued free access to the US and European markets and the ability to maintain sizable ckd exports to a number of Third World countries to be assembled by local firms.

Table 8.4: World Motor Vehicle Production, 1979 (Thousands)

	Total	Cars Only
1. United States	11,481	8,434
2. Japan	9,636	6,176
3. West Germany	4,250	3,933
4. France	3,613	3,222
5. USSR	2,173	1,314
6. Italy	1,632	1,481
7. Canada	1,632	988
8. UK	1,479	1,070
9. Brazil	1,128	962
10. Spain	1,123	966
11. Poland	483	357
12. Australia	459	403
13. Sweden	355	297
14. Belgium	325	283
15. Yugoslavia	315	285
16. Argentina	253	192
17. Czechoslovakia	226	175
18. South Korea	204	114
19. Netherlands	105	90
20. India	101	42
Total World*	41,027	30,811

*Only countries shown plus small amounts for Austria, Finland, Switzerland and Hungary. Figures for East Germany and Romania not available.
Source: SMMT.
Note: Local content requirements and the growing integration of national industries make unit production figures increasingly arbitrary and perhaps misleading.

Notes

1. *Financial Times* , 29 October 1979.

2. *Financial Times*, 12 January 1980.

3. Summarised in *Financial Times*, 27 November 1979. The Japanese advantage stemmed almost entirely from a labour cost per car of $1,010 less than in American plants. This easily absorbed ocean freight charges of $325 per unit and the other cost disadvantages of exporting to the US.

4. In 1973 Volvo made the decision to build an assembly plant in Virginia to supply the American market. The estimated cost was $150m and the initial output 30,000 cars a year. Construction of the plant was under way when the project was abandoned because of the shift in demand to small cars with the energy crisis, and also because of Volvo's straitened circumstances. However, the company continues to operate its small car assembly plant in Canada, established in 1963.

5. *Financial Times*, 23 May 1979.

6. *Financial Times*, 9 February 1978.

7. *Financial Times*, 30 July 1979.

8. *Financial Times*, 21 June 1979.

9. Jack Baranson, 'Integrated Automobiles for Latin America?', *Finance and Development*, vol. 5 (1968), p. 25.

10. Ibid., p. 25. National lists included items on which LAFTA members were to reduce their overall duties by 8 per cent a year for 12 years to get free trade at the end of the period.

11. Jack N. Behrman, *The Role of the International Companies in Latin American Integration: Autos and Petrochemicals* (Lexington Books, Lexington, Mass., 1972) p. 117.

12. Volkswagen may be an exception because of sizable exports from Volkswagen-Brazil to Africa and Volkswagen-Mexico to the US.

13. *Financial Times*, 8 October 1979.

14. *Financial Times*, 17 August 1979.

15. *Business Week*, 'To a Global Car', 20 November 1978, p. 103.

16. Ibid., p. 102.

9 MULTINATIONAL ENTERPRISES AND COMMUNIST COUNTRIES

In 1938 the Soviet Union produced 211,000 motor vehicles, the great majority being trucks. Output reached 2,151,000 units in 1978, of which 1,312,000 were cars. Total output for the rest of Eastern Europe before the second world war was less than 17,000, mostly from Czechoslovakia. By 1978 every country except Bulgaria was manufacturing cars and/or commercial vehicles, with the combined output being 1,253,588 units. It is no exaggeration to say that without the technical assistance obtained from the Western MNEs, a great deal of this expansion would not have taken place. Almost all the automotive MNEs have been engaged in attempts to negotiate agreements with Eastern Europe and China, even though most were never successfully concluded.

Strong technical and other links with Yugoslavia, Poland and the Soviet Union have placed Fiat in a dominant position in Eastern Europe. Since each of these countries produces Fiat-based vehicles and components, complementation to secure economies of scale and a broader model range is possible between them, and with Fiat itself. Fiat's links go far beyond the ordinary type of licensing agreement. It is almost a case of integration via commercial transactions rather than ownership. In a sense, plants in Yugoslavia and Poland can be considered part of the Fiat MNE network.

Yugoslavia was the first Communist country to seek automotive technical assistance from the West, and in 1954 a contract was signed between Zavodi Crvena Zastava (ZCZ) and Fiat for the granting of a licence and the provision of the necessary technical assistance to build up a motor industry from scratch. An extremely interesting insider's account of the resulting long-term relationship has been given by Prvoslav Rakovic, Director General of ZCZ.[1] He concluded that a joint venture with a foreign partner was preferable to a licensing agreement. After foreign capital participation became possible in Yugoslav enterprises, Fiat signed a new agreement in 1968 and invested $17 million, which gave it a 16.5 per cent share in ZCZ. Commenting on this agreement Mr Rakovic states, 'It can be frankly said that the contract for technical, managerial and financial collaboration between Zavodi Crvena Zastava and Fiat has opened a new chapter in such relations, transforming the old licenser/licensee relationship into a partnership and starting up a process of industrial collaboration in the proper sense of the term.'[2]

Great importance was attached to industrial collaboration, not only with Fiat but also with other interested foreign enterprises, involving the reciprocal exchange of parts, sub-assemblies, assemblies and semi-finished products. This was considered essential for a relatively small country such as Yugoslavia with its limited market, in order to make mass production and the introduction of modern technology possible. A developing country could substitute cheap labour for lack of experience, but cheap labour could not compensate for the other basic factors affecting costs − scale, modern technology and organisation of work. As well as the licence to produce Fiat models, as well as technical and managerial assistance, collaboration with Fiat also brought about the production and supply of inputs for each other. Exports to Fiat included, for example, stamped parts, electrical equipment, shock absorbers, batteries, forged parts and seats. In the agreement signed in 1971 with Fiat and its commercial vehicle subsidiary OM, ZCZ was to produce 58 per cent of the value of the vehicle and permanently import the remaining 42 per cent from OM. It was also to make 50 per cent of the vehicle for itself and for OM. The engines, gearboxes and other items would be supplied by OM while ZCZ made the front and rear axles, complete chassis, wheels, shock absorbers, batteries, etc. Industrial collaboration agreements were also entered into with the Polish motor industry (1966) and the Volga motor works in the USSR (1969). The Polish contract was concerned with two Fiat car models with many standardised features, such as the engine, transmission and suspension, so that sharing out the manufacturing process resulted in longer runs for one partner or the other. In the agreement with VAZ (USSR), the Yugoslav company undertook to produce certain parts designed to fit in with the ZCZ programme in return for a complete car model which would widen the range offered by the Yugoslav concern in its domestic market.

When such agreements are made with the licencing company, they also serve to ease the chronic foreign exchange problems facing most developing countries which are greatly aggravated when a motor industry is started. But improvement in the balance of payments of the developing country cannot be achieved solely by industrial collaboration. Exports too are needed. MNEs are sometimes criticised for restricting exports by subsidiaries or foreign licensees. 'Under the contracts concluded between Zavodi Crvena Zastava and Fiat the export of Zastava cars is regulated in such a way that Zavodi Crvena Zastava are not entitled to export cars to countries where Fiat has plants of its own or workshops for the assembly or production under licence of the cars in question, with the exception of the Eastern countries. Zavodi Crvena Zastava is entitled to export to other countries, on the understanding that in certain cases it must first reach agreement with Fiat.'[3] On the other hand, 'The organisation of car exports to third countries is a serious and responsible task, involving, among other things, considerable investment in facilities. Cooperation with a partner in a developed industrial country which has a well-organised network and a wealth of experience is very useful, and even essential.'[4] In fact ZCZ had not done much in the way of exports, partly because in the early years production capacity was small and domestic demand very high, and partly because, even in the early 1970s, short production runs meant its cost of production was much higher than its foreign competitors. However, the growing need for foreign exchange and for a market for the larger number of vehicles being produced was leading to steps to establish a position in foreign markets.

Finally, much emphasis was placed on the need for ZCZ to develop its own design and engineering capability. From giving mere assistance to Fiat in the early days of their relationship, ZCZ personnel were currently fully participating in study and design, analysis, the purchase of equipment, and in suggestions for changes or adaptation at ZCZ. Engineers and technicians in the ZCZ Technical Office at Fiat worked together with their Fiat counterparts so that the latter could transmit their experience directly. As a consequence of this policy, ZCZ was able to set up design and study departments which, in co-operation with Fiat's technical services, succeeded in developing and producing the Zastava 101 which, although derived from the Fiat model, had characteristics of its own in regard to the design itself and the technical solutions adopted. One of the most serious problems involved in producing under licence was the question of introducing the modifications and improvements made to vehicles and then continuing to design them after the licenser had ceased to do so.

That the relationship between Fiat and ZCZ is still a mutually satisfactory one is indicated by the new long-term agreement covering industrial co-operation signed in November 1978. Under its terms the Yugoslav company will build versions of the Fiat 131 Miafiori and 127 models in addition to its current range of Fiat 128s, 132s, and older 750s which are to be phased out. It is hoped that eventually Fiat will cease manufacturing the 128 model and instead take those produced by ZCZ in exchange for parts, components and finished cars of other models and sell them through its world-wide network. Total output at ZCZ is scheduled to rise to 320,000 cars and 20,000 light commercial vehicles a year by 1982 compared with the current production of 200,000 cars and 11,000 commercial vehicles. Fiat is to assist the company in obtaining finance from Italy for its development and will possibly transfer part of the manufacturing equipment. The deal calls for the exchange of cars and components between the two countries worth $1.2 billion each way during the period 1980 to 1986, starting from some $100 million in 1980 and rising to over $200 million in 1986. These exchanges have to be in balance. Fiat now accounts for three in four cars manufactured in Yugoslavia and two in three cars sold there and it intends to keep its market share.

Fiat's relationship with the Polish industry dates back to the 1930s when the little 508 car was assembled under licence. With the first postwar agreement in 1965, Fiat licensed the production of the 125 model (known as the 125P or Polski-Fiat) and provided technical assistance. The 125 ceased to be produced in Italy in 1972, but has continued to be made in Poland and exported to some 40 countries (excluding Italy under the licence agreement) because of its well-tried design and low price. A second co-operation agreement was concluded in 1971 which provided for the building of a factory in Silesia to produce a new Fiat model, the 126. In this case the licence forbade sales of the Polish-produced 126s in the West. Both agreements were once-only deals involving a lump-sum payment, with no royalty payments on sales of Fiat designs. Early models of the 126 were assembled from ckd kits imported from Italy and, even as late as 1973, approximately 15 per cent of the 125P components were still being supplied by Fiat.

In June 1979 a much more comprehensive and significant agreement was made which, in effect, reflected Fiat's aim of rationalising and integrating its international activities. As the cornerstone of a ten year co-operation programme, it provided for the production of two new vehicles in Poland. The first was to be the assembly from ckd packs, starting in 1981, of Fiat's new small car, the 'zero' model for sale in Poland. The second was to be the production of a new, multi-purpose vehicle, with versions for both agricultural and commercial use, jointly designed with Fiat. It would be powered either by petrol engines produced in Poland or diesel engines imported from Italy. At the same time, Poland will supply an unspecified number of the 126 model, the production of which Fiat proposes to phase out to concentrate on the 'zero'. The 126, as well as the new commercial vehicle, will be sold by Fiat dealers in Europe and certain other countries. Despite the fact that no foreign direct investment is involved, the Polish motor industry has become, to an appreciable extent, part of a MNE network.

Fiat's most dramatic move in Eastern Europe was, of course, associated with the Togliatti plant in the USSR. That country, after the war, had continued its policy of emphasising the production of trucks. Even as late as 1965 only some 200,000 passenger cars were made. The most popular model and the only one in volume production was the Moskvich, and this was derived from captured Opel plans and drawings. So great was the technology gap and so urgent was the need to meet public demand for private transport, that the Soviet Union once again sought help from the West to establish the base for a large-scale, modern car industry. Fiat not only helped to design, build and equip the huge Volga Automobile Works in Togliatti but also provided the car to be produced under licence – the Fiat 124, modified for Russian driving conditions and weather, and called the Zhiguli. What Fiat received for its design and the turn-key operation has never been disclosed. Planned output was 660,000 units a year in a plant said to have cost $800 million and to be probably the biggest integrated car production complex in the world, making practically everything apart from tyres, glass, some electrics and a few mechanical components. From 1966 to 1972 more than 2,000 Russians went to Turin to get plans, plant and equipment, and to undergo training, while some 1,000 Italian supervisory technicians were employed in Togliatti. Production started in 1970 when 28,000 cars were made. Output rose rapidly and by making fuller use of existing capacity annual production has exceeded 700,000 units.

The Russians insisted on having the right to export and Fiat is said to have agreed in order to get the job and in the belief that if they did not do so others would.[5] However, by 1975 the exports of the Russian Lada – a copy of the Fiat 124 – began to cause concern to the Italian company. Its Managing Director called for urgent action by the EEC to prevent the 'dumping' of cars at prices well below their actual cost value. He told a London press conference that he was particularly worried by the marketing policy of Russia and Poland who were selling copies of Fiat cars at retail prices hundreds of pounds cheaper than their Italian-made equivalents. At the same time he maintained that he did not regret either of the deals made with these countries and hoped they would stand Fiat in good stead when East European markets were opened to imported cars and components.[6]

Renault too has been active in Eastern Europe, particularly in

Romania since the signing of an agreement in 1967 for the assembly of its cars, the Renault 8 and 12. The original target was for an output of 50,000 R12s in 1973 with 60 per cent local content. At the same time Romania became the company's largest foreign subcontractor by undertaking to supply it with gearboxes, front and rear axle systems and other components. Most of these were incorporated in the Renault light van, the Estafette. A second agreement was signed in 1978 worth about £475 million which involved doubling the capacity of the car plant at Pitesti where the Renault models are made under licence, and constructing a factory for pick-up trucks. Capacity at the Pitesti plant will be increased from 75,000 vehicles a year to 150,000. Output of the Dacia (Renault 12, local content now 94 per cent) is to be reduced to 60,000 a year to make way for producing Renault's new medium-size saloon, the R18, with an installed capacity of 90,000 units. At the same time a new assembly plant will be built to produce 35,000 pick-up vehicles, initially with engines imported from Renault in France.

The French company's contract includes buying parts from the Romanian operation and it will expand its purchases of gearboxes and other parts for its vans. Renault is also to provide assistance in marketing the vehicles produced, through its networks in areas such as Africa and Asia, where the Romanian vehicles are considered well suited to local conditions.

Renault has also concluded deals with several other East European countries and Russia. It provided the latter with technical assistance for a major redevelopment of the Moskvich works in Moscow and supplied equipment for the plant. Further technical assistance was given from 1971 onwards for a diesel engine factory with an annual capacity of 250,000 units as part of the huge Kama river truck project. In Poland, Berliet and Polmot signed a ten-year co-operation agreement in 1972 providing for truck licences and technical assistance. The Czech firm, Avia, builds Saviem trucks under licence which have had 95 per cent local concent since 1974. Renault also approached the Czech government offering assistance in the development of a domestic car industry but nothing came of the informal offer. In 1976, the French company signed a co-operation agreement with the Bulgarian government and, more recently, is to provide East Germany's Wartburg car with Renault engines for units exported to the West. Heavy exhaust emissions had virtually excluded the German car with its domestic, two-stroke engine from Western markets. Finally, Renault provides engines for light commercial vehicles built by the Yugoslav firm, Industriya Motornich Vozil, and the latter also assembles Renault cars.

The two German MNEs have established links in Yugoslavia. Volks-wagen has a 49 per cent share in a joint venture with Tvornica Auto-mobile Sarajevo (TAS) which assembles the Golf. Plans for expanding capacity to 50,000 units a year have been under consideration. Daimler-Benz has licenced Fap-Famos to produce its vehicles and receives parts and components from what it refers to as 'our Yugoslav partner'.

Peugeot-Citroen has become active in Eastern Europe in recent years. Citroen itself, in 1972, formed a joint venture in Yugoslavia, Cimos, in which it had a 49 per cent share. The company assembles Citroen cars under licence and mass produces certain parts and assem-blies for itself and the French firm. Complete production lines were transferred from France for this purpose. Peugeot concluded an agreement in December 1978 with the Yugoslav firm Fabrika Amortizera Pristina to construct a factory to produce 50,000 Peugeot cars a year by 1981. The French company is to participate in the invest-ment. In 1976 Citroen signed an agreement with the Romanian govern-ment to construct an industrial complex at Craiva to manufacture a new car designed for the Romanian market. It will hold a 36 per cent interest in a FFr2.5 billion investment. Imports for the Romanian factory will be paid for by shipments of cars, sub-assemblies and engines. The cars will be sold in Western Europe by Citroen. Planned output is 130,000 vehicles a year. In 1978 Citroen was awarded a FFr1.6 billion contract by East Germany to construct a turn-key factory to begin production in 1981 of front-wheel drive transmission systems. Capacity output will be 675,000 units a year, over half of which are to be used in a new small car to be made jointly by East Germany and Czechoslovakia. Citroen has agreed to buy 300,000 transaxles a year from 1982 for use in its own cars. The British com-ponents firm, GKN, competed for the contract but dropped out in the later stages because it refused to enter a buy-back agreement with the East Germans. Peugeot-Citroen is also currently competing along with GKN, Fiat and Volvo for the largest industrial project East Germany has yet offered Western companies, a £500 million modernisation scheme for its truck industry. The government wants to pay with 100 per cent counter-purchases by Western companies of East German products, but it is not insisting on delivery output from the new truck component plants. Together, East Germany and Czechoslovakia are trying an independent solution without linking with a Western car firm as such.

The Swedish Volvo company entered a unique operation in Hungary in 1975 to assemble locally its cross-country vehicle, 3314. With two

Hungarian companies, Csespel Auto and Mogust, it jointly established a
new concern, Volcom Hungary, to be responsible for marketing the
vehicles, in which Volvo has a 52 per cent share. The Volvo Truck
Division provided complete technical information for the manufacture
of the 3314, the technical training required in design and production,
the tools of vital importance for assembly, and the major mechanical
components such as the engines and gearboxes. A considerable amount
of local manufacture was involved, especially regarding the bodies. The
production target the first year was 1,000 vehicles, many of which were
to be exported and sold through the Volvo dealer network.

Finally, several truck producers have made licensing and technical
agreements with one or more of the East European countries, notably,
the German firms, MAN and Magirus (now part of IVECO), and Steyr-
Daimler-Puch of Austria.

Notable for their absence are the American and Japanese MNEs,
although General Motors has a 49 per cent interest in a joint venture
in Yugoslavia, Industria Delova Automobila, which manufactures iron
castings and automotive components. The US firms have been involved
in negotiations with East European governments either directly or
indirectly through their European subsidiaries, but without success.
Ford-US held serious talks with the USSR concerning the Kama river
truck project but potential agreement was vetoed by the American
government. Ford of Europe negotiated with the Romanian government on a joint venture (Ford share 49 per cent) to build a truck plant
with a capacity of 50,000 vehicles but nothing materialised. More
recently General Motors came close to making a truck manufacturing
agreement with Poland but the negotiations broke down because all
efforts to secure international financing failed, including a loan request
to the US Export-Import Bank. The proposed deal reflected a very
significant change in General Motors' policy and warrants closer
examination.[7]

The plan called for GM to design a series of vehicles, ranging from
light vans equipped with 4-cylinder diesel engines to 5-ton trucks. These
were to be production engineered for a small truck facility in Lublin
then making light commercial vehicles using an obsolete 2000 cc
engine of the Warzawa automobile. The factory was to be modernised
and expanded according to GM specifications and design, and to have
an annual capacity of 100,000 units. The unique aspect of the agreement was that the vehicles to be manufactured were to be of an original
design meeting Polish specifications and not an existing GM design.
Production documentation was to take place at GM's UK subsidiary,

Vauxhall Motors, with the participation of Polish technicians. Approximately 100 GM design engineers from various parts of the world were to be assigned to work with and instruct their Polish counterparts. It was expected that GM would buy back between 15,000 and 18,000 light vans to be sold through its marketing channels. In turn Poland would have been granted exclusive marketing rights in Eastern Europe. The initial expansion was expected to cost about $600 million and the total investment eventually could have reached as much as $1 billion. There was to be virtually no capital outlay by GM let alone any equity investment.

Willingness to accept the proposals is a clear indication that the world's largest manufacturing MNE no longer considers ownership and managerial control indispensable to its overseas operations. It is now prepared to accept, under certain circumstances, the release of technology and production know-how to non-controlled affiliates in order to earn a return on these corporate assets. It is also willing to allow a non-controlled affiliate to become part of its international supply system.

It appears that both parties would have been satisfied to go ahead on the basis of these proposals had they been able to secure the necessary funds from international sources. At any rate, GM still seems to be interested in this type of agreement with East European countries and with China.

China

> We are hearing the Chinese use terms like joint ventures, which to us means joint ownership. If these types of arrangements can come to fruition, then I think there is a real opportunity that something could happen, but, if not, the prospects are substantially less. (Philip Caldwell, Vice Chairman and President, Ford Motor Company, 1979)[8]

Although fundamental changes in attitudes and institutions have been taking place in China in recent years, the present structure and state of its automotive industry are still largely the product of the political philosophy embodied in the ideas and policies of Chairman Mao regarding industry and technology.[9] As such it is unique. The general pattern followed by most developing countries has been to welcome foreign direct investment and to make extensive use of licensing arrangements in order to establish vehicle assembly, components, suppliers and supporting industries. Critics have charged that such policies have resulted in inappropriate designs, inefficient production techniques (in a setting of massive unemployment) and continuing dependence on foreigners for technology. More broadly, they have attacked the pattern of automotive consumption and the social values enshrined in the hierarchical production systems transferred from abroad. It was precisely all this that the Chinese sought to avoid.

They hoped to achieve this for industry in general by developing an indigenous technological capability at the shop floor level in each of the Chinese provinces, and by encouraging the technical creativity of the mass of the workers, particularly in medium- and small-scale enterprises. Efforts were made through worker innovation programmes to break the barriers between technician and worker as part of a general policy of attempting to unify mental and manual labour in society. Obviously direct foreign investment by foreigners in China was out of the question, but so too were conventional licensing arrangements since there was no desire slavishly to copy foreign designs and methods and, in any event, royalties were opposed on principle. The only technical interest in products from abroad was as prototypes, things to be altered and adapted to Chinese needs and production methods, largely through the ingenuity and skill of the workers whose creative energies would be released and spurred on by Chinese communist attitudes and institutions. The aim was to create a society that was both genuinely socialist and technologically self-sufficient.

As a consequence, the automotive industry (non-existent before 1949) developed a very fragmented structure. Vehicles are produced on a small scale in a minimum of thirteen locations, with most of the plants surrounded by even smaller manufacture and repair shops that serve as parts and components suppliers. The largest motor vehicle producing plant is at Changchun which has a current annual output of over 40,000 vehicles, mostly trucks, and this accounts for nearly half the country's entire production. It was built in 1956, admittedly with the aid of Soviet technicians, and had an initial capacity of 30,000 units. Several of the basic truck designs were developed in collaboration with the Russians, but after 1958 the Chinese industry was self-sufficient except for a small number of imported vehicles, mostly buses and specialised types not produced by the domestic firms.

It demonstrated that a large but very poor developing country could do without the MNEs and at the same time avoid a flood of imported vehicles. It meant small-scale production and low productivity by

Western standards, and waiting while commercial vehicle output was gradually increased by means of domestic know-how and resources. It meant simple and slow moving trucks (although said to be reliable, long-lived and easy to service). Above all it meant no private cars for any of the Chinese people.[10] But for a country in the early stages of industrialisation, faced with the task of feeding over 900 million people and finding useful employment for its huge, mostly rural, work-force, there is much to be said for such a policy. And to the extent that it is true that MNEs bring the wrong products and the wrong technology to developing countries, then excluding private cars and building up an indigenous technology capable of deriving suitable versions of imported vehicle prototypes and producing them with labour-intensive methods seems to make economic sense.

And yet in practice this approach has turned out to be incapable of meeting China's present needs for road transport, let alone the demands of 'a powerful, modern, socialist country by the end of the century', the goal of the present Chinese leadership. Motor industry output is stagnating. Current annual production is believed to total less than 100,000 units — probably nearer the 90,000 mark. This compares unfavourably with production levels in excess of 100,000 which it is understood were recorded in 1972 and 1973.[11] The industry has of course been adversely affected by the political upheavals of the 1970s, but it seems fair to say that the Chinese have taken the 'Maoist' motor industry about as far as it can go, that the time has come to introduce modern industrial systems which can produce efficiently at high volumes. That, at any rate, seems to be the conclusion of the present government, which also appears to be convinced that the move into higher volume production will require extensive foreign assistance.

For the past few years, practically every automotive MNE has been busy preparing plans for the modernisation of China's car and truck industry. In the spring of 1979, according to Chinese planning officials in Shanghai, General Motors, Ford, Chrysler, Citroen, Renault, Volks-wagen and Nissan were holding talks on bringing up to date China's main saloon car factory in Shanghai. In November of that year, Mr John Quick, a GM Vice President announced that his company was discussing a possible joint venture with China to manufacture heavy-duty trucks.[12] He identified GM's competitors for the contract as Ford, International Harvester, Renault, Volvo, Daimler-Benz and an unnamed Japanese company. GM's Japanese affiliate, Isuzu Motors, was conduct-ing separate negotiations for the construction of a light-duty truck plant, while Volkswagen was said to be the only company still interested in manufacturing passenger cars in China. In March 1980 Volkswagen announced that it was having talks with China about building a car assembly plant there. If successful, cars from the firm's lower- to medium-range, including the Golf, would be assembled. The company warned against expecting quick results and indicated that there were other international competitors.

Although no agreements have yet been announced between any of the Western MNEs and China, there can be little doubt some contracts will be made sooner or later. The government has clearly made up its mind to seek Western technological and perhaps financial assistance, and the MNEs are eager to provide it. The only question that remains, and it is a fascinating one about which nothing has yet been said, concerns the terms. The successors of Chairman Mao have him to thank for the strong bargaining position they are in, but he would not be pleased at what they are doing.

Summary and Conclusions

That socialist countries should seek economic assistance from capitalist countries, and in particular from Western MNEs, and that these 'agents of imperialism' should be willing and eager to provide it, is one of life's ironies. In this there is nothing unique about the motor industry. It is a development involving most of the major MNEs in a wide range of industries, and one which has been well documented.[13] Buyers and sellers have entered into mutually profitable arrangements in what amounts to a triumph of economics over ideology.

The overriding motive on the part of the socialist countries for business deals with foreign MNEs, as far as the motor industry was concerned, was to obtain fairly quickly the modern technology and know-how needed to meet the growing demand from consumers and industry for transport stemming from rising GNP and living standards. Passenger cars had been given a low priority up to the mid-1960s, and the relatively few that were produced were old-fashioned and generally inferior to Western models. Trucks had received more emphasis but nevertheless output was inadequate and the vehicles were not acceptable outside Eastern Europe. 'Even in countries like Finland, where there was considerable pressure forcing the Finns to accept Russian cars and trucks, they were not appreciated, and few people acquired them voluntarily. The Finns, who had to import Russian trucks, landed them on the docks and had mechanics take out the Russian engines and insert English Ford engines. This is the only way the trucks could be sold.'[14]

Faced with the very high research and development costs needed to close the automotive technological gap with the West, it was considered cheaper, and of course quicker, to buy the technology rather than to invest in finding out what others already knew. The resources thus saved could be used to adapt and improve the acquired technology, or for other purposes. Since MNEs not only possessed the technology but also had the personnel and resources required to transfer it on a large scale, they were the agents chosen.

For the MNE it was simply a question of 'profitability'. Excluded from selling built-up vehicles, denied the opportunity to invest except to a limited extent in Yugoslavia and possibly Romania, access to a significant and potentially large market could be gained by selling licences, technology and know-how. In itself this represented an extra return on existing knowledge and a help in financing the future research and development expenditure needed to remain competitive and one step ahead of licensees. But more importantly, it led to large sales of machine tools, machinery and equipment supplied directly by the licenser, or indirectly in his capacity as main contractor. And except in the case of the Soviet Union, it meant the sale of components over a longish period while the local industry was being established. Indirectly it might also lead to access to markets in some developing countries which preferred to do business with socialist states. Finally, licensees could be used as cheap and reliable sources of parts and components. Such immediate benefits outweighed any costs that might arise in the future from hastening the development of motor industries in socialist countries, industries which would sooner or later have come into being in any event.

The large-scale technological transfer to Eastern Europe has led to considerable regional integration between the motor industries there and in the West. In effect, individual socialist enterprises have become a part of a private MNE network although there are no ownership links except in the case of joint ventures in Yugoslavia. This has come about through the need to get economies of scale and to pay for the imported technology, equipment and components, either in hard currency or in automotive shipments to the MNE. The buy-back arrangements insisted on by the Eastern European producer inevitably makes him a member of the MNE 'team' during the life of the agreement. The strong economic pressures favouring integration suggest that the links will not be broken, that new, long-term agreements will be entered into. These same pressures are responsible for the trend toward regional integration within Eastern Europe. Again the links are not based on ownership.

Notes

1. Prvoslav Rakovic, *Development of the Automotive Industry in Developing Countries in Co-operation with Industries in the Developed Countries* (UNIDO, Vienna, ID/WG 136/4, 13 October 1972)

2. Ibid., pp. 24-5.

3. Ibid., p. 29.

4. Ibid., p. 30.

5. *Business Week*, 'Multinationals: A Fiat is a Lada is a Zastava', 12 February 1972.

6. *Financial Times*, 19 April 1975.

7. See Jack Baranson, *Technology and the Multinationals* (Lexington Books, Lexington, Mass., 1978), pp. 46-51.

8. *Financial Times*, 15 February 1979.

9. For probably the best account of the development of the Chinese industry up until the early 1970s see Jack Baranson, 'The Automotive Industry' in William W. Whitson (ed.), *Doing Business With China* (Praeger, New York, 1974), pp. 170-89.

10 At Changchun the Red Flag Model, a cumbersome and old-fashioned passenger car is made in strictly limited numbers for use by top members of the Chinese government. Several thousand cars are produced annually at the Shanghai factory consisting of two models, down-market from the Red Flag, which are for use by senior officials.

11. Economist Intelligence Unit, *Motor Business*, 'A Review of the Automotive Sector in China' vol. 93 (1st quarter 1978), p. 25.

12. *Financial Times*, 6 November 1979.

13. J. Wilczynski, *The Multinationals and East-West Relations* (Macmillan, London, 1976).

14. J. Wilner Sundelson, 'US Automotive Investments Abroad' in Charles P. Kindleberger (ed.), *The International Corporation* (MIT Press, Cambridge, Mass. and London, 1970), p. 250.

10 LABOUR'S RESPONSE TO THE MULTINATIONAL ENTERPRISE

> When there was a dispute of Ford workers in a Ford plant,
> Henry Ford met with the prime minister and served notice on
> the head of that soverign state that unless the dispute was
> settled in accordance with the terms the Ford Motor Company
> had offered, Ford would move its operations to Cologne,
> Germany. How do you resolve that? It was resolved because
> the German workers, who were part of a world trade union
> organisation, said we won't work on that.
>
> (Victor Reuther, United Auto Workers, retired, 1975)[1]

The MNE by definition invests in production facilities outside the home
country. Inescapably it takes its technology with it and, to some
extent, capital. The home trade union sees this as an immediate loss of
jobs. It fears also that an exodus of technology and capital will erode
the country's competitive strength leading to long-term employment
losses and a diminution of labour's share in the national income. Perhaps, most of all, the union is concerned over a weakening in its
bargaining power in dealings with the MNE. The latter, as an international organisation, always has resources which cannot be reached by
the nation-bound trade union. The existence of these 'extra-territorial'
resources gives the MNE alternatives which strengthens its bargaining
position.

MNE decisions as to where it will invest, introduce new models,
start new ventures, or gradually run down existing investments, are
bargaining cards the national firm does not possess. It was a card that
Henry Ford II played at the time of the 1971 strike at Ford-UK plants.
'I could not in good conscience recommend to my Board any new capital expenditure in Britain.'[2] Moreover, when it comes to a strike, the
union cannot bring the activities of an MNE to a complete halt as is
the case with a national company. The MNE may be able to supply
affected customers from its overseas factories and, in any event, 'business as usual' elsewhere means that all its income is not choked off and
a lengthy strike is more easily endured. Less dramatic, but of importance, is the MNE's ability to withhold information about its overseas
activities and its intra-company transactions. Without an intimate
knowledge of the operations of the MNE as a whole the union is

handicapped in its negotiations with these organisations.

It might be thought that trade unions in host countries would welcome MNEs on the grounds that the home country's loss — jobs, technology, capital — would be their gain. Initially this may be so, but once the MNE is established locally, the most important concern becomes the company's relative mobility and its effect on relative bargaining positions. This concern is accentuated in the case of a host country union since the bulk of the MNE's operations will be outside its domain. In particular, negotiating with local management over investment seems pointless since these and other strategic decisions will be made by the parent company in its home country.

Since union antagonism toward the MNE stems largely from the latter's relative mobility and its effect on relative bargaining positions, labour's response to the MNE has taken the form of both national and international efforts to reduce the mobility of the MNE or to increase labour's ability to counter that mobility.[3]

National Efforts

The most comprehensive attempt by national labour to check the power of MNEs culminated in the 1971 Burke-Hartke bill in the US, sponsored by the AFL-CIO. The bill sought to legislate four major new constraints on MNEs. It called for increased taxation of their foreign income, presidential licensing of all foreign direct investments and exports of technology, more complete corporate disclosures of international activities and the curtailment of US imports, especially those produced abroad with American-made components, so as partly to prevent US firms from meeting domestic demand through foreign production. Except for some minor changes in taxation this was rejected by both the administration and Congress.

In 1969 and 1970, two major US unions challenged foreign direct investment under the authority of the National Labor Relations Act, which compels business to bargain with labour over its investment decisions that affect employees in the bargaining unit. Both attempts failed. One was made by the United Auto Workers and attacked Ford Motors' decision to produce Pinto engines and gearboxes at its English and German subsidiaries. Although this attempt to block the Ford move was not successful, a year or so later the company, for whatever reasons, announced a change in plans — European Pinto engines would be phased out by 1973 in favour of a new engine plant at Lima, Ohio.

Sweden is the only other home country in which labour has made a major effort to check the power of MNEs through legislation. In 1974 laws were adopted requiring government approval for all capital out-flows for foreign direct investment by Swedish-based firms. Corporate applications must be accompanied by statements on the proposed investment by the trade unions concerned. No applications have yet been denied and it is too early to judge its effectiveness from labour's standpoint. Volvo's application in 1977 to build a truck and bus plant in Brazil had the support of its unions, mainly on the grounds that major components would be supplied from Sweden. The required Brazilian content can now be as low as 72 per cent, provided 25 per cent of production is exported.

In Germany, and to some extent elsewhere in Europe, another route has been followed to increase the power of labour over the MNE. Unions have sought national and EEC legislation giving them equal representation with management on all supervisory boards – Mitbestim-mung, or co-determination. The motor industry provides the most successful example of co-determination on foreign investment decisions. In 1975 Volkswagen workers opposed the company's pro-posed investment in the US, helped delay the project and forced the retirement of the management that proposed it. And in 1978, Herman Rebhan, General Secretary of the International Metalworkers Federa-tion in Geneva, was appointed as a union nominee to the supervisory board of Ford-Germany.

When MNEs are involved in strikes, the nation-bound trade unions can close down all local plants but cannot directly affect operations elsewhere in the MNE network. Nevertheless, there are effective steps the unions can take, and the lengthy Ford-UK strike in 1978 provides an interesting example of the tactics used by both sides.

When Ford integrated its European operations after Ford of Europe was formed, its plants in the major producing countries became depend-ent on each other for manufactured inputs. The company realised of course that this would make it more vulnerable in case of a dispute. So the changes made were designed to give flexibility during strikes. Many components, sub-assemblies and even complete cars can be either dual-sourced or substituted by similar products made elsewhere. Those that cannot, can be stockpiled in anticipation of labour trouble. It was said that in this case Ford, at a cost of several million dollars, had stockpiled an average of 55 days supply of essential UK compon-ents, including parts in transit.[4] This compares with the company's normal stock level of 20 days.

The dispute began with unofficial walkouts by men in several parts of the country while the existing wage agreement still had a month to run. This was how the previous major, national Ford strike in 1971 had begun – no doubt the union response to stockpiling, aimed at affecting continental production as quickly as possible. The next step after the strike became official was to prevent Ford imports of built-up cars from Europe, which then accounted for a third of the company's sales in the UK. The Transport and General Workers Union, which had a large membership at Ford, officially requested its dockers and delivery drivers to refuse to handle Ford shipments. They were supported by the seamens' unions so that all imports and exports of the company's products were effectively halted. By the end of the fifth week of the dispute, the shortage of UK supplies began to cause cutbacks in production in Ford plants in Belgium, Germany and Spain. The strike lasted nine weeks – oddly enough, the same duration as the one in 1971.

International Efforts

To bargain more effectively with the MNE, the national trade unions needed to know about the company's international activities, and they needed at times to collaborate with unions in other countries. To meet this need they turned to the International Trade Secretariats, international organisations uniting national unions with membership in similar sectoral employment such as metalworkers, postal workers, miners, chemical workers, etc. Seventeen such secretariats are in existence, among them the International Metalworkers' Federation (IMF) now organised in separate departments, one of which is concerned with the automotive industry. It is said to be the strongest secretariat in terms of financial support, leadership and staff.

The IMF has gradually created a number of world auto councils, one for each of the major American, European and Japanese automotive MNEs[5] composed of trade unionists directly involved in these companies who come together to co-operate in information gathering and strategy planning. At their disposal are detailed and sophisticated data on profits and the financial position of the companies, and a computer bank on wages and working conditions at 47 representative plants of 15 world automotive firms. The national trade union negotiator is no longer handicapped by ignorance of what the MNE is doing elsewhere, and has become fully aware of the importance of looking at the global operations of the firm in framing labour's position on wages and other issues.

As far as transnational union collaboration is concerned, the IMF has tried to assist host country unions to resolve specific problems with data and technical advice or via home union pressure on the parent company of the MNE. It has also initiated multinational union conferences where information is exchanged. Recent actions cited by the IMF include efforts in support of strikers in Brazil at Volkswagen, General Motors, Chrysler and Saab-Scania by way of home unions in late 1978 and April 1979. Reasonably successful results were claimed at Volkswagen and Saab-Scania. It is maintained that, partly as a result of IMF-sponsored interventions, Ford and General Motors in the Port Elizabeth area of South Africa recognise a black union (the UAW of South Africa). In June 1979 a useful encounter between Volkswagen management and black trade unionists took place in Wolfsburg. Home union pressures have been sought on Ford and Chrysler regarding their Spanish operations over a period of years. The IMF has initiated talks on several occasions between the Chrysler parent company and the Union General de Trabajo, and has been in frequent touch with Ford-Europe on behalf of its Spanish affiliate. Several multinational union meetings were arranged in 1978 to consider possible joint industrial action to preserve jobs threatened by the takeover of Chrysler-Europe's operations by Peugeot-Citroen.

It can be seen from this that the IMF's role has consisted in furnishing information and technical advice to its affiliated members; and in action in the form of private initiatives to resolve specific problems, largely with the help of home unions, and the arranging of multinational union conferences for discussion purposes. At no time has the IMF engaged in collective bargaining negotiations with MNEs on behalf of its members. The day when multinational collective bargaining takes place, with a single multinational union composed of members from all relevant countries confronting a MNE, seems very far off indeed.[6] There are many reasons for this.

To begin with, MNEs in the motor industry are almost unanimous in their opposition to transnational collective bargaining.[7] The response of General Motors to a recent ILO questionnaire no doubt is representative of their views and is worth quoting in part. After indicating that its subsidiary operations are essentially local enterprises that are for the most part locally controlled from a labour-relations point of view, the statement continues:

Labour relations is practical business. General Motors experience has

shown there is no valid reason for the imposition of international
bargaining and/or consultation with labour relations management in
the home office of the Corporation or for any other kind or degree
of transnational bargaining.[8]

Clearly General Motors feels strongly on this issue. But in the past
many companies who were just as adamantly opposed to bargaining
with national trade unions, were forced to change their minds when
confronted by a strong, organised and united labour force. And they
have lived with the consequences (more or less happily) ever after. It is
the weakness of international labour rather than the strength of company opposition to transnational bargaining that is primarily responsible for the inability of such bargaining to get off the ground.

There are fundamental structural differences among labour organisations in different countries which make the multinationalisation of
labour extremely difficult. Trade unions outside North America,
particularly in the car industry, are rarely organised on an industrial
basis. In Britain the industry is highly craft-orientated but also includes
a section of a general workers' union. In Japan it is organised in company unions. Then too the degree of unionisation differs between
countries and this may result in differences in union strategy. The UAW
has virtually 100 per cent of the American and Canadian workers
organised compared to 35 per cent or less in some Western European
countries. Most important of all is the existence of rivalry between
trade unions based largely on ideological differences.

The Chrysler/Peugeot-Citroen council meeting in London in 1978
provides a good illustration of this rivalry and how political schisms
have impaired joint union confrontation of MNEs.[9] Present were delegates from the IMF's affiliated unions in a number of countries, including
France and Spain. The French representatives were from the Christian
Democratic union, the Confederation Francaise Democratique du
Travail (CFDT) and the Socialist/Social Democratic union, Confederation Generale du Travail-Force Ouvriere (CGI-FO), while the Spanish
delegates were from Social Democratic and Christian Democratic
unions comprising the Union General de Trabajo (UGT). They represent a minority of the workers in the industry in both countries. Also in
London were members of their rival unions, both closely allied with the
Communist Party, the Confederation Generale du Travail (CGT) and
the Comisiones Obreras (CCOD). These unions do not represent much
more of the workforce in the two countries but they play an important
role in trade union affairs nationally. The CGT did its best to get

admitted to the meeting; they invited the Spanish unions to meet separately with them; they invited British shop stewards to discuss employment with them; they cajoled and threatened but without success. They were not affiliates of the IMF, and despite the urgings of the British unions only IMF delegates were allowed to participate.

Excluded from the work of the secretariats, the CGT and the Confederazione Generale Italiana del Lavoro (CGIL, also allied with the Communist Party) have attempted to create what have been referred to as 'underground' world company councils by organising shop stewards' committees from the various European countries. They were designed to undermine or discredit the activities of the company councils of the secretariats. The European operations of Ford have been one of the targets.

Labour unity against the MNE is further weakened by the trend toward European regional collaboration since the second world war, culminating in the formation of a European Trade Union Confederation (ETUC) in 1973 which decided that it too must have a direct role in confronting MNEs. Affiliates of the CGIL were invited to join from the start, and moves to include the CGT have since been made. The ETUC has created six industrial committees (one of which is the European Metalworkers Federation) which are supported and subsidised by the EEC Commission. These Euro-secretariats, although they are loosely connected with the international trade secretariats and share some common membership. represent a direct challenge to them and to their world company councils.[10]

In addition to creating rivals to the international secretariats, the ETUC has also been active within the EEC in fostering the future establishment of a body made up of European Works Councils which will engage in Europe-wide collective bargaining. It has insisted that only its affiliates participate in these Works Councils and that it will nominate the representatives of the workers on the boards of directors of European companies. A European Trade Union Research Institute has been created to assist in building up trade union participation in corporate affairs. Co-operation between European regional labour organisations and the international trade secretariats, such as the IMF, whose major affiliates include large contingents from North America and Japan, will not be easy.

But the main obstacle to effective international trade union collaboration lies not in the opposition from MNEs to transnational bargaining, nor in structural handicaps, but in the conflict of interests between unions in the different countries in which the MNEs operate. The

British and German trade unionists welcomed Ford's decision in 1970 to produce Pinto engines and gearboxes in Europe; the American UAW attacked it. In 1974 the Japanese Automotive workers rejected UAW requests for their help in persuading Japanese firms to accept voluntary export restraints on their sales to the US. More importantly, labour unions in developed countries view with alarm the continuing shift of automotive production to low-wage developing countries. This is not how their fellow workers at the receiving end look at it.

The trade union is really in the same position as the nation-state. Both realise that an international organisation is logically the answer but neither is ready to surrender its sovereignty to a world body. World labour solidarity has as much reality as international solidarity as displayed in the United Nations. But the idea behind the United Nations lives on, and the multinational trade union is not a dead issue.

Notes

1. Jon P. Gunnermann (ed.), *The Nation-state and Transcontinental Corporation in Conflict* (Praeger, New York, 1975), p. 52.

2. *Financial Times*, 10 September 1977.

3. C. Fred Bergston, Thomas Horst and Theodore H. Moran, *American Multinationals and American Interests* (The Brookings Institution, Washington, DC, 1978), p. 110.

4. *Financial Times*, 26 September 1978.

5. There is no auto council for Fiat as the Italian unions are not affiliated to the IMF.

6. The only significant and successful case of international union action in the motor industry was the gaining of identical pay and working conditions for American and Canadian workers in 1970. But this was a special case because the union concerned, the UAW, has members in both countries. The IMF was not involved.

7. Fiat has expressed a dissenting view. 'The Fiat company is in favour of transnational collective bargaining tending to standardise the regulations in the metal industries covering individual employer-worker relations and their collective aspect, provided national bargaining defines their technical and economic content. This applies especially to integrated regions such as the European Economic Community.' International Labour Office, *Social and Labour Practices of Some European-based Multinationals in the Metal Trades* (ILO, Geneva, 1976), p. 92.

8. International Labour Office, *Social and Labour Practices of Some US-based Multinationals in the Metal Trades* (ILO, Geneva, 1977), p. 147.

9. Economist Intelligence Unit, *Multinational Business*, 'The Changing Structure of Trade Union Response to the Multinational Company' vol. 4, (1978), pp. 11-12.

10. Ibid., p. 14.

11 THE SURVIVORS

This industry is pitiless to the weak. (Jean Parayre, Head of
Peugeot-Citroen)[1]

The history of the motor industry in the major producing countries is
uniformly one of growing concentration of production, brought about
by merger, acquisitions and the competitive elimination of firms. As a
result, the typical national industry has become composed of three or
four mass producers and a handful of small-scale, specialist manufacturers of cars and of heavy trucks. Any industry in which a small number of firms accounts for a large proportion of total output is labelled
an oligopolistic industry. In such an industry the barriers to new
entrants are formidable and there is a high degree of interdependence
among the survivors. Each knows that the consequences of any decision depends heavily on the reactions of the others. To reduce the
attendant risk and uncertainty, and to increase profits, it is generally
argued that the major firms will resort to collusion. Its most usual form
is an agreement, or tacit understanding, to avoid price competition.
Rivalry then centres on product differentiation, which may be costly
for consumers. Hence pinning the label 'oligopolistic' on the motor
industry conjures up a picture of cozy, non-price competition, excess
profits, proliferation of models, frequent model changes and far too
much advertising and selling expenditure.

Unfortunately labels tend to stick and one which was applied in the
past with some justification to the mature American industry, dominated by General Motors, Ford and Chrysler, is widely used to charac-
terise the motor industry of today. It hardly seems appropriate. Ten
giant firms from six different countries are fiercely competing for
shares in the world market. Some dozen more are still in the running,
not counting enterprises in the Soviet Union and Eastern Europe. With
more or less free trade in motor vehicles throughout the developed
world, every producing country in the market economies has undergone
substantial import penetration except Japan. Most companies would
have been delighted to earn normal returns let alone excess profits. And
there have been major casualties in the ranks of the MNEs.

Saved by the State

British Leyland

> If we are efficient and effective, we can be profitable. But unless we
> collaborate along the Honda lines I do not think there is much hope.
> (Sir Michael Edwardes, BL Chairman, March 1980)[2]

In 1973 British Leyland was the tenth largest producer of motor
vehicles in the world, with an output of almost 1.2 million units and
total sales of $2.8 billion. It had subsidiaries in 33 countries, most of
them small assembly plants but there were manufacturing subsidiaries
in Australia, Spain and Italy. Just one year later it had to be rescued
from bankruptcy by the government and it was nationalised in 1975.

The company's deteriorating position at home forced it to start
liquidating its loss-making manufacturing activities overseas even before
the financial crunch came. The Australian subsidiary had lost over
$A50 million over the three years to 1974 and the P76, a model
specially designed for the Australian market at a cost of $A25 million,
had not been a success. By the end of 1974 manufacturing had ceased
and the main plant in Sydney had been sold to the government which
intended to use the site for a housing estate. Early in 1974 it was
announced that the Spanish subsidiary, Authi, which was said to have
lost money since its acquisition by British Leyland in 1969, would be
sold to General Motors. However, the negotiations, which involved the
Spanish government, were not successful and the main assembly plant
was finally purchased by SEAT in 1975. In the same year the Italian
subsidiary which had only been acquired in 1972, was liquidated.

The management claimed that its difficulties were caused by the
energy crisis, the 'collapse' of the world car market, and the 3-day
week brought on by the strike of the UK miners. But its troubles were
much more deep-seated than that. Ever since British Leyland was
formed in 1968 through Leyland Motors' merger with British Motor
Holdings, its profits had been wholly inadequate and insufficient to
finance the investment necessary to introduce new models when
required and to maintain the business on a profitable basis. To make
matters worse nearly all the profits were distributed as dividends
instead of being used to finance new investment. Moreover, a substantial proportion of the fixed assets were old and fully written down so
that its depreciation charge was an inadequate measure of what should
have been spent on capital equipment. Even working capital had been
run down to critical levels.

Indeed the first step hastily taken by the government in December 1974 was to guarantee a British Leyland overdraft of £50 million for working capital while it considered the company's request for long-term support for its investment programme. The Ryder Committee set up by the government to investigate the affairs of the company concluded that its survival as a full-line producer of cars and commercial vehicles (which it recommended) would require a massive investment and that the government would have to finance much of it. In inflated price terms, the committee estimated that £2.8 billion would be needed over the eight-year period to 1982, half of which would have to be public money and the remainder internally generated within the company.

The Ryder proposals were quickly accepted by the government but the forecasts on which they were based proved to be hopelessly optimistic. This is not the place to go into the subsequent trials and tribulations of British Leyland (now BL). Suffice it to say that car production at 504,000 units in 1979 was down to almost half that of the peak year 1972, and the company's share of the UK car market fell from 40 per cent in 1968 to just under 20 per cent in 1979. The figures for commercial vehicle production show a similar pattern of decline. To make matters worse, replacements for the ageing model range are being delayed by a shortage of engineering resources and uncertainty over finance. The Mini Metro, at a cost of £280 million, finally reached the market in the autumn of 1980. But the replacement for the Allegro/Marina models, a middle range car code-named LC10, may not be introduced until 1983 by which time the estimated cost will be some £400 to £500 million. With its new model range, including the Honda car, the company hopes to increase car output to an annual 900,000 units by 1984. Even this will be a long way short of the 2 million which some industry observers believe will be the minimum necessary for survival in the world volume car market during the eighties. Hence the Chairman's statement at the beginning of this section and echoed by Roy Horrocks, Chairman and Managing Director of the Austin Morris division, 'The benefits of rational collaboration can be enormous. In the face of the mountainous sums the American industry is investing in research and design every smaller manufacturer must think in terms of pooled resources.'[3] It is certain too that Leyland Vehicles, the truck and bus division, with an output of only 28,000 units in 1978 will need a partnership with a foreign company if it is to re-establish itself as a significant world producer.

The survival of BL, at least in its present form, is far from assured. But there can be no doubt that its future depends on the establishment of co-operative agreements with other manufacturers. Whether this can be done, and whether the agreements will be successful without financial links between the partners, remains to be seen.

Chrysler

> Chrysler owes its success over the years to its ability to overcome the disadvantages of size. As a result, even though it is the smallest of the three full-line automobile manufacturers, Chrysler is a large and strong company. (John Ricardo, Chairman and Lee A. Iacocca, President, Chrysler Corporation, 1978)[4]

In 1973 Chrysler was the third largest automotive producer in the world and the eighth largest manufacturing corporation in the market economies, with subsidiaries in 26 countries. It produced over 3.2 million cars and trucks world-wide and its total sales were almost $8 billion. Five years later the company had sold, or was in the process of selling, virtually all of its overseas assets save the operations in Canada and Mexico, and total production had fallen to 1.6 million units. During 1979 it had to seek government assistance to avert bankruptcy.

As in the case of British Leyland, the fundamental weakness of the parent company led to the disposal of the bulk of Chrysler's overseas operations which for the most part had been unprofitable. It was a dramatic development in the history of the industry and marked the end of a vainglorious attempt to rival Ford and General Motors overseas. The company's entire European facilities were sold to Peugeot-Citroen for $300 million in cash and an equity holding of nearly 15 per cent in the French company which took over almost $400 million in debt. The Argentine subsidiary was sold to Volkswagen which also acquired a two-thirds interest in Chrysler-Brazil. Mitsubishi purchased a 30 per cent share in the Australian subsidiary, with an option to acquire more later on. Local interests took over 75 per cent of Chrysler-South Africa, and the company's equity in the joint venture in Turkey was purchased by its Turkish partners. The company did, however, hold on to its 15 per cent share in Mitsubishi.

Most observers lay the blame for Chrysler's predicament squarely on the shoulders of management. The company is paying now for years of underspending on its capital needs at home while it invested abroad in loss-making operations. In general its models lacked wide appeal in the American market and time and again were copies, two or three years later, of successful Ford and General Motors designs. A drastic cost-cutting campaign in the autumn of 1974 resulted in the departure

of thousands of designers and engineers with an effect on future car
development which was nearly fatal. When the company belatedly
decided in 1975 that it must produce a subcompact car in the US it
had to rely on Volkswagen for the engines and manual transmissions.
Limited supplies from Volkswagen crippled the sales of the successful
Horizon/Omni the first small, front-wheel drive car to be manufactured
in America.

The management estimated in 1976 that the company would have
to spend $7.5 billion on new models, machinery and equipment, and
new factories in order to survive as a full-line producer. In 1979
Chrysler lost over $1 billion and, not only could it not afford the rescue
plan, it urgently needed help to avoid imminent bankruptcy. That help
could only be provided by the US government. In pleading its case the
company argued that its problems resulted largely from the government
standards for new cars which were forcing the US industry to undertake
billions of dollars of capital investment, dollars which Chrysler simply
could not afford. It pointed, with the help of the UAW, to the 200,000
to 300,000 Chrysler workers, dealers and suppliers who would become
unemployed if the company did not receive assistance. Its Chairman con-
tended that Ford and General Motors would not pick up Chrysler's
customers and that import penetration would rise to over 30 per cent.
To those familiar with the plight of Chrysler-UK in 1975, this will have
a familiar ring.

Despite misgivings in some quarters, the government finally agreed
to what has been referred to as 'the biggest corporate bail-out in US
business history'.[5] Chrysler was to receive $1.5 billion in loan guaran-
tees to help to stave off certain bankruptcy, provided it could raise $2
billion in non-guaranteed money by selling off assets, getting extra
credit from lenders and 'other concessions' from persons with an
economic stake in the company. The 200 or more banks to whom
Chrysler owes money are seeking a solution which minimises the
amount of new money Chrysler borrows. That solution, when it comes,
will almost certainly mean a greatly slimmed-down Chrysler Corporation.

Volvo Car BV (formerly DAF)

(Pulling Volvo Holland round) was one of the toughest jobs in the
automotive world. But we still have a fair chance of doing it. (Hakan
Frisinger, President, Volvo Car, 1980)[6]

Not a major casualty, of course, but an instructive example of the difficulties a small, democratic country encounters in trying to retain an independent foothold in the motor industry.

The Dutch automotive company, DAF, was established by the Van Dorne brothers after the war. It produced its first truck in 1950 and more than half its output subsequently went to the Dutch army. The first car, the Daffodil, was introduced in 1959, with its unique, belt-driven automatic transmission which was the secret of its survival. This was much cheaper and simpler than conventional automatic transmissions and enabled the car to be sold at a higher price than its rivals, concealing its cost handicap from small-scale production. Nevertheless, the car side of the business was probably only marginally profitable, certainly not enough to finance the new model development and expansion essential for long-run survival.

A financial link with an MNE seemed to be the answer and in 1972 the car and truck business was split, with Volvo taking a one-third interest in the former and International Harvester a similar share in the latter. The Dutch government held a share in both parts. In 1974 Volvo increased its participation to 75 per cent (the government held 25 per cent) and changed the name of the company to Volvo Car BV. For a number of reasons, including the introduction of an unsuccessful model, the enterprise sustained heavy losses, and it seems fair to say that, without considerable financial assistance from the Dutch government, it would have been abandoned by Volvo.

In 1977 a state loan of £23.8 million was made to Volvo Car BV for investment purposes, not to cover losses. At the time the Swedish company was anxious for the government to increase its stake, but the offer was rejected. But the following year the government did increase its holding to 45 per cent with a cash injection of £18.3 million thereby reducing Volvo's share to 55 per cent. The government also promised to provide financial support up to £32 million to 1980. A third rescue package was decided upon in 1979, with the government putting up $76 million and Volvo $39 million for new product development. It was hoped that retained profits after the company came out of the red in 1982 would finance about two-thirds of the development cost.

The conditions attached to the original agreement and those added to the various aid packages reflect the typical fears of a host country in dealing with a MNE. A seven man supervisory board was established with two government representatives, one employee representative and four from Volvo. Six of the seven must approve major decisions such as large-scale dismissals, liquidation or mergers. An agreement in principle was obtained on a change in the original policy of centralising decision making in Sweden to give the Dutch subsidiary greater freedom to decide its own policies. Unease over transfer prices led to the requirement that Volvo must deliver components to the subsidiary at cost prices. The main concern of the Dutch unions was that Volvo's need to rationalise operations would reduce the subsidiary, which had the capacity to develop and build models from scratch, to the role of supplier of components to the parent company. Hence the Dutch government's insistence that most of the development work on the new model to succeed the 343 should be done in the Netherlands. Plans to name a percentage figure in the contract were dropped, but in principle as much work as possible will be carried out in the subsidiary. Volvo also agreed not to develop a middle range car similar to the 343 outside Holland. Moreover, the Swedish company did not obtain the rights to a new transmissions system which it had, mistakenly, thought was part of the deal. As part owner of the enterprise, the Dutch government clearly has more leverage than did the British government in its dealings with Chrysler-UK. It remains to be seen, however, to what extent the tail can wag the dog.

The Volume Producers

Arbitrarily taking an annual capacity of 100,000 units as the minimum for a volume-producer, there are just 25 such firms in the market economies, and they account for over 98 per cent of the non-Communist world's total production of motor vehicles. The remainder is made up of production by relatively small manufacturers of heavy trucks and of specialist cars such as Rolls-Royce. But the industry is a good deal more concentrated then this suggests. As shown in Table 11.1, four firms produce half the world total, and the eight largest companies produce nearly three quarters. Including the production of the Communist countries does not significantly alter the picture, since they account for only some 8 per cent of the world total.

The eight firms shown in the table are the industry giants, each capable of producing at least two million units annually. The figure of two million has become a significant one in industry circles and, with the exception of Chrysler, there is an output gap of one million units or more between these producers and those in Table 11.2.

Table 11.1: The Eight Largest Producers, Output and World Share, 1979 (Thousands)

	Home	Foreign	Total	World Share* Per Cent
1. General Motors	7,292**	1,377	8,669	22.9
2. Ford	3,559**	1,991	5,550	14.7
3. Toyota	2,996	4	3,000	7.9
4. Volkswagen	1,720	860	2,580	6.8
5. Nissan	2,380	51	2,431	6.4
6. Peugeot-Citroen	2,002	396	2,398	6.3
7. Renault	1,591	351	1,942	5.1
8. Fiat	1,382	507	1,889	5.0
Total			28,459	75.1

* Excludes Communist countries.
** Includes Canada.
Source: SMMT.

Table 11.2: Other Volume Producers, Output, 1979 (Thousands)

	Output*	Financial Links
9. Chrysler	1,517	
10. Toyo Kogyo	971	Ford
11. Mitsubishi Motors	939	Chrysler
12. Honda	802	
13. Daimler-Benz	687	
14. BL	628	
15. Isuzu	425	General Motors
16. American Motors	395	Renault
17. Daihatsu	366	Toyota
18. Suzuki	345	
19. Volvo	336	Renault
20. Fuji	334	Nissan
21. BMW	328	
22. Alfa Romeo	210	Nissan
23. International Harvester	136	
24. Saab-Scania	113	
25. Hyundai Motor	110	
Total	8,742	

* Includes foreign production, if any.
Source: SMMT production figures (except for Hyundai).

Nearly half the firms in the 'second division' have financial links with one of the eight leading producers while a number have specialised in the manufacture of heavy trucks and/or 'up-market' cars. Many have co-operation agreements with other companies. Notable is the presence of seven Japanese companies in this group, nurtured by a massive postwar growth in demand in a sheltered home market so that industry concentration has been much less in Japan than elsewhere.

Prospects for the 1980s

Only companies which operated on a world scale, with an annual capacity of at least 2 m. vehicles would be contestants in the world market battle of the 1980s. (Donald Petersen, Executive Vice President, Ford, 1979)[7]

It's going to be a hell of a dog fight. Some noses are going to get bloodied. (William O. Bourke, Executive Vice President, Ford, 1978)[8]

The idea that a yearly production of 2m vehicles was essential for survival for a major group was first publicly expressed back in 1969 by Giovanni Agnelli of Fiat.[9] Since then it has become a widely-quoted figure. Mr Agnelli also forecast at that time that by 1980 there would be ten major groups surviving in the world — three American, two Japanese and five European. If, on the criterion of value of sales (rather than unit production), Chrysler and Daimler-Benz are added to Table 11.1, then the forecast was exactly right for 1979.

But the struggle for survival is far from over. There will be more changes. Already Chrysler has ceased to be a main contender and its continuation as an independent producer is in doubt. The fate of that company is a reminder that even in the motor industry, size is not everything. Of the other leading companies, Fiat, losing its firm grip on its home market and beset by labour problems, may not be able to maintain its position as a major contestant in the world market in the 1980s. The biggest question mark, however, surrounds the two Japanese producers.

They have the volume but they do not 'operate on a world scale', that is, they are not MNEs in the sense that they control a global network of production facilities, with an appreciable proportion of their total output manufactured outside Japan. If this is a necessary condition for survival as a major world producer, then we may expect extensive foreign direct investment by the Japanese companies to match the world-wide facilities of their main rivals. At this late stage in the development of the industry this may not be easy, especially if Japanese superiority is primarily based on location-specific advantages rather than firm-specific advantages.

There is always the possibility that one or two firms in Table 11.2 may break into the 'first division', perhaps with the aid of a technological breakthrough. At the moment, Toyo Kogyo, Mitsubishi and Honda seem to be the most likely candidates. The rest will survive as junior partners of the major companies or, at least for a time, in a comfortable niche as specialist producers. But one thing is certain, when the dog-fight is over, there will be fewer dogs.

Notes

1. *Financial Times*, 8 October 1979, Survey of the European Motor Industry.
2. *Financial Times*, 18 March 1980.
3. *Financial Times*, 12 April 1979.
4. Chrysler Corporation, *Annual Report*, 1978.
5. *Financial Times*, 2 November 1979.
6. *Financial Times*, 22 February 1980.
7. *Financial Times*, 30 July 1979.
8. *Business Week*, 20 November 1978, p. 102.
9. *Financial Times*, 6 December 1969.

PART THREE

MOTOR INDUSTRY CASE STUDIES

12 CONDITIONS OF PRODUCTION

However commonplace the motor car has become, it is, nevertheless, a complex, highly sophisticated product. To design, develop and plan for the production of a unique model destined for the mass market takes roughly three years and calls for the co-ordinated efforts of numerous highly-trained and experienced personnel with a wide range of skills. The ability to perform this critical function is still limited to firms in less than ten countries.

Given the product, more countries are, of course, capable of carrying out the manufacturing process. That process is especially notable for two features. First, the dependence of the car manufacturer on a range of ancillary industries for basic materials, and on a host of specialised firms for some of the 4,000 or so separate items contained in each car. Typically, some 60 per cent of the cost of a car represents inputs purchased by the vehicle manufacturer from outside sources. There must be suppliers of steel, iron, aluminium and other metals, rubber, plastics, glass and textiles; together with companies producing parts, components and accessories not normally made by the manufacturer himself — tyres, brake linings, batteries, electrical equipment, carburettors, sparking plugs, fuel injection pumps, windscreen wipers, locks, door handles, etc., etc. Obviously the efficiency of any motor industry is heavily dependent on the efficiency of the suppliers to the manufacturers of the final product.

The other outstanding feature of the manufacturing process is the very great significance of economies of scale. Few industries have been so profoundly influenced by such economies as has the motor industry. They go a long way towards explaining why the production of motor vehicles is highly concentrated in the major industrial countries, and even why less than a dozen giant companies in those countries account for the bulk of the world's output of automotive products. The use of capital-intensive, mass-production techniques, which reduce unit costs at high volumes, is made possible by the existence of large markets and is encouraged by relatively high labour costs, conditions found in the advanced industrial nations.

Developed Countries

> We sell the same things everywhere and minimise the number of
> locations in which we make them. (George Lacey, Managing Director,
> Chrysler-UK, 1978)[1]

> It is true that one major gamble — say with a new car — could break
> a small company like Volvo. (Pehr Gyllenhammar, Managing Direc-
> tor, Volvo, 1975)[2]

The main processes performed by motor manufacturers in the mid-
1970s which gave rise to significant technical economies of scale consisted of the casting and forging, machining and pressing of metals,
largely iron and steel,[3] and the assembly of sub-assemblies into the final
product. The economies came primarily from the spreading of the
heavy initial fixed costs, e.g. tooling, design, building and testing of
prototypes; and the use of highly specialised and mechanised equipment. A number of attempts have been made to estimate the extent to
which unit costs of production fall as the scale of operations is
increased. The conclusions have varied considerably, partly because of
measurement problems and partly because some writers have tried to
determine the 'optimum' volume (i.e., the point at which unit costs
would cease to fall) and others have sought the minimum efficient scale
(mes), the level below which the manufacturer is placed at a serious cost
disadvantage in relation to larger competitors. For all practical purposes, the latter is what matters.

Table 12.1 is taken from a major, authoritative study of the British
Motor industry and is based on techniques used in 1974 in volume car
production. It indicates that foundry work, that is, the casting of
engine blocks, casings for axles, brakes and transmissions, etc., is a
relatively small-scale operation,[4] that the mes of final assembly plants
has increased considerably since the early postwar years, due primarily
to the growing use of robot welding machines for body assembly; and
that it is in the machining and assembling of the engines, transmissions
and axles, the 'powertrain', that economies of scale are most pronounced. It is here that the use of specialised equipment and automa-
tion pays off at high volumes, making 500,000 identical units a year the
mes for that process, based on a powertrain life 'well beyond the seven
to eight year period normally accorded a volume car'.

Table 12.1: Economies of Scale in Car Production

Manufacturing Operation	Minimum Efficient Size (Identical units per plant per year)
Casting of engine block	100,000
Engine and transmission machining and assembly	500,000
Final assembly	250,000

Source: Central Policy Review Staff, *The Future of the British Car Industry*, p. 16.

Possible economies in the body shop are discussed in the Report but no attempt is made to give a figure for the mes for stampings. However, it is not difficult to determine the theoretical optimum level of output for this process. The huge presses themselves are expensive pieces of equipment, but they can be used for all models and they have an extremely long life, remaining fully competitive for up to 30 years. Ideally, they should be worked continuously, without having to stop to change the dies inserted in them which shape each body panel or part of a particular model. The optimum *annual* output is then the operative speed of the presses, which are capable of some 2m stampings a year. The optimum *total* output of the model is determined by the physical life of the dies. On this the Report states, 'For each model a set of high-volume dies costs around £15 million (1974 prices) and is capable of producing as many as 7 million stampings before replacement.'[5] The latter figure seems high, but if accepted it means the optimum for pressings is 2m a year for 3½ years.

Few individual models come anywhere near achieving the optimum, but no estimates of the cost penalty associated with smaller volumes are available. As far as the unit capital cost of the dies is concerned, the penalty appears to be slight. Using the above figures, the optimum unit cost of the dies would be £2.50. If the total production of the model were 2m (say 250,000 a year for eight years) the unit cost of the dies would be increased by only £5. However, the much smaller annual volume would involve fairly frequent changing of the dies (which can be expensive and time-consuming) in order to use the presses as much as possible. Even so one source maintains that few manufacturers achieve even 50 per cent utilisation of their presses.[6] This suggests that the cost penalties of not achieving the annual optimum volume for one model are appreciably greater than failing to reach the optimum total volume.

Lacking an estimate for the mes for pressings, the CPRS Report implies that 500,000 units a year is the mes for producing a single model, that figure being determined by economies of scale in producing the powertrain.

But the mes is considerably higher than that for the volume producer of cars because of the heavy risks involved in relying on one model, and because of the need to produce a range of models to cover each of the major segments of the market. At least three basic models (with minor variations) are called for, and if these were completely different from each other it would raise the mes to 1,500,000 units a year. To the extent that the models share common body panels, parts and mechanical components, this figure can be reduced. But the Report concludes that,

> individual firms with average annual production below 750,000 vehicles will find it difficult if not impossible to compete in volume car markets.[7]

This figure provides a good, solid benchmark for any economic assessment of firms and industries. The mes is certainly not lower than this. There are grounds for believing it is higher. Other studies made in the 1970s suggest a higher figure[8] as do statements made by industry spokesmen. Moreover, the huge and growing costs of research and development (not included in estimates of technical economies of scale) needed to comply with fuel economy, safety and pollution standards favours the larger companies. General Motors spent $1.6 billion on research and development in 1978. Spread over its output of 9.3m vehicles, it amounted to $172 per unit. The same sum spent by a firm with a production of 2m vehicles would add $800 to the cost of each. Small wonder that even firms of this size are interested in joint research and development schemes and in getting government help to finance research and development.

Developing Countries

Almost without exception, the technological gap and diseconomy of scale make it impossible for a developing country to enter the world market with a unique vehicle which has been developed, designed, manufactured and marketed by its nationals. The transplantation of manufacturing operations from developed to developing country is both achievable and viable. However, even this possibility seems impractical (measured by standards of reasonable accomplishment) without the assistance of multinational firms. (UNIDO, 1969)[9]

The production characteristics of the motor industry as indicated in the preceding section — large scale, capital-intensive, a complex product, requiring a wide range of high-quality inputs from numerous suppliers, top-grade engineering and managerial skills — would seem to make it a highly unlikely industry for a newly-industrialising country to seek to establish. Yet half a dozen or more have done so in the past 20 years and most developing countries have encouraged local assembly of vehicles incorporating some local content.

Nothing is to be gained by refusing to accept the fact that developing countries are dependent on the developed nations for motor industry technology; there is no question of 'going it alone'. What is at issue is the method by which the technology is transferred and the suitability of that technology. As to the former, the basic choice for the developing country is between acquiring the technology through incoming foreign direct investment or through the market. Foreign direct investment brings a package containing capital, technology, managerial and marketing expertise, perhaps even market outlets. On the other hand, it may be possible for the developing country to obtain one or more of the contents of the package through the market to work with indigenous resources, thereby avoiding foreign ownership and control. Capital to finance domestic projects might be obtained from abroad, from national or international institutions. Technical and other knowledge might be transferred through licensing agreements and through hiring experienced foreign engineers and managers who would in time train local personnel to take over. Or, if trained personnel are available to receive the specialised knowledge, a 'turn-key' operation along the lines of the USSR-Fiat arrangement might be a possibility. Assuming that these market options are available to developing countries (and for many they may not be) which is preferable from their standpoint — foreign direct investment or the market?

The Case for Foreign Direct Investment

A recent study of the transfer of manufacturing within MNEs provides two detailed examples from the overseas operations of Ford-US.[10] The first concerns Ford-South Africa, a wholly-owned subsidiary established in 1923. The second relates to Ford-Lio Ho in Taiwan, a joint venture initiated in 1972 in which Ford has a 70 per cent share. In both cases, a precise account is given of just how technology has been transferred to the subsidiaries from the parent company and from other Ford companies throughout the world. Knowledge was provided not only in a general, systematic way, but also from time to time in solving specific problems which arose in the subsidiaries. There was much interchange of personnel and the emphasis was on face-to-face exchange of know-how. The reader is left with the impression that each subsidiary unhesitatingly gets all the technical help it requests, and that Ford-US does all it can to ensure that every one of its subsidiaries is an efficient member of the Ford network.

Ford-SA illustrates an important characteristic of the parent company-subsidiary relationship, namely, that the technology transfer is continuous and changing in nature as the affiliate expands and develops, and as new models and processes appear. The assembly plant set up at Port Elizabeth in 1923 represented the first technical assistance to South Africa by Ford. The production line for the Model T 'was a small-scale version of the Detroit factory'. Over the years the plant expanded and received continuing assistance from a variety of sources within the organisation. With the government's introduction of local content requirements in the early 1960s came the decision to initiate local manufacture of engines and this led to a major transfer of technology. The manufacturing staff in Ford-US developed the entire plant construction, layout and processes, all based on the company's worldwide experience. A specialist engineer was dispatched from Ford-Canada to oversee the construction of the building. Some 40 people were sent to South Africa between 1962-4, mostly from Ford-US, but Britain, Australia and Canada were represented. These expatriates held the positions of project manager, plant manager, manufacturing engineers, plant and equipment maintenance, production maintenance, materials control and quality control engineers. Within a few years after engine production commenced, South Africans had taken over all these positions. The setting up of a second assembly plant specially for the Cortina at Straundale in 1973 brought more technical assistance from Ford-US. Officials in the South African company estimated that if they had had to buy this information outside the organisation, the plant would have been delayed at least a year. Moreover, it would have required an additional 240 man-months and cost another $300,000 or more in the mere construction phase.

Some indication that this transfer of technology has been highly successful is provided by the numerous attempts made by competitors to secure the services of Ford-SA officials with technical skills and managerial know-how in using Ford methods and systems, by offering

promotion and higher salaries. The Managing Director was bid away
after being with the company for 41 years, and the process has extended through the plant manager level to quality control technicians into
the work force. In this connection, two locally-owned licensees of
Japanese companies supply an example of the relative merits of technology transfer from parent company to subsidiary compared to that
from licenser to licensee. 'Both Toyota and Datsun have pirated Ford
officials, partly because they found it so difficult to obtain technical
assistance and managerial know-how from the Japanese licenser.'[11]

Of great significance also was the technology transfer from Ford-SA
to its suppliers, and to local dealers and garages. Assistance to suppliers
was on both a regular basis and to meet immediate problems, involving
manufacturing processes, scheduling, quality control, cost control,
organisational structure, purchasing analysis and packaging. Service is
a serious problem in South Africa for mechanics are scarce and turnover
of garage mechanics is high. Ford-SA prepares and distributes a 'Regis-
tered Technicians Programme' under which it sends out monthly
booklets as material for a correspondence course. This is followed up
by visits to garages and dealers' service departments. In addition Ford
offers one-week training courses in Pretoria and Port Elizabeth every
two weeks covering all aspects of mechanical and electrical maintenance, transmission repair, and requisition of parts and accessories.
Special one-week courses on all aspects of repair and maintenance are
provided on demand for government departments and for vehicle fleet
owners. Some are offered to engineer-trainers who must constantly
instruct newly-hired mechanics. During 1973, over 1,000 mechanics
attended training programmes held outside the company by Ford technicians.

The case study of Ford-Lio Ho presents another detailed account of
just how technology is transferred within an MNE to which the interested reader is referred. The fact that, in this case, the subsidiary is not
wholly-owned, appears to make no difference to the parent company in
this respect. Of particular note is the contrast between the technical
assistance supplied to an independent company under licence, and that
provided by a majority owner.

Lio Ho was a licensee of Toyota from 1968 to 1972. It was a new
company, formed specifically to produce Toyotas in a plant constructed solely for that purpose. The owners were the Tsung brothers, highly
successful textile manufacturers, who ran an engineering and technical
school for their textile and other interests. The workers for the car
plant were drawn mostly from this school and were sent to Toyota in

Japan to learn their jobs. They were taught some foundry skills and assembly of the car and engine, but the emphasis was on the technique needed for a specific job such as spray painting or machining of engine parts. None were taught inspection or analysis of problems and having learned the production processes they returned to Taiwan. Japanese engineers were sent to help set up the engine line and three others delegated to stay in Taiwan — a chief engineer, one for the engine plant and one for the foundry. In addition, three technicians remained to check on problems of metal, paint and inspection in the assembly process. These men solved problems by themselves or obtained help from the sole distributor in Taiwan associated with Toyota. There was little communication with Toyota in Japan since the Japanese personnel considered telexes too expensive. As production began, parts validation was carried out mainly in Japan. Two complete engines were sent on the commencement of assembly and corrections were returned on each and every part. One new model was introduced during the four years and Toyota sent three men to train Chinese on inspection and assembly procedures and they stayed two or three months. No more than five such officials visited the firm throughout the period of the licence.

According to the testimony of the Lio Ho engineers, much more technical expertise was needed if they were to be able to handle the problems arising in the plant or to produce a range of models. They noted two significant gaps in their training aside from problem analysis. No attention was given to manufacturing engineering or to supply management since Toyota made all the decisions and simply left Lio Ho to carry out assembly operations on the ckd models sent to it. The engineers would have liked much more technical assistance and the managers wanted to produce a higher-class Toyota. Their only consolation was that their main competitor, Yue Loong, had been treated in the same way by Nissan since 1953. As a consequence, Lio Ho concluded that it could not get what it wanted from *any* vehicle manufacturer as long as it remained a licensee.

In the meantime the Taiwan government had decided that it could not build up the kind of motor industry it wanted if it continued its policy of relying solely on licensing. Virtually all vehicle manufacture had been developed in technical co-operation with Japanese firms but under Chinese ownership and control. Parts manufacturing too had been done under licence, with minority foreign equity in some cases. As in other developing countries, progressive import substitution had led to rising costs, poor quality, proliferation of models and plants in a limited market, and idle capacity. The solution was seen to be specialised production for world markets of parts and components with relatively high labour content such as foundry items, and certain low-volume items. Export production would call for the whole-hearted and continuous commitment of scarce technical and managerial personnel by MNEs. However, it was recognised that such firms would be unwilling to commit the necessary production and marketing capabilities unless they were allowed equity participation, the only assurance of an adequate return on such a commitment. Hence the decision of the government to open the industry to foreign investment, although it wanted Chinese to keep at least a minority position.

In summary, a strong case is made in support of the view that technology transfer within the MNE is vastly superior to such transfer through other channels. The subsidiary has ready and continuing access to the entire technical know-how of the parent company and to the knowledge and experience of the other affiliates as well. Moreover, every step of the process is included, from the initial proposal and planning stage, through product design, plant design and construction, start-up, value engineering and controls, product development; and external support in the form of a flow of technology to suppliers, educational institutions, maintenance and repair shops and customers. This range of knowledge, it is maintained, is simply not available to independent firms through licensing or the hiring of the services of managers and engineers in world markets.

Given that most of the technology transferred within the MNE is derived from knowledge and experience already available in one part of the system, the additional cost of using it in some other part is relatively small. In practice, most of this technical assistance appears to be 'donated' by the parent company or, to a lesser extent, by other affiliates, and no attempt is made to estimate the cost. In cases where overseas personnel are requested by and remain with a subsidiary for six months or more, the subsidiary would pay the salary and expenses involved. One example was given where the cost of the technology transfer was included in the price of the ckd deliveries. (This may happen also under a licencing agreement.) Sometimes the parent company develops new knowledge from scratch for a specific subsidiary. This happened in the case of the induction process in Ford-Brazil's foundry. Precise records were kept by Ford-US of the man-hours spent in its gestation and transfer. Presumably the subsidiary would be charged for this. But it would not reflect the total cost for, in the case of Ford-Brazil, this 'would have included a portion of corporate overhead (40-50 per cent of the time of the manufacturing staff alone) and the expertise drawn on here would not be costable.'[12]

This does not mean, of course, that the subsidiary (and the host nation) gets valuable technical assistance free or at very little cost to itself. It pays for it in the profits remitted to the parent company, perhaps also in royalties or in the price of ckd shipments, machinery, equipment and other items supplied by the parent concern. In other words, the cost of the technology is inextricably bound up with the cost of the whole 'package' and leads to the wider, much more complex, question of the net benefits to the host country of foreign direct investment.

The Case for the Market: South Korea

> It will not be long before you guys too own automobiles. (Chung Se Yung, President, Hyundai Motor Company, at a mass assembly of his production workers, 1979)[13]

In writing about MNEs economists sometimes suggest that developing countries explore the possibility of 'breaking open the package', that is, as an alternative to accepting foreign direct investment, domestic firms borrow foreign capital, licence foreign technology and hire experienced key technical and managerial personnel from abroad. The Hyundai Motor Company did just that.

It was established in 1967 by the Hyundai group which has wide interests in Korea — engineering, shipbuilding, construction and international trading. Initially the motor company assembled ckd kits from Ford-UK, supplemented with local items. Output in 1973 was a mere 7,000 units, less than half the capacity. Encouraged by the government, the company made the decision to develop and manufacture its own car model. A public company was formed with 100 per cent Korean equity and most of the money to finance the project was borrowed overseas. Barclays Bank provided £17m and money was also obtained from the French Banque de Suez and Japan's Export Import Bank. The top management team was hired, led by George Turnbull, former Managing Director of British Leyland, who brought six senior British engineers with him from the UK motor industry on a three-year contract. The design and the technology for the car, called the Pony, was purchased from abroad. The design from Giorgetto Giugiaro in Italy, the engine and gearbox from Mitsubishi in Japan, and many of the components from Britain, including Girling brakes, Burman steering and Smith's instruments. A high local content was planned from the start, with Hyundai manufacturing the engines and gearbox under licence, and local suppliers the components – all under licence. The car is now said to be 95 per cent manufactured in Korea.

The plant was laid out to produce 100,000 cars a year, with its own foundry, forge, press shops and engine works. However, the initial plan was cut back so that the plant was tooled-up to produce 56,000 units a year. Although Korean wages were less than half those of Japan, the techniques adopted were simply scaled-down versions of those used in the West. Work began in January 1975 on a green-field site at Ulsan, on the coast 250 miles from Seoul and, incredibly, the car was on sale in May 1976. Output of the Pony has risen from 30,000 in 1976 to about 110,000 in 1979, of which over 20,000 were exported to over 40 countries. The company is now entirely run by Koreans.

Success for Hyundai, and for the South Korean industry as a whole, depends very much on government support. The South Korean authorities are clearly following the Japanese model, with a protected, booming home market providing the volume and the profits needed to enable the industry to be competitive in export markets. The level of Korean incomes has reached that of the Japanese in the early 1960s when domestic sales of cars began to expand rapidly in that country. Moreover, extremely high taxes on car purchase and ownership has kept demand artificially low, given the size of the South Korean population and the level of incomes. These taxes can be progressively reduced, if necessary, to ensure that domestic demand matches the growing supply of vehicles. As part of its plan for the industry, the government encourages exports, although it is admitted that every Pony is sold abroad at a loss. Home market sales of the car, for which there has been a six-month's waiting list, subsidises the exports and, in addition, the government allows Hyundai to import one Ford Granada ckd kit for local assembly and sale at very high prices for every five Ponies exported.

The government's plans for the future of the industry are very ambitious, as they must be if the country is to become a major exporter of motor vehicles, the goal of the authorities. Apart from Hyundai (which also produces trucks and buses) the industry consists of two other assembler/manufacturers – the Saehan Motor Company, a joint venture in which General Motors owns 50 per cent, and Kia, an independent company with strong technical links with Honda. The former assembles the Opel Rekord and the Isuzu Gemini, has an engine plant with a capacity of 50,000 units a year, and produces a wide range of trucks and buses. General Motors' South Korean partner is the Daewoo group which bought its 50 per cent stake in 1978 from the Korean

Development Bank. Saehan is expected to develop its own model as a rival to the Pony. The American company has great plans for its South Korean affiliates and is linking it with its world car network. The third producer, Kia, manufactures a former Mazda model under licence from Toyo Kogyo and is also an important maker of commercial vehicles. In 1978 the capacity of each of these companies was about half that of Hyundai, making total industry capacity 278,000 units. All three will have to expand rapidly to meet the government's targets – 1m vehicles in 1981, half of which are to be exported. For 1986 the goal is 2m made up of 1.4m cars, 0.4m commercial vehicles and 0.2m buses, of which 1.4m are to be exported.

For its part, Hyundai is now in the process of extending its plant at Ulsan to increase the capacity to 250,000 units by 1981 (200,000 Ponies, 20,000 Mark IV Cortinas and Granada kits and 30,000 trucks and buses). This despite the fact that the plant, built on former paddy fields is slowly sinking so that some of the shops are flooded when it rains. The company hopes to solve the problem by putting down concrete pylons 20 metres deep and re-siting some of the buildings. But it is production as usual while this construction is being carried out. In the meantime plans are being made for another plant to be constructed not far from Seoul for completion in 1984. It will be financed by an issue of shares on the Korean stock exchange.

Another model will be produced in the new plant, said to be somewhat larger than the Pony, front-wheel-drive, most likely designed to present a challenge in the Ford Cortina class. The design consultant is again Giorgetto Giugiaro, but where the technology for the new vehicle will come from is not yet known. In preparation for its new plant, Hyundai has been talking to a number of major European manufacturers, including Renault and Volkswagen. It is seeking to buy technology, not to negotiate for a joint venture partnership.

In his report to the government on the future of the Korean motor industry, Mr Turnbull stressed that the government would have to play an active supporting role if it wanted to see a fully viable industry with substantial export potential.[14] The high taxes should be reduced as quickly as possible and other changes made to bring about a rapid expansion of domestic demand. The consequent high volume production would enable prices to be reduced, would result in improved quality, and would generate profits sufficient to finance the heavy investments that must take place. Of particular urgency was an increase in the volume and quality of suppliers of parts and components to the vehicle producers. To bring this about the government was urged to consider 'actively encouraging participation by foreign companies in equity on a minority basis. This will put less strain on the internal financing and strengthen the supporting technical assistance agreements. Government to be more flexible on terms for foreign technical partners, e.g., length of T/A agreements and percentage of royalty.'[15]

Although neither Hyundai nor the industry as a whole has achieved the ambitious production targets set, the rapid development of the company and the industry is impressive. Hyundai has shown that it is possible for a firm in a developing country to 'break open the package' and produce acceptable motor vehicles. On the other hand, companies in the components sector appear to have done less well on this basis. And it remains to be seen whether Hyundai can acquire front-wheel-drive technology without accepting a foreign partner. Moreover, if it is to become a major world competitor, it must develop its own capacity to design and engineer a range of new cars requiring new parts and components. In short, the Pony is a dark horse that has yet to jump the major international hurdles.

As an independent company, in a relatively poor developing country, Hyundai's choice of product and techniques of production are of interest. Apparently no thought was given to producing a low-cost vehicle suitable for Asian markets and other similar markets. The product was to be a sophisticated passenger car, designed to sell in the world's major producing countries as well as at home. As for the techniques of production, the Japanese pattern would be followed. When rates of pay in Japan were much lower than in other developed countries, capital equipment was purchased which made the Japanese more capital intensive than many of their competitors. As a result Japan is still competitive despite its very high labour costs today. The moral — even when labour costs are low, buy the best capital equipment, scaled down of course where smaller volumes are needed. This is discussed further in the following section.

Suitability of Techniques and Products

Almost all of the world's research and development takes place in the wealthy industrialised countries, the bulk of it in the parent companies of the MNEs. The innovations are designed to meet the needs of advanced societies. New production processes are capital intensive, reflecting relatively cheap capital and expensive labour plus an abundance of highly-skilled labour. New products are elaborate and sophisticated, aimed at affluent consumers. What do poor countries want with automated car factories or sports cars designed for rich teenagers? Why not substitute cheap and abundant labour for scarce capital? Why not produce cars without all the frills considered essential by wealthy consumers, perhaps a means of family transport halfway between a car and a bicycle?

Much of this criticism is wide of the mark as far as the cost of producing conventional automobiles is concerned. Economies of scale are of such overriding importance that the level of output largely determines the techniques used, with differences in wage rates having relatively little to do with the choice. In other words, given the necessary managerial and technical capabilities, the highly automated plants of America would be duplicated in countries such as Mexico, Nigeria and South Korea if the markets in each were large enough to absorb the planned output. In fact this is what happened in the case of the Ford engine plant in Ipananga, Brazil, which was directly copied from one of the new American factories. Twenty Brazilians were sent to the US for training 'which facilitated the direct translation of the Lima, Ohio engine plant into a new Brazilian facility for 2.3 litre engines using high technology.'[16] Ford's decision to establish a manufacturing plant in Spain was made at a time when wages there were significantly below EEC levels and this was one of the factors which influenced Ford to produce in that country. Nevertheless, it set up a plant operating on the same scale and using as sophisticated machine tools and equipment as comparable plants in most developed motor markets; and similarly for the transmission plant in Bordeaux, France, at a time when the level of French wages was well below that of the US. 'The layout, processing and tooling were duplicated from Ford-US plus all the improvements that had been developed but not yet implemented there. Bordeaux, therefore, obtained the absolute latest in developments, which US engineers would like to have had but could not yet afford to adopt.'[17]

From the MNE's point of view, the capital-intensive technology is the least-cost method to use in high-volume production, more or less regardless of what the wage levels are, and hence is the 'appropriate' technology. It may not seem so to the developing country with a large and growing mass of unemployed. But with high levels of output, capital-intensive techniques in the motor industry are capital-saving as well as labour-saving, so that employing more labour and less mechanisation at these levels would increase the capital cost and total cost. There must be more 'appropriate' ways of providing employment in developing countries than doing that.

Of course, the problem for most of these countries is not one of choosing the most appropriate technology for the mass production of automobiles, but rather of adopting techniques capable of turning out much smaller volumes for restricted markets, without increasing costs too much. Obviously, the high technology of the industrialised nations would not be suitable, for the capital cost per unit would be astronomical at very low outputs. Hence the MNE 'scales down' its operations for small markets, and in doing so automatically increases the labour content per unit.

Broadly speaking this is done by drawing on methods and layouts used in earlier periods by the parent company. Where possible these are modified to allow for subsequent improvements. For the Ford Company:

> some 90 per cent of its US studies and the work of its manufacturing staff is directly usable abroad in some affiliate, so that foreign engineering in developing countries consists in 're-do's of earlier operations in the United States; for example, circa 1940s for Ford-Lio Ho in Taiwan. The Brazilian engine plant was originally set up on a 1940 model Ford plant, producing 18/hour instead of 125/hour; however, it used technology for 125/hour and cut down the scale by segmenting the line and shifting workers from one phase to the next moving along with the engines; eight breaks were introduced and all workers were trained for each step.[18]

But there is a cost penalty to 'scaling down' as indicated by Jack Baranson in a comment based on his experience with the World Bank and as a consultant.

> The critical factor was scale. For motor vehicle and parts manufacture, for example, it was pathetic to see engineers breaking down processes in L.D.C. plants because they could not use automatic transfer machines. They inevitably ended up with a higher capital/output ratio for the lower scales.[19]

For the developing country, the crucial question is how far can the scaling down process go before local manufacture becomes uneconomic? A rough guide is given in Table 12.2. Another source is in broad agreement with this. Referring to a simple, sturdy, inexpensive 'vehicle for the masses', it indicates that at 50,000 cars a year and almost 100 per cent local content, the price might be 1.4 times that of mass-produced vehicles. At an annual output of 200,000 units and 100 per cent local content, the price would be competitive in world markets. At 300,000 units per annum the factory has reached European standards.[20] The figures apply to one model, allowing for variations to include private cars, vans and a jeep-like vehicle. The cost includes fees for licences and technical assistance but nothing for research and development. With perhaps one or two exceptions, no developing country has the technical resources to design and develop its own vehicles and, if it did, output would have to be considerably higher to finance it. A third source suggests, on the criterion that 'the cost of the vehicles will not be too different from the world price', complete domestic production is feasible when total demand exceeds 100,000 cars and 50,000 commercial vehicles a year.[21]

Table 12.2: Minimum Volume Production for Developing Countries

	Annual Sales		
	Assembly	Manufacture (1 type)	Remarks
Bus bodies		300	Cheap labour
Truck and bus chassis	2,500	6,000	5 tonners
Tractors	3,000	10,000	36-65 hp
Passenger cars (medium)	20,000	50,000	Excluding production of body panels
		200,000	Including production of body panels

Source: A.S. El Darwich, 'The Establishment of an Automotive Industry in Developing Countries' in UNIDO, *Establishment and Development of Automotive Industries in Developing Countries*, Part II, p. 60.

All studies stress the need for standardisation in the industry, and the necessity for the developing country to restrict the number of manufacturers and models, for few have a domestic market of over 200,000 vehicles a year. This creates a dilemma for governments and their advisers in industrial matters. The economics of the motor industry calls for a protected market and a monopoly, or at most an oligopoly in such countries. But these are industrial structures about which economists tend to be highly critical.

The large minimum size of domestic market needed to support a viable motor industry, combined with a lack of the prerequisites for the establishment of such an industry, has restricted most developing countries to the assembly of imported kits and the incorporation of some local materials and parts. For this stage of manufacture, relatively little capital investment is required and the cost penalty of small-scale, labour-intensive techniques is limited.

Initially, the assembly may be semi-knocked down (skd) and this does not require any special machinery. The bodywork comes as a completely welded shell, already painted, and the engine and other main mechanical components arrive pre-assembled. These parts are brought to an assembly station, simply screwed together and the interior fittings and trim added. Between skd and ckd there are various intermediate stages. For ckd assembly the imports from the manufacturer are made up of separate body parts which must be welded together and painted, and mechanical parts of engines and other major components are built up on sub-assembly lines. Line assembly is used, the vehicle or unit being transported from one assembly station to another by means of mechanically-driven conveyor belts. Such a plant must have expensive welding, body building and paint shops, and requires more skilled workers than simple assembly. With ckd assembly the stage is set for the gradual incorporation of local materials, parts and components when these become available.

But even for assembly, the scale of operations cannot be ignored. Import of complete vehicles is preferable where annual demand is less than about 10,000 for cars and 5,000 for commercial vehicles.[22] At smaller volumes, skd assembly is more suitable but should be considered only as a temporary stage in which an organisational nucleus is formed, labour recruited and trained, sales and service departments established and the groundwork prepared for the move to ckd assembly. The reason for this is that skd assembly is not economic, it increases cost and has to be protected by tariffs discriminating against built-up imports. With ckd assembly, bulk orders reduce the high import costs of skd shipments and the higher volume reduces local assembly costs. In other words, unless local demand is, or is expected to be, high enough to absorb at least 10,000 cars and/or 5,000 trucks a year, local assembly is not economically justified.

However, even if the local assembly plant can compete successfully without tariff protection against built-up vehicles (and this is unlikely) the developing country does not gain a great deal other than through the additional employment created in the assembly plant itself. There is little or no reduction in the import cost of the vehicle, since the packing materials and labour cost of preparing the shipments cost as much or more than complete assembly in the manufacturer's own plant. Hence there is little saving in foreign exchange (other than on transport costs). Most important, no impetus is given to industrialisation as all the inputs come from abroad. Thus, just as skd assembly should be considered only as a stepping stone to ckd assembly, so should the latter be recognised as no more than an essential stage in a move to manufacture a significant part or all of the country's requirements for motor vehicles. As a gathering of industry specialists from all over the world attending a seminar arranged by UNIDO put it, 'The integration of vehicle-assembly manufacture does not in itself make a significant contribution to cost reduction or to manufacturing integration and should therefore be delayed until clear evidence is available that the subsequent continuance of manufacturing integration will proceed smoothly and without excessive cost and quality problems.'[23] Up to a point, this can be done even though annual demand for cars is well below the minimum needed for efficient production of the whole vehicle. Where there are existing producers of paint, glass, textiles, plastic, rubber fittings, screws, nuts, pipes, cables, wire, small metal stampings, etc. for industry in general, it should be possible to supply many of the requirements of the motor manufacturers at reasonable prices. The same should be true of tyres, batteries and other replacement parts, and the manufacture of these should preferably be established before assembly is undertaken. Other items, such as mufflers, filters, water pumps, brake drums, bushings and some electrical components can be readily made, and with relatively little capital investment. All in all it should be possible for quite a few developing countries to increase the local content of their automobile production to around 40 per cent of total cost without an undue cost handicap. But even this cannot be done without a drastic limitation in the number of manufacturers and models, and much standardisation on the part of the suppliers of the manufacturers.

For most developing countries, to attempt to increase the local content much further by manufacturing the engine and other major mechanical components, the sheet steel and the main body pressings, is utterly uneconomic. Low volume production of these items inevitably means a high-cost industry turning out expensive, poor quality vehicles which can only be sold in heavily protected markets. For most, the dilemma posed by a small domestic market remains – high-cost manufacture of complete vehicles or the high foreign exchange costs of importing some 60 per cent of their vehicle requirements. One possible way out is through specialisation and trade and in recent years developing countries have begun to turn to this as a solution to the problem of scale. The aim is for one country to produce engines for a regional group of states, another transmissions, another body panels, etc., each using its export proceeds to pay for the major components it does not produce itself. Final assembly would take place in all the member countries in the group. MNEs, with their 'world cars' and international networks of affiliates, have been in an ideal position to foster this development and have been eager to do so. The political difficulties of such international integration of production are great, but the economic pressures are pushing developing countries in that direction.

Everything that has been said thus far concerning production techniques and minimum scales of production and assembly in developing countries pertains to motor vehicles of conventional design. The conclusion is that sophisticated products call for sophisticated techniques. In other words, the high quality vehicles generated in the industrialised countries require mass-production techniques and machine precision if they are to be manufactured efficiently. Why then not design a much simpler, low-cost motor vehicle, which could be produced efficiently at relatively small volumes, substituting plentiful labour for scarce capital?

A move in that direction was made by the MNEs in the early 1970s. Various versions of what is sometimes referred to as the Asian Utility Vehicle, a relatively low-cost four-wheeler, first appeared in the Philippines. Its forerunner there was the Jeepney, a modified version of United States army surplus jeeps which were practically the only form of motorised transport in the Philippines in the immediate postwar years. The Jeepney was introduced by a local concern, Francisco Motors, which still produces it, usually powered by an Isuzu diesel engine imported along with the transmission, drive train and wheels. The lead in the design of the Asian Utility Vehicle came from Ford and General Motors, both of which had subsidiaries in the Philippines and viewed the development in a wider context. It is assembled locally from mechanical components supplied by the manufacturer, and chassis and body parts fabricated locally following the manufacturer's design and instructions. The vehicle has been designed for simplicity and ease of local manufacture in small job shops where brake presses and simple welding jigs replace the stamping dies and automated equipment of the supplying manufacturer. The result is a rugged vehicle which combines the economies and performance of mass-produced mechanical components with small-scale, labour-intensive, simple bodywork and assembly, at a price considerably below that of conventional cars or trucks. Even so, in relation to income per head in these countries, they are still expensive and sales have been limited.

This development has been generally welcomed by those critical of MNEs for supplying 'unsuitable' products to developing countries and producing them locally using 'inappropriate' techniques. Nevertheless, it is argued by some that the move has not gone far enough (as the limited market for Asian Utility Vehicles shows) and that what is needed is something much simpler and less conventional to replace the more primitive forms of transport operated by animal or human power. The Expert Group Meeting on Manufacture of Low-Cost Vehicles in Developing Countries, held in Melbourne, Australia in February 1976, concluded, 'The problems in designing a vehicle that could provide better and cheaper transport than the bullock cart and the tractor yet would provide some draught power were obviously considerable and possibly intractable.'[24] Nevertheless the Group pointed out that the low-cost vehicles currently in use were derived essentially from those originally designed for considerably more advanced countries; that this was just as true of the Indian three-wheelers (still basically the same as their Italian predecessors) as for the Asian Utility Vehicle, and that more radical designs might be contemplated. One thing seems certain — if a completely new, low-cost vehicle of the type envisaged does appear, it will originate in the developing countries themselves. It is hard to imagine Detroit turning out motorised bullock carts.

Notes

1. *Financial Times*, 28 April 1978.
2. *The Times*, 24 February 1975.
3. Gerald Bloomfield, *The World Automotive Industry* (David & Charles, Newton Abbot, 1978), p. 34.
4. On the other hand, Mr T.N. Beckett, Managing Director, Ford-UK has stated that the optimum output for a foundry could be as high as 2 million engines per year. Parliament (Commons), *Fourteenth Report of the Expenditure Committee, 1974-75, The Motor Vehicle Industry* (HMSO, London, 1975), p. 37.
5. Central Policy Review Staff, *The Future of the British Car Industry* (HMSO, London, 1975), p. 14.
6. Krish Bhaskar, *The Future of the World Motor Industry* (Kogan Page, London, 1980), p. 51.
7. Central Policy Review Staff, *The Future of the British Car Industry*, p. 23.
8. L.J. White, *The Automobile Industry Since 1945* (Harvard University Press, Cambridge, Mass., 1971) (800,000, two models only); C.F. Pratten, *Economies of Scale in Manufacturing Industry* (Cambridge University Press, Cambridge, 1971) (1,000,000 mes); D.G. Rhys, *The Motor Industry: An Economic Survey* (Butterworths, London, 1972) (2,000,000 optimum).
9. United Nations Industrial Development Organisation, *Establishment and Development of Automotive Industries in Developing Countries*, Report and Proceedings of Seminar held in Karlovy Vary, Czechoslovakia, 24 February-14 March 1969, Part I, Report of the Seminar (UN, New York, 1970), p. 67.
10. Jack N. Behrman and Harvey W. Wallender, *Transfers of Manufacturing Technology Within Multinational Enterprises* (Ballinger Publishing Co., Cambridge, Mass., 1976).
11. Ibid., p. 81.

12. Ibid., p. 29.

13. *Financial Times*, 2 April 1979.

14. G.H. Turnbull, *The Future of the Korean Car Industry* (March, 1976). I am grateful to Mr Turnbull for letting me have a copy of his report and for discussing his experience in South Korea with me.

15. Ibid., p. 4.

16. Behrman & Wallender, *Transfers of Manufacturing Technology Within Multinational Enterprises*, p. 33.

17. Ibid., p. 40.

18. Ibid., pp. 33-4.

19. Jack Baranson, 'Bridging the Technological Gap Between Rich and Poor Countries' in G. Ranis (ed.), *The Gap Between Rich and Poor Countries* (Macmillan, London, 1972), p. 361.

20. G.L. Malleret (Director of Production Facilities, Foreign Countries Division, Citroen), 'Importance and Practical Aspects of Technical Cooperation in the Establishment or Development of a Motor Vehicle Industry in Foreign Countries' in United Nations Industrial Development Organisation, *Part II, Proceedings of the Seminar*, p. 4.

21. United Nations Industrial Development Organisation, *The Motor Vehicle Industry* (United Nations, New York, 1972), p. 18.

22. Ibid., p. 18

23. United Nations Industrial Development Organisation, *Establishment and Development of Automotive Industries in Developing Countries*, Part I, Report of the Seminar, p. 73.

24. United Nations Industrial Development Organisation, *The Manufacture of Low-Cost Vehicles in Developing Countries* (United Nations, New York, 1978), p. 21.

In this category, the UK as a mature host country, and the US as a mature home country, provide an interesting contrast. In the former, an indigenous motor industry was undermined by the presence of foreign subsidiaries. In the latter, a strong domestic industry gave birth to the world's largest MNEs. They are alike in that, in more recent years, the industry in both countries has been seriously threatened by imports.

United Kingdom

Just 25 years ago this country, with an output of over one million motor vehicles, was the world's second largest producer and the world's leading exporter. Today it ranks eighth in production, fifth as an exporter, and over half its domestic market for cars has been captured by foreign exporters. Any assessment of the role of MNEs in this highly industrialised host country must be made against this background of relative and, since 1972, absolute decline.

Competition and Industrial Structure

> We do not have the volume to compete with the real giants in the cheap end of the market. (John Barber, BL Deputy Chairman and Managing Director, October 1975)[1]

When vehicle production was resumed after the second world war, there were some 20 manufacturers in all, with six concerns accounting for 90 per cent of the domestic market. By 1968 there were four major companies and a handful of specialist firms such as Rolls-Royce and Lotus supplying less than one per cent of the total output. There was nothing unusual about this concentration of production. It had taken place in every country with a mature motor industry. What was remarkable was that three of the four were subsidiaries of American MNEs. The fourth, the only nationally-owned volume producer, was British Leyland. It was by far the largest in terms of UK assets and was responsible for somewhat more than 40 per cent of the total domestic production of cars and commercial vehicles. The behaviour and comparative performance of each of these companies during the following decade,

a period of intense competition especially after the entry of the UK
into the EEC, is worth examining in some detail.

Table 13.1: UK Car Production and Company Shares, 1968, 1973,
1978, 1979 (Thousands)

	1968		1973		1978		1979	
	Units	Per Cent	Units	Per Cent	Units	Per Cent	Units	Per Cent
British Leyland/BL	818.3	45.0	875.8	50.1	611.6	50.0	503.8	47.1
Ford	553.7	30.4	453.4	25.9	324.4	26.5	398.7	37.2
Chrysler/Talbot	189.1	10.4	265.4	15.2	196.5	16.1	103.0	9.6
Vauxhall	244.8	13.5	138.4	7.9	84.0	6.9	58.8	5.5
Other	10.0	0.7	14.3	0.9	6.4	0.5	6.2	0.6
Total	1,815.9	100.0	1,747.3	100.0	1,229.9	100.0	1,070.5	100.0

Source: SMMT.

As reflected in Table 13.1, all four firms have suffered a serious fall
in annual output since 1968. Using a volume of 750,000 cars a year as
the benchmark, every one of them is producing at an output at which
any independent company 'will find it difficult if not impossible to compete in volume car markets'. Indeed, the figures for Talbot and Vauxhall
are derisory. BL has, despite all its troubles, maintained its share of about
half of the total UK output of cars. Ford has significantly increased its
share at the expense of Vauxhall.

Table 13.2 reveals that the American companies were no more successful than British Leyland in meeting the growing challenge to the UK
market from imports, with vehicles produced in Britain. Where the
foreign MNEs scored was in their greater ability to bolster their poor

Table 13.2: Company Shares of New Car Registrations in UK, 1968,
1973, 1977, 1978, 1979 (Figures in Parentheses Reflect Captive Imports)

	1968	1973	1977	1978	1979
British Leyland/BL	40.6	31.9	23.5 (24.3)	22.5 (23.5)	18.7 (19.6)
Ford	27.3	22.6	19.1 (25.7)	16.0 (24.7)	14.5 (28.3)
Vauxhall	13.2	8.0	6.1 (10.4)	6.0 (8.2)	5.6 (8.2)
Chrysler/Talbot	10.2	9.7 (11.5)	4.9 (6.0)	6.2 (7.1)	4.8 (11.0)*
Imports	8.3	25.7 (1.8)	45.4 (12.8)	49.3 (12.8)	56.3 (23.5)

*Includes Citroen and Peugeot imports.
Source: SMMT.

performance with captive imports from their subsidiaries on the Continent. Such imports for 1979 were: Ford (236,824), Peugeot-Citroen/ Talbot (108,354) and Vauxhall (44,822) compared to BL's 16,751 from its Belgian subsidiary. Captive imports have been growing in recent years and in 1979 amounted to 42.5 per cent of the total imports which were 406,751 cars.

Car Exports

Table 13.3 gives a clear indication of the influence of deliberate policy decisions on the part of the parent companies involved. There were no exports from the American subsidiaries to the US, the home country (which in effect now includes Canada), nor did these companies compete seriously in Continental Europe against affiliates there. On the other hand, British Leyland, as the home-based MNE with no manufacturing subsidiaries in the two main overseas markets, exported more than the three US subsidiaries put together. Vauxhall's performance was particularly dismal and it was announced in 1979 that the company was withdrawing from the European market. Chrysler's export record would be just as poor were it not for its long-term contract to supply Iran National with ckd kits, a contract initially obtained by its predecessor Rootes. Ford's exports to Europe, while noticeably better than those of the other two American companies, nevertheless did little to offset its captive imports.

As far as the US market is concerned, it should be mentioned that the door has not always been closed to exports from American subsidiaries in Britain; that they did have the opportunity earlier to participate in the postwar boom in small cars there. Up to the 1970s, the UK was the sole source of captive imports by Ford-US. Over 120,000 English Fords were sold in America during the period 1956 to 1960, and over 80,000 in the years 1966 to 1970. Since then Ford-US imports have consisted of German-built Capris and the Fiesta from Spain. General Motors sold 40,000 Vauxhalls and 55,000 Opels in the two years 1959 and 1960 and subsequently chose Germany as the sole source of its imports of small cars, although in turn these have been replaced by imports from its Japanese associate Isuzu. Chrysler dropped the French Simca in 1971 in favour of Chrysler-UK's Avenger (Cricket in the US) and the Colt from Mitsubishi. By the end of 1973, there were 98,000 Colts sold as against 46,000 Crickets and the latter ceased to be imported.

In short, the UK subsidiaries of the American firms have not always been excluded from the US market, nor have they been treated any

Table 13.3: UK Manufacturers Exports of Cars, 1975-1979 (Thousands)

	British Leyland					Chrysler/Talbot					Ford					Vauxhall				
	1975	76	77	78	79	1975	76	77	78	79	1975	76	77	78	79	1975	76	77	78	79
Europe																				
EEC	103	151	168	159	120	12	12	12	32	25	36	32	53	28	23	12	16	12	6	5
EFTA	19	28	18	10	5	5	5	5	5	1	5	7	10	2	5	5	6	6	1	1
Other	3	7	4	3	2	1	1	1	2	1	2	3	8	6	7	–	–	1	1	1
America																				
Canada	11	14	4	7	5	–	–	–	–	–	–	–	–	–	–	–	–	–	–	–
US	63	75	63	49	46	–	–	–	–	–	–	–	–	–	–	–	–	–	–	–
Other	2	2	2	1	1	3	5	6	1	1	4	4	7	4	6	–	–	–	–	–
Asia																				
Iran	–	1	–	–	–	136	72	100	84	31	–	–	–	–	–	–	–	–	–	–
Other	5	4	7	7	4	1	1	–	–	–	28	25	30	34	40	–	–	–	1	1
Africa																				
South Africa	8	4	5	8	1	2	–	1	–	–	7	–	23	–	–	–	–	–	–	–
Other	4	4	4	2	1	1	–	1	–	–	1	2	2	2	–	–	–	1	1	–
Oceania																				
Australia	5	5	5	4	5	–	–	–	–	–	8	18	5	6	14	–	–	–	–	–
New Zealand	11	15	9	5	5	8	5	2	3	3	12	9	9	8	11	3	7	2	2	2
World	234	309	290	256	196	170	102	128	129	62	104	100	148	89	105	21	30	22	10	9

Source: SMMT.

differently than other affiliates. When the British subsidiaries had the right model at the right time to fit the overall strategy of the parent company and could supply that model in the amounts required, they could export to the US and their sales were facilitated by the use that could be made of the parent company's distribution network. When these conditions were no longer met, the exports ceased. The policy of the American MNEs has been to use their foreign subsidiaries only as sporadic, marginal suppliers to the American market to fill the small-car gap in their model range. Such a policy means that no US subsidiary can hope to gain a significant and continuing share of total sales in America. Only independent European and Japanese firms can hope to do that.

Commercial Vehicles

Similar data for commercial vehicles indicate that Ford-UK and Vauxhall have performed considerably better in this sector than has BL. To an important extent this reflects the historical decision of the American parent companies to concentrate their European CV production in Britain. Ford has greatly increased its share of a fairly constant UK total output of around 400,000 units, and even captured a slightly larger share of UK sales, despite the rise in imports to 23 per cent of the total. (Captive CV imports have been insignificant as would be expected.) BL's share fell by over 40 per cent.

With little or no CV production capacity on the Continent, both Ford and Vauxhall exported more CVs to Europe than did BL, Ford appreciably more. The two American companies each exported a higher proportion of their CV production than did the British company and Ford's exports world-wide were only slightly less than BL's. Chrysler's UK production of CVs has never been very significant and, with CV production capacity in France and Spain, its exports from the UK have been minimal.

It seems fair to say from this that British exports of commercial vehicles would have been less, and imports more, had not Detroit centred its European production of these vehicles in the UK. Nationalistic critics of MNEs tend to overlook the decisions, 'over which they have no control' which favour the host country, and only to see those which do not.

To sum up: on the criteria of production, exports and competitiveness, the four UK manufacturers performed badly in comparison with their European and Japanese rivals. Compared to each other there is not a great deal of difference. BL did rather better with cars, Ford and

Vauxhall rather better with commercial vehicles. There seems little doubt that car exports by the American subsidiaries were restricted as a result of parent company policy.[2]

Profitability

The ultimate test of the performance of a commercial firm is, of course, its ability to make profits, in this case at least enough profits to enable worn-out or inefficient equipment to be replaced, to develop new models as needed, and to increase capacity when conditions warrant. Of the four companies, only Ford-UK can perhaps be said to have passed the test. In 1975 British Leyland's financial problems became so great that it had to be rescued by the government, nationalised and given massive injections of public funds to enable it to survive. Three years later and after receiving financial help from the British government, Chrysler-UK's mounting losses and the desperate plight of the parent company, led to its sale to Peugeot-Citroen along with the other assets of Chrysler-US in Europe. It is probable that loss-making Vauxhall would not have survived either had it not been for the 'deep pocket' of General Motors. As for Ford, although the company made money, it never achieved the Ford profit target and earnings remained far below those of Ford-Germany.

The more or less common fate of British Leyland and the three foreign subsidiaries strongly suggests that adverse factors in the UK economy were primarily responsible for the industry's lack of competitiveness, that location factors rather than company characteristics were decisive. The relatively slow rate of economic growth and faster rate of inflation, government stop-go policies, poor labour relations, lack of confidence, and a deep-seated air of malaise and dissatisfaction throughout society as a whole, might be cited. In addition, the motor industry faced problems which could only be overcome by drastic changes in its industrial structure.

Integration

Put bluntly, by the late 1970s not one of the car manufacturers, considered as an independent producer, had a sufficient volume to be able to compete successfully in volume car markets in the long run. Even with efficient management, more investment in modernising plant and equipment, good labour relations and work practices, the UK car manufacturers could not match the unit production costs of their competitors, nor could they afford the overhead expense of designing, developing and maintaining the range of models demanded in international markets. Even British Leyland had fallen well below the minimum of 750,000 cars a year and the others were nowhere near that figure.

Under these circumstances, and given the continuation of free trade, there was only one course of action which offered the chance of survival to the UK manufacturers — European integration. To be successful such a policy must involve the specialisation and exchange of components and final products so that each can be produced at something like the optimum scale, and so that the cost of developing new models can be spread over many more units. It means the joint design and development of new models and also dependence on a foreign source for the production and supply of some essential components and probably part of the model range. This is the road taken by Ford-UK ever since Ford-Europe was established. That policy more than anything else explains the relative success of the British subsidiary. It also had the right models at the right time but this too owes something to integration. Belatedly General Motors has taken the same road and is integrating its Vauxhall and Opel plants. It is to be hoped that Peugeot-Citroen will genuinely integrate Talbot-UK into its European operations and not regard Britain as an offshore assembly plant with some spare manufacturing capacity to duplicate what is done on the Continent.

Given the need to integrate, the presence of three MNEs may well turn out to be advantageous to Britain. It is obviously a great deal easier to integrate operations under common ownership, in the family so to speak. For a shrunken BL, things are more difficult. Although still an MNE of sorts, it has no overseas manufacturing subsidiary with which to integrate. Its link with Honda will provide it with a badly-needed new model in mid-1981 but it is not a solution to its basic problem — relatively small size.

Integration on the scale needed to make the UK industry viable means, of course, the end of a 'national' motor industry, which was the goal of all industrialised countries and still is the goal of some developing nations. It means that Ford-UK, Vauxhall, Talbot and even BL cease to be independent units and make economic sense only as integral parts of European organisations. What was the reaction of the British government to this development and the events leading up to it?

The Government and the Motor Industry

The way the economies of the world are going makes it inevitable that there is going to be closer involvement between the major industries and Government. We are already heavily dependent on

Government for the whole future planning of our business. (Lord
Stokes, Chairman and Chief Executive, BLMC, May 1975)[3]

The two main aims of government policy were to ensure the survival of
a British-owned firm holding a dominant position in the domestic market, and to maintain employment in the industry. When these goals
conflicted, employment was given priority. Closely associated with both
goals was a continuing concern over the effect of structural changes on
the balance of payments. With one major exception the government
reacted to events rather than initiated changes as economic forces
brought about growing concentration.

The move by Chrysler to take over a majority share in Rootes in
1967 provided the first example of the government's intentions. The
American company had purchased 30 per cent of the voting stock and
50 per cent of the non-voting stock of Rootes in 1964 without opposition from the Conservative government. In the following year, a Labour
government allowed Chrysler to increase its holding to 45 per cent of
the voting and 66 per cent of the non-voting stock. After three years
in which losses increased steeply, Rootes faced bankruptcy and its only
hope of survival was as part of a larger organisation. The government's
reaction was to encourage British firms to take it over and the British
Motor Corporation and Leyland were consulted. Neither was interested.
The government considered nationalisation of Rootes but rejected the
idea on the grounds that the company, severed from its already existing
links with Chrysler, would not be viable. Confronted with the choice
between the bankruptcy of Rootes involving immediate and considerable unemployment or more foreign ownership, the government
accepted the Chrysler takeover.

The decision was taken with full awareness of its long-term consequences as Mr Wedgwood Benn, Minister of Technology, made clear in
the House of Commons. 'Our doubts about this did not arise from anti-
American feeling, but from the anxiety that Britain, looking ahead over
a period of years, might not be able to sustain three large American
corporations and a British corporation when the United States which is
three times our size and has a much larger output can only sustain three
corporations.'[4]

But if the UK could only sustain two, or at most three, firms,
which of the four would eventually be eliminated? The recently established Chrysler subsidiary? And where was the surviving British mass-
producer? It arrived just one year later, largely on the initiative of the
government with the merger of BMH and Leyland. Commenting on this

merger in March 1970 in the House of Commons, Mr Wedgwood Benn stated, 'Whereas there is a strong overlap of interests with national companies operating entirely or principally on a United Kingdom basis, this is not exactly the same in the case of international companies . . . It was exactly for this reason that the government, with the help of the Industrial Reorganisation Corporation, played a very significant part in bringing about the merger between Leyland and BMH.'[5]

Five years later the government's protégé faced bankruptcy or a drastic curtailment of its activities. The Ryder Committee appointed by the government to look into the affairs of British Leyland considered that the company should remain as a major volume producer. It estima- ted that this would require some £2.8 billion in inflated price terms over the coming eight years 'and a very large part of the funds required could only come from the government'. The conclusions of the Ryder Report were accepted by the government and Harold Wilson, Prime Minister, commented in the House of Commons, 'The Government have decided that Britain must remain in the world league so far as a British- owned automobile industry is concerned.'[6] Moreover, not to do so, he indicated, would endanger one million jobs, have a disastrous effect on the balance of payments, and cause a major loss of confidence in British industry at home and abroad. Under the circumstances, the nationalisa- tion of British Leyland was inevitable.

Only six months later the Chrysler Corporation announced that it was reconsidering the future of its unprofitable British subsidiary and shortly afterwards declared that it saw liquidation as the only alterna- tive to the transfer of the complete ownership of Chrysler-UK to the British government, or the transfer of at least 80 per cent, with Chrysler maintaining a minority interest. It might be thought that a government, which had recently decided to maintain a British-owned enterprise in existence at great cost to the taxpayer, would welcome the withdrawal of one of the three foreign MNEs in the industry. Instead it chose to prop up one of the weakest subsidiaries of an ailing American MNE by taking on a contingent liability of £162.5 million over the period 1976 to 1979.[7] Once again the goal of maintaining employment (at least in the short run) was given top priority. Also of importance in the deci- sion was the adverse effect on the balance of payments if the long-term contract to supply ckd vehicles to Iran were to be lost as a consequence of the withdrawal from the UK by Chrysler. In this connection, some weight was given as well to the possible political consequences of breaking the Iranian contract.

The government seriously considered the possibility of taking over

Chrysler-UK but rejected the idea. As the Secretary of State for Industry put it, 'As a Government-owned company we saw no return of profitability because it would be so small and it would not be integrated, which I think is a crucial factor.'[8] Integrating the company with British Leyland was quickly ruled out on the grounds that the latter could not cope with Chrysler's problems on top of its own vast reorganisation programme. Since neither Ford nor Vauxhall were interested in acquiring any significant part of the assets of Chrysler-UK, the only integration possible was within the Chrysler organisation itself, in particular, integration with Chrysler's other European plants, which the company claimed had not been done because it could not afford it. Again, in the words of the Secretary of State for Industry, 'Part of the support operation was to ensure that Chrysler UK would be firmly locked into the world wide operations of the Chrysler Corporation. If we cannot achieve that, there is not much hope for the company.'[9]

The Central Policy Review Staff's Report published on 16 December 1975, the day on which the terms of the government's agreement with Chrysler were announced, could hardly be said to support the government's decision to aid Chrysler-UK, but it clearly regarded integration of the operations of most if not all the British volume car manufacturers with those of similar producers in Europe as essential if the UK industry were to remain viable. In essence the Report maintained that only by the drastic reduction in the number of models, powertrains (engines, transmissions, axles) and plants could UK manufacturers hope to achieve the economies of scale needed to be competitive in the mass market. But if they did that they would not have the range of models every volume producer had to have to survive. The only way of combining the two requirements was for each UK company to integrate design and development, production, and marketing activities with one or more European counterparts.

Although in accord with the Report over the need for integration, the government's decision ignored the CPRS's insistence on the necessity to reduce capacity in the industry. Even on the most optimistic assumption of the demand for UK-produced cars up to 1985, it was estimated that the industry had an excess capacity of at least 400,000 cars a year. One of the Report's five main conclusions was that, 'There are too many manufacturers with too many models, too many plants and too much capacity.'[10] The withdrawal of Chrysler-UK would have gone a long way toward overcoming these weaknesses. It meant one less manufacturer in the UK industry (a foreign MNE at that) bringing its structure more into line with competing European countries. Automatically there would have been fewer models and plants, and capacity would have been reduced by 320,000 cars a year. Government-owned British Leyland and the other UK producers would have benefited provided, of course, they were able to increase output enough to prevent imports from filling the gap left by Chrysler-UK.

Aginst those advantages was the stark fact that the liquidation of Chrysler meant the direct loss of 25,000 jobs and perhaps double that figure if Chrysler's suppliers could find no alternative orders. Moreover, the unemployment would be heavily concentrated in the Coventry and Glasgow areas. Rather than face the economic and political consequences, the government gave financial assistance to enable the subsidiary of a foreign MNE to stay in business with, admittedly, a slimmed-down labour force of 17,000.[11]

In doing so, great stress was given by the government to the need to integrate Chrysler-UK with the world-wide operations of the Chrysler Corporation and this was reflected in the parent company's Declaration of Intent. Although the Secretary of State for Industry's comments on just what was implied by this integration were vague and general, a subsequent parliamentary inquiry into the affairs of Chrysler-UK not only forcefully put the case for integration but spelt out exactly what the Expenditure Committee felt integration must mean if Chrysler-UK was to survive. In its view, integration of design and development, technology, managerial know-how and markets was not enough. It must extend to production, to the integration of Chrysler-UK's manufacturing facilities with those of Chrysler-France and Chrysler-Spain in order to get the significant economies of scale denied a small, national producer. Even with integration Chrysler-Europe would be smaller than most of its European rivals and would have to have less variety in major mechanical components and body shells, and would have to source them from single plants. As an example it was suggested that the UK and French operations could make two cars each of a four-model integrated range, and one engine made entirely at Stoke, and another at Poissy. Genuine integration would involve the two-way flow of parts between the UK and France and shared use of facilities. Without that the UK operation might be regarded simply as spare assembly capacity which could be dispensed with if necessary without upsetting the rest of the Chrysler operations in Europe. With genuine integration Chrysler-UK would be the sole source of supply for certain major items. It would cease to make sense as an independent economic unit but would stand or fall with the success or failure of Chrysler-Europe.

In the event, the US parent company, itself now in dire financial straits, could not afford Chrysler-Europe, whatever its prospects, and sold out to Peugeot-Citroen two and a half years later. The sale was subject to the approval of the British government as far as Chrysler-UK was concerned but, given the unwillingness to see the company liquidated or to integrate it with BL, the government had no option but to accept once Peugeot-Citroen had agreed to take over all the Chrysler Corporation's obligations with regard to Chrysler-UK and the government. A Declaration of Intent was obtained from the French company, similar to that secured previously from the Chrysler Corporation and not legally binding. Among other things the company promised to provide continued employment at all Chrysler-UK's facilities 'to the extent consistent with prevailing economic conditions'. And a familiar note was sounded with, 'That in accordance with the desire to integrate, CUK's products and model ranges will be planned as an integral part of PSA's overall product and marketing plan so that CUK's production and capacity will be complementary to, and have a specific and definable position within, the total strategy of PSA.'[12]

As a truly integrated part of the world's fifth largest producer in the industry, Chrysler-UK would no longer be hampered by the high costs of a small-scale manufacturer. Whether such integration would take place remained to be seen, with much depending on the strategic plans of the French company as well as on labour relations and productivity in the British plants.

As for BL, there is ample evidence to show that it is not large enough to stand on its own feet as an international competitor, nor is it, as a nationalised company, behaving any differently than its MNE rivals with regard to the need to integrate. Whether that need can be met by means of co-operative deals with other producers, avoiding equity ties, remains to be seen.

The Multinationals: An Assessment

At this point the reader may be expecting a practical application of the theoretical analysis contained in Chapter 2, perhaps even an elaborate cost-benefit approach. If so he will be disappointed. The practical and conceptual limitations of cost-benefit analysis, in this context at any rate, are such that any conclusions emerging from it regarding UK welfare would convince neither the reader nor the writer. Similarly with the simpler approach in Chapter 2, which is really designed to explain *how* foreign direct investment might benefit the host country. To attempt to quantify the gain (or loss) from an additional X pounds of foreign investment in the British motor industry would not only be impossible but irrelevant. It is not a question of a little bit more or a little bit less, but rather a question of whether the UK should have a motor industry at all and, if so, whether the presence of foreign MNEs benefits the country or not.

Even to suggest the possibility of Britain without a motor industry may seem outrageous to some, but the industrial structure in every country changes over time as new and expanding industries replace declining ones. Few would deny that the UK motor industry has been going downhill for the past decade or more. Moreover, the general view is that for the government (for employment or balance of payments reasons), to preserve a declining industry which has no prospect of achieving viability, would be a waste of resources. On the other hand, the short-run consequences of a rapid and complete run-down of the motor industry would be severe, and it might be argued that the country simply could not afford in the long-run to be completely dependent on imports to meet its automotive needs.

If this had been the case in 1978, Britain's trade deficit would have increased (other things being equal) by some £8 billion. This figure is made up of a decrease in exports of £3.9 billion, an increase in vehicle imports of £2.8 billion and in replacement parts and components of £1.3 billion.[13] Since £3 billion was actually spent on automotive imports in 1978, the total foreign exchange cost of supplying Britain's entire automotive needs from abroad would have been around £11 billion. To meet this annual charge on the balance of payments (which would increase in real terms as the number of vehicles in use rose) exports would have to increase by one-third, with no increase in imports.

The effect on employment would be equally severe. Total employment in the industry in 1974 was estimated to be 1.3 million, including 450,000 engaged in selling, service and repair.[14] The latter would of course retain their jobs but (allowing for some shrinkage in employment in the industry by 1978) there would be some 800,000 additional unemployed, ignoring the multiplier effect. Much of that would be concentrated in the West Midlands, Merseyside and Glasgow.

Broadly speaking, replacing the motor industry would be the equivalent of reallocating roughly 10 per cent of the country's industrial production[15] to one or more highly competitive industries capable of bringing in overseas earnings equivalent to at least £8 billion (at 1978 prices) every year. It would be a daunting task even if the decline in the motor industry were gradual and some of the parts, accessories and components sector survived. Rather than undertake it, it seems almost certain that any government will seek to preserve the industry, either by accepting the international integration which is essential if the vehicle manufacturers are to survive under free trade conditions (and also the parts and components producers whose fortunes are linked with the vehicle manufacturers), or by protecting the industry from foreign competition with tariffs and other measures. Thus far successive governments have chosen a policy of international integration. This has implications for the balance of payments, employment, efficiency, technological development and innovation.

Prior to 1970 it was generally safe to conclude that a company's exports of vehicles (assembled and in ckd form) represented its trade contribution to the balance of payments, since the import content of those vehicles was small. Integration, which necessarily involves the intra-company specialisation and exchange of parts, components and finished vehicles, profoundly alters the situation as can be seen in Table 13.4

Table 13.4: Company Balance of Payments 1978 (£ Million)

	Exports*		Captive Imports**		A		Component Imports		Net Balance
BL	910	—	35	=	875 —		N/A	=	N/A
Ford	775	—	327	=	448 —		N/A	=	N/A
Vauxhall	229	—	126	=	103 —		N/A	=	N/A
Chrysler	209	—	52	=	157 —		57	=	100*

Source: *Company Reports.
   **Estimated using unit import values of cars and CVs.

The contrast between BL and Ford stands out. The British company, basically non-integrated so that there is little to subtract from column A in the way of component imports, made a major positive contribution to the country's balance of payments. On the other hand, Ford's fairly high exports are to an important extent offset by imports, although just how much to deduct for component imports is not known to the outsider. It could be that the entire amount should be subtracted for the company has been criticised in the past by government officials for its policy of balancing trade in components,[16] and the value of its trade in built-up vehicles actually did roughly balance in 1978. One can only speculate on Vauxhall's net contribution but it is not likely to be significant. Admirably, Chrysler did disclose a net figure. However, this was heavily dependent on the Iranian contract and, if Peugeot and Citroen UK sales are included as captive imports in subsequent years (as they should be), the net balance will be negative. In short, the MNEs are not likely to provide much net foreign exchange as time goes on taking into account the cost of servicing the investments. In comparing this with BL's far superior performance in this respect, it must be borne in mind that the latter has been highly subsidised by the taxpayer, and that if the company is to survive without such help in the future it must become more internationally integrated. If and when it does, its 'balance of payments' will become more like that of its UK competitors.

As far as employment is concerned, under normal conditions the integration of production should help to maintain employment even though unit output falls. Table 13.5 suggests that this has been happening. Employment at Vauxhall barely changed despite a fall in volume of 40 per cent from 1974 to 1979. At Ford, employment increased roughly in line with the growth in unit output. The shedding of labour by Chrysler was part of the government's rescue plan and, in any case, Chrysler was not an integrated company. In short, integration, in itself, has not meant fewer jobs.

But of course employment cannot be maintained under normal demand conditions in future if the vehicle firms are not efficient. Integration will remove the handicap of scale under which they have been operating and this is a necessary condition of their survival under free trade conditions. It also provides a breathing space and the opportunity to overcome the other locational factors which are undermining the international competitiveness of UK-based firms. Integration alone cannot ensure the efficiency needed to halt the decline of the industry.

Table 13.5: Vehicle Manufacturers' Average Weekly Employment in UK, 1974, 1978, 1979 (Thousands)

	1974	1978	1979
BL	173	169	155
Ford	70	74	76
Chrysler/Talbot	31	25	24
Vauxhall	34	33	33
Total	308	301	288

Source: SMMT.

Finally, there is the impact of integration on technological development and innovation. The costs of initiating new models and of meeting fuel consumption, pollution and safety standards have risen enormously, and the enhanced ability provided by integration to spread these costs over a much wider output is a tremendous help for the UK-based firm. As indicated earlier, BL admits it cannot afford the massive sums required and is looking for partners with whom to share such costs. Even the larger, more successful European MNEs have found it desirable to pool research resources. Volkswagen, Peugeot-Citroen-Talbot and Renault, together with Fiat, Volvo and BL have recently formed a joint research committee to co-ordinate research into such things as combustion technology, corrosion, surface treatment, motor vehicle batteries, quality control, computerised engineering methods and the properties of new materials. The work will be performed within the existing research organisations of the partners and by universities and research institutes. The agreement, covering the manner in which the work will be organised and how costs are to be shared, is now being examined by the EEC authorities. The partners maintain that their competitive position will not be altered since all final product development will be carried out individually and outside the co-operation project. If the European Commission approves the agreement, the industry will have taken a significant step forward in sharing the costs of advanced, long-term, technological research.

As far as research and development (and design and engineering) *within* the MNE is concerned, integration has implications for the location of these activities, and for host country policy with regard to it. The American MNEs, in common with others, have always heavily concentrated such work in the home country (and main market), with overseas research and development largely confined to adapting products, processes and techniques to local conditions. Such a policy makes economic sense, nevertheless Britain and other host countries have tried to persuade foreign MNEs to do more of their research and development locally. Yet no matter where the innovation or new knowledge originates, it is the parent company that decides what is to be done with it and where, and the parent company profits most by it. Whether, from the standpoint of the host country, this is a wise use of highly-trained and scarce design and engineering talent is questionable. The era of the 'world car' and General Motors' project centre concept highlights the issue. The latter involves the formation of an engineering group to shepherd each new car through its development, bringing together experts in design, manufacturing, assembly, customer service or marketing. The experts may come from Vauxhall, Opel or any overseas subsidiary as well as the US and has all the earmarks of a 'brain drain'.

Conclusion

The severe short-run costs of a collapse of the British motor industry and serious doubts about the ability of the economy to effect the major structural changes needed to finance the import of most of the country's automotive needs, strongly suggests that Britain will continue to have a motor industry — with free trade if possible, with protection if need be. International integration of production and the widespread sharing of innovation costs is essential if vehicle manufacture is to be viable under free trade conditions. The three foreign MNEs with subsidiaries in the UK have the volume, world-wide, to support the necessary research and development, and for them to integrate UK and Continental operations would be entirely an internal matter. For BL, integration presents a much more difficult task, one which seems likely, sooner or later, to require financial links with one or more partners.

But the integration must be genuine, a mutual specialisation and exchange between the UK and the Continent. If the MNEs view Britain merely as an offshore ckd assembly plant for sales in the UK then there is no domestic base for the all important parts and components sector which does have export potential. Should that happen the imposition of local content requirements seems probable. These in turn could lead to demands for complete protection from imports.

Some would like to see tariffs and quotas now which would preserve the bulk of the home market for UK producers. This would undoubtedly maintain employment and prevent deficits in automotive trade. But the costs to those outside the industry would be high, not only because the home market is too small for four manufacturers to produce efficiently but also because the captive market would enable trade unions to push up wages and their employers to push up prices. Nor would BL's chances of survival be improved since it would have to bear the full cost of new models and innovations while the UK subsidiaries of its MNE rivals would not. And, of course, protection invites retaliation from trading partners so that jobs and foreign exchange earnings in other UK industries might be lost.

In short, the end of the British motor industry is not nigh, as some observers have predicted. International integration offers a path to survival and in this the MNEs with subsidiaries in the UK have a crucial role to play. And if the path of protection is ultimately resorted to —

those MNE subsidiaries will still be there. In the former case they will be efficient and internationally competitive; in the latter, inefficient, high cost — but with built-in profits.

United States

The US is of interest primarily as a home country of automotive MNEs. It was from here that large-scale overseas investment originated, culminating years later in the world-wide networks of General Motors, Ford and Chrysler in the early 1970s. If the same exodus of technology, managerial know-how and capital had occurred simultaneously in a broad range of US industries, theory strongly suggests that this would have had an adverse effect on the country's welfare — although it seems impossible to provide convincing empirical proof of this conclusion. Within the framework of a single industry the welfare issue only becomes manageable if welfare can be boiled down to the question — did this foreign investment weaken or strengthen the *domestic* activities of the US motor industry?

The overseas investment was certainly not made at the expense of investment at home. For the most part it was financed from retained profits earned abroad and foreign borrowings so that the actual outflow of dollars was relatively small. But if the home industry was not handicapped by a shortage of capital, perhaps it was undermined by the diffusion of Detroit's technological and managerial superiority which made the foreign investment possible in the first place? Theory suggests that 'superior knowledge' cannot be kept inside a foreign subsidiary, that sooner or later it becomes available to the host country via external economies. But the American firms never had superiority in basic automobile technology, after all the internal combustion engine was first developed in Europe. Their advantage lay in their knowledge of large-scale production and distribution. The European firms may have acquired this knowledge somewhat sooner because of the presence of American subsidiaries but it is something they would have gained anyway as output expanded. The Japanese companies picked it up quickly enough without local competition from US firms. And it is inevitable that the larger, more industrialised developing countries will acquire the same knowledge, if not from American firms then from European or Japanese companies.

Turning to trade, US exports have not been displaced by production abroad by American companies nor have domestic sales been reduced to any extent because of imports from overseas subsidiaries. As indicated in Part Two, American foreign investment was almost always defensive, made in response to tariffs and other measures designed to protect and encourage the development of local motor industries. The US subsidiaries supplied markets closed to American exports, and exported to third markets the smaller, cheaper, European-type cars which could not be competitively produced in America at that time. Indeed had it not been for the foreign investment, US exports would have been appreciably less than they actually were, partly because of the stimulus it gave to the export of parts and components, and partly because of the existence of a world-wide sales and distribution network outside the US, the mainstay of which was overseas production. On the import side, as we have seen, only limited and sporadic use was made of captive imports to meet the growing US demand for small cars. In effect, they were treated as a stop-gap measure until the American industry could be geared to produce, at first compacts then sub-compacts. Moreover, the decision to manufacture the latter in the US was taken at a time when the available evidence on costs suggested that it would have been cheaper to make them in Europe.

In short, it was not the overseas investment by the American companies that was responsible for stagnant exports and for the growing vulnerability of the home market to imports, but a refusal to give a large section of the American public what it wanted, namely European-type cars, until forced to do so by foreign competition and government fuel requirements.

A Declining Industry?

I frankly don't see how we're going to meet foreign competition. We've only seen the beginning. We may become a service nation one day because our manufacturers could not compete with foreigners. (Henry Ford II, Chairman, Ford Motor Company, 1974)[17]

In the closing years of the 1970s, the American automobile industry was in trouble. It had been unable to stem the tide of imports, which captured 21.8 per cent of the US market in 1979 and 27 per cent in the early months of 1980. Three quarters of the imports came from Japan, and the Ford company claimed that the Japanese were able to land a car in Detroit for $700 to $800 less than the cost to Ford because of lower labour costs and a currently favourable yen-dollar exchange rate.[18] As market shares and profitability declined, future government and market-dictated fuel economy requirements forced the American firms to spend billions of dollars at a time of what appeared to be a general and world-wide recession. Of the four US car producers only General Motors seemed to be financially secure. 'Little' American Motors was in the process of being taken over by Renault. Chrysler had been forced to sell all its production facilities outside North America and narrowly escaped bankruptcy with the aid of a loan guarantee from the government totalling $1.5 billion. Ford's losses on its North American automotive operations were anticipated to be $2.5 billion, it had borrowed over $1 billion from its UK and German subsidiaries, and there was talk of the company becoming a second Chrysler.

Was this essentially a short-term crisis brought about by a major shift in demand in the US to small cars, or was it the consequence of a long-term declining trend? The product cycle hypothesis, at least in its early form, suggests the latter. A recent article maintains that the history of the industry in the US supports the product cycle concept and that the American firms face 'a slow, but continuing erosion of margins and market shares'.[19] For automotive companies, this is a recipe for disaster so that the statement implies the eventual end of the US motor industry.

If it collapsed tomorrow it would mean an extra import bill of $93.8 billion, and over 60 per cent of the earnings from total US exports would have to be earmarked to pay for the country's automotive requirements.[20] Something like 2 million people would lose their jobs, the equivalent of one-tenth of total employment in manufacturing industry.[21] A government willing to put up $1.5 billion to save one company, Chrysler, seems bound to do much more to save a whole industry. However, the pattern of spending on new plant and equipment by US firms strongly suggests that this will not be necessary.

Table 13.6 is hardly a picture of an industry in decline. It reflects massive re-equipment in the US for the purpose of supplying the domestic market with a new generation of fuel-efficient cars. The equally huge investment overseas is primarily for the development of an international network to produce engines and other components for 'world cars'. Production will be integrated on a global basis aimed at obtaining scale economies and spreading the very large research and development expenditure (incurred almost entirely in the US) over a world-wide output. As such it has the ingredients for success, not failure.

Allocation of Investment

We recognise the balance of payments issue. But we feel strongly that if developing countries want to take advantage of economy of scale, then they must establish their local content regulations with the idea in mind to allow certain import-export credits. For this reason we would like governments to give us the responsibility of having our operation provide a balance of payments surplus. (Alex Cunningham, General Motors executive in charge of overseas operations, 1979)[22]

Of the total capital expenditure planned for 1980 of $12.5 billion, only $715 million or 5.7 per cent is going to developing countries. Nearly half the latter figure will be spent in neighbouring Mexico. Relatively high-cost Germany is receiving over half the $2.9 billion allocated to Europe (as against $400 million in relatively low-wage Spain). Canada, with the same industry wage level as the US is getting $2.1 billion. This is not the behaviour predicted by the product cycle hypothesis for a mature, oligopolistic industry with a standardised product forced to shift to low-cost locations.[23]

Table 13.6: Expenditure on New Plant and Equipment by US Firms, 1974-1980 ($ Billion)

	Foreign Affiliates (Transportation Equipment)**	Domestic (Motor Vehicles)
1974	1.6	2.7
1975	1.4	2.0
1976	1.4	2.4
1977	1.8	4.0
1978	2.2	4.6
1979*	3.8	5.4
1980*	6.1	6.4

*Latest plans.
**Almost entirely motor vehicles.
Source: *Survey of Current Business*, March 1980 and earlier issues.

Costs matter, of course, but in a capital-intensive industry do relative wage costs matter all that much? Perhaps industry spokesmen have been right all along and it is markets, not low wages, that carry most weight in location decisions. And to retain markets it is often necessary to export from the country in question for balance of payments reasons. Canada is getting $2.1 billion in US investment at a time when that country has had a large trade deficit in automotive products with

America for a number of years. Mexico obtains more US investment than any other developing country after passing legislation in 1977 which goes into effect in 1982 and limits the value of imports by producers in Mexico to no more than the value of the products they export. Without imported car bodies the Mexican market is lost. Ford invests in a major new engine plant in the UK at a time when its UK subsidiary is ceasing to be a net exporter of built-up cars. General Motors is building four overseas engine plants for its 1982 'world car' – in Australia, Brazil, Austria and Japan. Two-thirds of Australian output will be shipped to Europe and the Brazilian plant will also ship the bulk of its production to Europe. Markets matter and most countries are concerned over their balance of payments.

Foreign Investment in the US

As the world's largest single market, the US has attracted relatively little foreign investment in production facilities, and even that not until the last half of the 1970s. But this is what one would expect from the history of the motor industry and from the theory of foreign direct investment. Firms have always preferred exports to overseas investment, rarely resorting to the latter unless there were tariffs or other barriers to exports. Prewar America had tariffs but foreign companies had no superior knowledge, i.e., no firm-specific advantage to enable them to compete in the US. Postwar America reduced tariffs to a mere three per cent on cars and first Volkswagen and then the Japanese firms proved that a significant share of a huge foreign market could be captured without producing in that market. Their success with exports reflected firm-specific advantages in the form of small-car technology and quality control, advantages which would make investment in the US possible. Given free trade, the investment decision then hinged largely on location-specific advantages which, for most of the postwar years, favoured production at home and exports because of lower wages and favourable exchange rates against the dollar. With the eventual rise in German wages, relative to those in the US and the appreciation of the mark, Volkswagen concluded it would have to produce in America. Under less pressure from location-specific factors, Renault, partly because it lacks the capital, is pursuing a low-risk strategy by entering the US market via a minority interest in American Motors and Mack. For the Japanese producers, the location-specific factors including certain attitudes and institutions peculiar to Japan are still favourable to that country, hence the reluctance of Toyota and Nissan to manufacture in the US despite considerable American pressure to do so.

Honda is a special case. As a thrusting newcomer it can only hope to become a major producer in world terms by pursuing a high-risk strategy, relying on innovation and rapidly expanding overseas sales. Moreover, unlike its main Japanese rivals, it has no land for further growth at home and land prices for suitable factory sites in Japan are astronomical compared to Ohio.

Whether Chrysler can survive as an independent company remains in doubt and in its slimmed-down state must present a tempting target to foreign firms seeking to establish themselves in the US market. Mitsubishi? Peugeot-Citroen? Volkswagen? An outsider? Whoever it may be, will be taking a bold step, one which is bound to alter appreciably the 'balance of power' among the survivors.

European and Japanese investment in America does fit the product cycle hypothesis. Their past environments led to innovations of a material-saving, capital-saving and space-saving nature. This led, in this case, to small-car technology and growing exports followed by foreign investment when that involved location-specific advantages. But as Raymond Vernon points out, the product cycle hypothesis also predicts that this innovation advantage will only be temporary. As US firms confront similar factor cost conditions in a home market no longer much different from the home markets in Europe and Japan, they can be expected to introduce a stream of innovations of the same type as their rivals.[24]

Home Sweet Home Country

The importance to the MNE of a solid base in its home market can scarcely be exaggerated. Without that it could never become an MNE. It was the existence of the huge American market in the early days of the industry that gave the US firms their head start in building up what has come to be called a global network. It was Volkswagen's home market that enabled it to overcome the barriers that had blocked new entry into the US industry for decades. The German company will be happy to achieve its target of 5 per cent of the American car market (450,000-500,000 per annum), but no domestic newcomer could survive on that volume. Kaiser-Fraser tried under the unusually favourable postwar demand conditions but was unsuccessful. It subsequently tried to produce in Argentina and Brazil without a home base, which doomed the venture from the start.

It is in the home country that the great bulk of research and development work takes place and the highly crucial design decisions for 'world cars' are made, aided by experts drawn from the subsidiaries.

Indeed it is in the headquarters in the home country that all the big decisions are made and the world-wide operations of the firm are co-ordinated. In arriving at those decisions the MNE may not always see eye to eye with its home government but the relationship is necessarily a close one. When there are significant policy differences between home and host country governments, there is little doubt which side the MNE will be on.

And when the MNE finds itself in serious difficulty, it retreats to the home country as Chrysler demonstrated so dramatically, sacrificing its overseas 'empire' to give the parent company a chance to survive — with a helping hand from the home government. Adversity reveals the MNE in its true colours.

Notes

1. *The Times*, 31 October 1975.

2. A parliamentary inquiry into the British motor industry revealed much evidence to suggest that of the four companies only British Leyland is able to export world-wide without any restrictions of parent-company policy or model design. *Fourteenth Report from the Expenditure Committee*, Session 1974-1975, 'The Motor Vehicle Industry' (HMSO, London, 6 August 1975), p. 111.

3. Ibid., p. 57.

4. Quoted in Michael Hodges, *Multinational Corporations and National Government* (Saxon House, Farnborough, 1974), p. 205.

5. Ibid., p. 212.

6. *Financial Times*, 25 April 1976.

7. £72.5m allocated toward losses incurred through 1979, £55.0m medium-term loan to finance capital expenditure and model development and £35.0m as a guarantee against bank loans to Chrysler-UK.

8. *Eighth Report from the Expenditure Committee*, Session 1975-76, 'Public Expenditure on Chrysler UK Ltd.' Volume 1 — Report (HMSO, London, 22 July 1976), p. 63.

9. *The Times*, 12 December 1975.

10. Central Policy Review Staff, *The Future of the British Car Industry* (HMSO, London, 1975), p. v.

11. In view of what subsequently happened to Chrysler-UK, it is interesting to note one reporter's comments at the time. In his opinion, whether the company was viable or not in the long term was not really at the centre of the argument. His impression was that almost no Cabinet Minister (except Mr Lever) gave the company more than three or four years at the most. Hence they refused to take any equity in the business and were not too worried by the argument that any real success by Chrysler had to be at the expense of British Leyland. *Financial Times*, 19 December 1975.

12. *The Times*, 29 September 1978.

13. The £2.8 billion cost of replacing home vehicle production is simply that production times the unit value of car imports (£2,204) and for CVs (£5,596) in 1978. The import cost of home replacement demand for accessories, parts and components assumes that 25 per cent of the net output of the motor industry (MLH 381) is for replacements, with three-quarters of this going to the UK market.

(See National Economic Development Office, *Motors* (NEDO, London, 1973), p. 26)

14. *Fourteenth Report from the Expenditure Committee*, Session 1974-75, 'The Motor Vehicle Industry', p. 16.

15. National Economic Development Office, *The Effect of Government Economic Policy on the Motor Industry* (NEDO, London, 1968), p. 6.

16. Hodges, *Multinational Corporations and National Government*, p. 220.

17. Louis Turner, *Multinational Companies and the Third World* (Allen Lane, London, 1974), p. 202.

18. *Financial Times*, 5 June 1980.

19. Louis T. Wells, Jr, 'The International Product Life Cycle and United States Regulation of the Automobile Industry' in Douglas H. Ginsberg and William J. Abernathy (eds.), *Government, Technology and the Future of the Automobile* (McGraw Hill, New York, 1980), p. 292.

20. 1979 ($ billion):

    64.0 Domestic output new autos

     7.4 Parts exports

    22.4 Parts output domestic use (vehicles in use x $150)

    93.8 Required increase in imports

    22.1 Present cost of imports

  115.9 Total import bill to meet all requirements

(Source: *Survey of Current Business*, March 1980).

21. The Harvard economist, Wassily Leontief has estimated that for every job lost in the motor vehicle and equipment industry (SIC 371), 1.5 additional jobs would be lost in related industries. Taking 800,000 as the 1979 employment in SIC 371 this gives the total loss as 2 million. *Effects of Motor Vehicles Manufactured Outside the United States on Domestic Employment*, Statement of the Motor Vehicle Manufacturers' Association of the United States, Inc, before the Subcommittee on Labor Standards of the House Education and Labor Committee. Presented by W.D. Eberle, President and Chief Executive Officer MVMA (5 March 1975), p. 22.

22. *Financial Times*, 14 August 1979.

23. In a recent article, the author of the product cycle hypothesis specifically mentions that automobile firms need to integrate their global production facilities, and that to get economies of scale they are likely to establish various component plants in both advanced and developing countries, and to cross-haul between plants for the assembly of final products. That pattern he admits is at variance with product-cycle expectations. Raymond Vernon, 'The Product Cycle Hypothesis in a New International Environment', *Oxford Bulletin of Economics and Statistics*, vol. 41, no. 4 (November 1979), pp. 255-67.

24. Ibid., p. 266. Hence the product cycle hypothesis does not necessarily predict that American firms face 'a slow but steady erosion of margins and market shares' as Wells claims. (See Note 19.)

14 RICH DEVELOPING COUNTRIES

Canada

The interest in Canada centres on the United States-Canada Automotive Trade Agreement of 1965 — the reasons for it and the economic consequences.

In a sense the Canadian motor industry was the creation of the Canadian government. Its policy of tariff protection coupled with the encouragement of foreign investment inevitably resulted in an industry almost entirely owned and controlled by the much larger American firms just over the border. During the postwar years preceding the Agreement it was an inefficient industry by international standards, primarily because of small-scale production, and this largely precluded exports. The limited domestic market, in which new registrations of passenger cars averaged some 450,000 units a year in the decade prior to 1965, was not large enough to enable even one volume producer to be competitive. But there were four producers — American Motors, Chrysler, Ford and General Motors. It was the familiar picture of oligopolistic competition in a sheltered market, with each firm producing a range of models and so further fragmenting that market. Despite a level of wages 30 per cent lower than in the US, factory list prices of certain popular models made in both countries were 18 per cent higher in Canada. They would have been appreciably higher than that had not 40 per cent of the value of the Canadian-built cars (50 per cent for trucks) consisted of components produced in high-volume plants in America and imported duty free, providing the equivalent was not obtainable in Canada.

But if the relatively low Canadian content helped to keep costs and prices down, it placed a heavy burden on the country's balance of payments since offsetting automotive exports to the US were ruled out by the higher Canadian prices. Moreover, the deficit was bound to increase over the years with the normal growth in the Canadian market. For the eleven years up to and including 1964, Canada's automotive trade deficit with the US averaged slightly more than US $400 million a year and this was responsible for the major part of its adverse merchandise trade balance with America. At the same time Canada's automotive production and employment had failed to expand with the growth of the economy let alone act as a stimulus to that growth.

For the government to have done nothing would have meant to accept, at best, a stagnating industry, costly in terms of resources and foreign exchange. To have adopted free trade would have brought considerably cheaper cars to the Canadian consumer – at the direct cost of 70,000 jobs and what many would regard as an intolerable burden on the balance of payments which importing all the country's automotive requirements would entail. To have appreciably raised the local content requirements would have brought more jobs and a reduction in the trade deficit – at the cost of reduced efficiency and higher prices, which in turn would have led to higher tariffs and the complete isolation of the Canadian market. How to get much of the efficiency benefits of free trade without destroying the Canadian industry?

The Automotive Agreement

This provided for generally duty-free passage of automobiles and parts between the US and Canada with a few exceptions, notably tyres and replacement parts. But on the Canadian side, only manufacturers of motor vehicles could escape paying duty, and for this privilege their freedom of action was limited in a number of ways.

In general terms,[1] they were required to maintain the same ratio of Canadian assembly to Canadian sales as prevailed in 1964, hence if the value of such sales increased over the years, the value of Canadian production (including production for export) would have to increase proportionately. Secondly, they were required to keep the value of the local content of vehicles built in Canada from falling below the level in 1964 in *absolute* dollar terms. This gave some protection to Canadian parts manufacturers. However, as output expanded, this condition would become less important and, since content included assembly work, it would be possible to decrease the total of Canadian parts in locally built vehicles. These two conditions were part of the treaty itself and ensured approximately the same sort of growth in automotive assembly that would have occurred under pre-existing protection, and also provided for the maintenance of the same level of local content.

The third requirement took the form of a letter of intent from each of the foreign manufacturers in Canada regarding the overall volume of Canadian production and it is not entirely clear how legally binding these letters are. They committed the manufacturers by 1968 to increase the Canadian value added in vehicles and original parts by CAN $260 million (in addition to an amount equal to 60 per cent of the growth in the value of Canadian car sales [50 per cent for trucks] something that would have occurred anyway under the pre-existing tariff).

Imports of vehicles or original parts by the foreign parent, either from its Canadian subsidiary or from independent Canadian car parts firms would count towards the fulfillment of these conditions.

Under these controlled free trade conditions, significant economies of scale became possible. Manufacturers could specialise in perhaps only one or two models in their Canadian factories, producing them for the entire North American market, and could supplement their sales in Canada with US-built models imported duty free. Specialisation in assembly would automatically lead to standardisation of single parts, e.g. one or two sizes. And lastly, with growth it would gradually become possible to specialise between parts, e.g. wheels from the US and batteries from Canada and vice versa. It was expected that the gains from specialisation would far outweigh any possible rise in costs associated with the CAN $260 million increase in local content.

How the Agreement has Worked

Despite some criticism, the Agreement met with general approval on both sides of the border during the years of expansion up until the end of 1973. US production increased by 25 per cent to a total of 12.7 million units, while Canadian output more than doubled to reach a record 1.6 million vehicles. This was accompanied by sizable increases in employment in the two countries. The effect on trade was spectacular. From an exchange of a mere 37,000 units in 1964, the total rose to 1,694 million in 1973, reflecting the large-scale integration and reallocation of production between the two countries aimed at securing economies of scale, particularly in Canada. In spite of the large increase in domestic production, Canada's trade deficit in automotive products with the US was less in 1973 than in 1964, although still sizable at US $426 million.

These developments are reflected in Table 14.1 which presents the trade balance in value terms from 1964 to 1978. Production and employment fluctuated in the intervening years between 1973 and 1978, but were slightly higher at the end of the period than at the beginning. In the five year period following 1973, the value of automotive trade nearly doubled to reach US $21.5 billion. From the Canadian standpoint, the balance of that trade was unsatisfactory, resulting as it did in a cumulative deficit of US $5.6 billion. An annual deficit ranging from US $2 billion to US $3 billion in the trade in parts was responsible, heavily offsetting a favourable balance in the exchange of built-up vehicles. Since 1978, the size of the deficit appears to have mounted considerably, causing increasing alarm in government circles.

Table 14.1: US-Canada Trade in Automotive Products, 1964, 1973-1978 (US $ Millions)

	1964	1973	1974	1975	1976	1977	1978**
US Exports							
Cars	34	1,439	1,657	2,142	2,354	2,655	2,613
Trucks	23	643	916	922	985	1,057	1,158
Parts*	583	3,644	4,203	4,579	5,666	6,578	7,193
Total Exports	640	5,726	6,776	7,643	9,005	10,290	10,964
US Imports							
Cars	18	2,272	2,595	2,809	3,477	3,795	4,129
Trucks	4	789	887	917	1,363	1,841	2,036
Parts*	54	2,240	2,062	2,075	3,149	3,631	4,327
Total Imports	76	5,301	5,544	5,801	7,989	9,267	10,492
Net Balance	+564	+425	+1,232	+1,842	+1,016	+1,023	+472

*Includes tyres and tubes.
**Preliminary.
Source: Thirteenth Annual Report of the President to the Congress on the Operation of the Automotive Products Trade Act of 1965.

But if the balance of payments situation has proved disappointing in more recent years, progress has been made toward the fundamental goal behind the Agreement, namely, to lower costs in the Canadian industry in relation to the larger, more efficient American one. On this there is no direct evidence available to the outsider. However, several attempts have been made to indicate indirectly that this has happened by showing a narrowing of the factory list price differential for equivalent car models produced in both countries (which unfortunately is affected by changes in the exchange rate, differing rates of inflation, and the extent to which cost reductions are passed on in the factory list prices – as well as the all-important productivity gains). General Motors showed a narrowing of the differential for the years 1964 to 1973 by comparing the US $ price with the CAN $ price,[2] *The Economist* for the years 1964 to 1969 by comparing the US price with the Canadian price converted into US $ at the exchange rate prevailing in 1964[3] and the President's Report to Congress for the model years 1977 to 1979 by converting the Canadian price at the current rate of exchange.[4] None is entirely satisfactory but, as shown in Table 14.2, they all point to the same conclusion – that the price differential has narrowed significantly. At the same time, the Canadian worker gained 'wage parity' with his American counterpart, so that it seems reasonable to conclude that the productivity of the Canadian industry has been appreciably improved as a result of the Agreement.

Table 14.2: Canadian Price Differential – Per Cent Over (Under) US Price, 1964, 1973, 1977-1979

	CAN $ = US $	CAN $ = US $0.925	CAN $ converted US $ current rate
1964	18.2	9.3	9.3
1973	11.1	2.8	11.1
Subcompact			
1977	5.3	(2.6)	4.2
1978	4.0	(3.8)	(5.3)
1979	4.2	(3.4)	(11.9)
Popular 4-door sedan			
1977	6.5	(1.5)	5.1
1978	7.3	1.4	(2.3)
1979	10.3	2.0	(6.7)

Source: see Notes 2-4.

Nevertheless, there is considerable criticism in Canada of the results of the Agreement. In addition to complaints over the trade deficit, there is the contention that the Canadian share of new investment and employment has been less than half of what should be expected. No doubt the Canadian government will be pressing the American producers of parts, as well as the vehicle manufacturers themselves, to expand parts and components production in Canada. Since North America is now a single automotive market, optimum-sized plants can be established in Ontario as well as in Ohio. Hence for the American companies the investment decision is largely an administrative and political one. In the long run, it is quite possible that a rough, overall balance in automotive trade between the two countries will emerge. Pressure to bring this about will be accompanied by inducements. For example, in 1978 the Ford Motor Company was offered $70 million to $75 million to establish an engine plant in southern Ontario, with part of this to be paid by the Federal Canadian government, much to the annoyance of the US administration. An arrangement was made with Volkswagen-US whereby the government agreed to lower tariffs on the importation into Canada of Volkswagens made in the US by roughly the same proportion by which the German car company increased its purchase of Canadian-made car parts throughout its global manufacturing operations. Even near-bankrupt Chrysler was given US $170 million in Federal loan guarantees in return for the company's agreement to maintain its Canadian workforce at 9 per cent of the level in Chrysler-US during 1980-1, and 11 per cent in 1982-6. In addition there was a commitment by the American company to build a Chrysler research centre at Windsor, Ontario, for which Ontario would pay half the capital cost.

Thus far there seems to be little support in Canada for scrapping the 1965 Agreement and the critics are seeking to improve and expand the domestic industry within the framework of the treaty. However, if negotiation and inducements to invest fail to bring about the changes considered essential for the future of the industry, there will be growing agitation to convert existing assembly plants into fully-integrated and self-sufficient operations (even if still foreign-owned). Such a policy would involve heavy costs in unscrambling the production and marketing links established with the US during the 15 years of the Agreement. More important, would a 'national' Canadian motor industry provide a satisfactory solution to the problem? The experience of the Australian motor industry suggests not.[5]

Australia

> To operate economically by world standards a motor manufacturer
> in Australia would probably need to build 250,000 to 300,000 units
> per year of one model on a two-shift basis. The market needs four to
> five different models, so you could calculate that one company
> might get by with an absolute minimum output of 500,000 units
> per year. (Finance Director, General Motors-Holden, 1979)[6]

> It costs twice as much to make most things in Australia as it does in
> Japan. (Local Manager of Toyota in Australia)[7]

By the beginning of the 1960s, the government's programme for
promoting the local manufacture of motor vehicles introduced shortly
after the second world war had run into difficulties. General Motors-
Holden, Ford, Chrysler, the British Motor Corporation (BMC) and
Volkswagen were each producing at least one model with a high local
content. However, increasing competition as the buyers' market
receded, the swing in demand to small cars, and a surge of built-up
imports from Japan despite the tariff, led them to introduce a wider
range of models and optional features such as automatic transmissions.
These inevitably had a relatively low level of local content, in the early
days at least, and imports of vehicle components rose rapidly, aided by
the abolition of import licensing controls in 1960. This rise in imports
led the government to introduce a new policy for the industry, the aim
of which was to induce the main manufacturers to produce virtually
the whole of their vehicles in Australia and the rest to assemble vehicles
locally with significant amounts of Australian content.

    Under Plan A, aimed at the relatively large-scale manufacturers, the
firm agreed, for each basic model submitted under the Plan, to raise the
local content by stages from an initial 40 per cent to 95 per cent within
five years (later increased to seven). During the transition period, the
company would be allowed by-law immunity from duty on the imports
of the appropriate percentage. The Small Volume (SV) Plan prescribed
the minimum local content percentage assemblers would have to
achieve to qualify for remission of duties. For a model with an annual
sales volume of up to 2,500 this was 45 per cent, beyond that to 5,000,
50 per cent, and exceeding that and up to 7,500 units, 60 per cent.
Entrants under the SV Plan were given 12 to 18 months to raise the
local content up to the level chosen. Importers of built-up cars would
continue to be subject to the 35 per cent general duty or the 25 per cent

British preferential duty. However, this would be increased if the market share of these imports exceeded 7.5 per cent.

The policy aimed to limit the growing market share of the Japanese producers and to give the local manufacturers a chance to build virtually the whole of their major models in Australia. It was not a success. Despite an increase in the tariff to 45 per cent, the share of the Japanese companies continued to rise as they introduced new models and sold built-up cars when their quotas for assembled vehicles were filled under the SV Plan. This undermined the position of the Plan A manufacturers, particularly with regard to their small-car entrants, models which had to remain largely unchanged for lengthy periods if local production were to be profitable. First Volkswagen and then British Leyland abandoned manufacturing and reverted to imports and assembly. Both Ford and Chrysler introduced new small car models from their overseas product ranges under SV Plans.

In 1974 just prior to British Leyland's withdrawal from manufacturing, the Industries Assistance Commission issued a report which was highly critical of the Australian motor industry and government policies towards it.[8] Costs of production, it concluded, were 'significantly higher' than in the major producing countries. It maintained that the cost disadvantages sprang primarily from unexploited economies of scale. 'The Australian market supports about four times as many stamping and engine manufacturing plants, twice as many transmission and axle plants, and twice as many assembly plants as would be compatible with an efficient industry structure.'[9] Moreover, it was government policy in the form of a high tariff and local content plans which was responsible for the unsatisfactory structure, in that it encouraged fragmentation of the market and provided relatively more assistance to uneconomic low volume production than to the large volume manufacturers. The remedy proposed was drastic — the gradual abandonment of the local content plans together with the eventual reduction in the tariff to 25 per cent. It anticipated that three local manufacturers with a high local content (but free to source locally-expensive components abroad) would be able profitably to supply practically all of the medium car market and most of the upper end of the light car market using a large number of components common to the medium vehicles. At the lower end of the light car market, manufacturers could be expected to operate profitably at fairly low levels of local content. However, it was admitted that a substantial proportion of that market would be met by imports, primarily from Japan. The Report estimated that some 15,000 jobs would be eliminated during the phase out of the uneconomic sections of the industry (which included parts of the components sector) over a ten-year period, but that this would largely be offset by the creation of about 13,000 new jobs from normal growth in the remaining efficient sections.

Although the government rejected for the most part the recommendations of the Industries Assistance Commission, its new long-term policy for the motor industry introduced at the end of 1974 did encourage specialisation in the production of components and international complementation by the MNE subsidiaries in Australia to improve the efficiency of the industry. The local content concept was retained but only at the single, more flexible, level of 85 per cent. And that could be calculated over the whole range of the manufacturer's output rather than on a single model as in the past. Moreover, a local subsidiary would be able to earn 'credits' towards duty concessions if it had a significant Australian component adopted for use by its parent company or an associate, thus generating large-scale exports. The credits would then allow it to have more than 15 per cent foreign content in the finished cars produced in Australia. At the same time further protection was given to the manufacturers in the form of a higher tariff (general-assembled cars 44 per cent, ckd 36 per cent) and shortly afterwards a quota on imports limiting them to 20 per cent of the market.

Of major importance for the future of the Australian industry was the entrance in 1976 of Nissan and Toyota as manufacturers under the 85 per cent local content plan. This represented another instance of foreign investment taking place to retain an export market that would be lost otherwise. The acceptance of the two Japanese companies as local manufacturers made international complementation even more essential if Australia was not to remain a high-cost producing country. Five firms manufacturing solely for the limited domestic market would be two, perhaps three, too many.

In March 1979 the government took a concrete step towards encouraging complementation when it agreed that companies would be able to offset five percentage points from their local content targets by exporting a similar amount of Australian-made components as from March 1982. The decision meant that General Motors-Holden would go ahead with its plan to build a new factory for the production of 4-cylinder engines with a capacity of some 240,000 engines a year. One-third of the output would be used for a new front-wheel drive car to be put on the Australian market in 1982, the remaining two-thirds would be exported to affiliates in Germany and the US. The company's

Finance Director thinks that the car will be at least A$1,000 cheaper than if the engine plant had been built to supply the Australian market alone.[10] Nissan had put forward a similar plan to the government in the spring of 1978. It proposed exporting engines from its newly-installed and highly automated Melbourne factory if allowed in return to import some additional components from Japan, and presumably this will go ahead in 1982. The Managing Director of Mitsubishi Motors-Australia (formerly Chrysler-Australia which was bought out by the Japanese group in April 1980) who was formerly Managing Director in charge of production in the parent company, is reported as saying that the long-term prospects for product sharing between the Australian and Japanese motor industries are good.

But complementation means nothing so far to the Australian buyer confronted with one of the most heavily protected motor vehicle industries in the world. The Industries Assistance Commission estimated recently that Australians pay double the price of a new car compared to their counterparts in major overseas vehicle markets. Four-fifths of the cars they buy must be 'made in Australia'. The remainder are mostly highly-desired Japanese imports on which the tariff was increased in August 1978 from 45 per cent to 57.5 per cent, an incredibly high level for a country at Australia's level of industrialisation.

Notes

1. For the specific terms and a detailed analysis of the Trade Agreement see Paul Wonnacott and R.J. Wonnacott, 'The Automotive Agreement of 1965', *Canadian Journal of Economics*, vol. 33, no. 2 (May 1967), pp. 269-84.

2. Thomas A. Murphy, *The Economic Impact of the Multinational Corporation*, Statement presented to the Subcommittee on International Trade of the US Senate Committee on Finance, Washington, DC, (27 February 1973), p. 19.

3. *Motor Business*, 'The Canada-US Automotive Agreement: Results 1965-1970 and Future Outlook', no. 63 (Autumn 1970) p. 33.

4. *Thirteenth Annual Report of the President to the Congress on the Operation of the Automotive Products Trade Act of 1965* (US Government Printing Office, Washington, DC, April 1980), tables 6 and 7, pp. 39-40.

5. Even though the Australian domestic market is only half that of Canada, the two countries are sufficiently alike to put them in the same 'league' as far as establishing an independent motor industry is concerned.

6. *Financial Times*, 4 September 1979.

7. *Financial Times*, 4 September 1979.

8. Industries Assistance Commission Report, *Passenger Motor Vehicles, Etc.* (Australian Government Publishing Service, Canberra, 1974).

9. Ibid., p. 2.

10. *Financial Times*, 4 September 1979.

15 POOR DEVELOPING COUNTRIES

Brazil and India, alike in a number of respects, make an interesting contrast. Brazil welcomed the MNEs with open arms, while India for the most part kept free of foreign direct investment.

Brazil

The world's greatest success story as far as the establishment of a domestic automotive industry is concerned. Or was it? A number of Latin American economists, sociologists and political scientists think not. For them it is not a national achievement but part of a process of dependent industrialisation, the benefits of which go largely to foreigners. It is useful to view Brazil's motor industry in this wider framework and to look at it through the lens of 'dependencia'.

According to this approach, economic development in Brazil (or Latin America as a whole) cannot be understood in isolation but must be seen in relation to the international economy of which it is an integral part. The country's external relationships have conditioned its economic growth, making it largely dependent on developments in the industrialised nations. After political independence in the nineteenth century this took the traditional form of reliance on an increasing demand for primary exports. But the internal growth and increase in local wealth was concentrated in modern enclaves, ports particularly, and there was little integration with the economy as a whole. This phase of foreign-orientated development ended with the world-wide depression of the 1930s, which drastically reduced export earnings and the ability to import manufactured goods. This stimulated a policy of import-substituting industrialisation, mainly initiated by Brazilian entrepreneurs, which was seen as a means of reducing the country's dependence on the world economy. However, further industrialisation after the second world war involved a major penetration of Brazil's economic structure by foreign capital and technology through the direct investments and licensing agreements of MNEs. In the process, new industries which had not attracted local capital were pioneered while others were denationalised by means of the acquisition and competitive elimination of indigenous firms. As a consequence, the Brazilian entrepreneurial class was eroded, with much of its talents being absorbed in a new international managerial class thus excluding the possibility of self-sustained national development.

The foreign companies were exploiting a local demand for the same sophisticated consumer goods being produced in the advanced countries, a demand arising from a relatively small group of economically elite created by the very unequal distribution of income typical of many developing countries. Local production of these products called for capital-intensive techniques, requiring imported machinery, equipment and intermediate goods. It also meant that more and more of the benefits of industrialisation went to foreigners in the form of profits, royalties, management fees and other payments.

Although this dependent industrialisation has succeeded in transforming and modernising Brazil's economic structure and greatly increased the country's GNP, it has done so to a large extent at the expense of the poorest half of the population. For these people the 'economic miracle' has meant the same old poverty, unemployment, squalor and neglect; with their protests being met by political and military repression. Neither they, nor another large section of the population not much better off, can afford to buy the kind of goods produced by the foreign subsidiaries. This means that after a relatively short period of growth, industry will lose its dynamic impulse unless exports of manufactures can be rapidly increased. In the meantime there are chronic balance of payments deficits accompanied by growing international indebtedness. For economic growth to continue in Brazil, MNEs must be willing to go on investing, international bankers must be willing to extend more and more credit, and the industrial nations must be willing to take increasing amounts of manufactured exports from Brazil. Without this kind of support from the centre, the model of dependent development cannot survive.[1]

The Automotive Industry and 'Dependencia'

A recent study by Rhys Owen Jenkins[2] has attempted to analyse the mechanism of dependent industrialisation in Latin America using the motor industry to provide concrete evidence showing how developments in the international industry have conditioned what has happened in Latin America.

During the postwar period the long-established national motor industries in the major producing countries became concentrated and internationalised. From the late 1950s onwards this was caused by greatly increased competition as the rate of growth in demand declined and tariffs in the developed world were lowered. What emerged from this was a dozen or so very large firms which dominated the industry and competed with each other on a world-wide basis. It was oligopolistic competition in the international automotive industry that was responsible for the rapid expansion of assembly and manufacturing operations in the underdeveloped countries, and especially for the proliferation of companies in a number of small markets. Admittedly, in practice, the investment decisions of these firms were complicated by the role played by host governments. The outcome, nevertheless, was the transmission of the oligopolistic structure of the international industry to the small, protected markets of individual Latin American countries.

Oligopolistic competition in a restricted market is characterised by non-price competition, market fragmentation as more and more models are introduced, high costs and prices because the firms cannot take advantage of economies of scale, a consequent inability to export, low capacity utilisation and only limited employment creation. The catalogue of economic evils would be the same regardless of whether the firms were owned by nationals or by foreigners since the harmful consequences stem from the structure itself. The point is that the structure was imposed on the Latin American countries from the outside. Furthermore, any further changes in that structure depend on developments in the international industry rather than on the Latin American countries themselves.

One change already wrought by the local operations of the MNEs has been the denationalisation of the new industries. Indigenous firms found it difficult to make the move from importing or assembly to manufacturing because of the much higher capital requirements and the need to obtain foreign technology. Some, usually licensees, were acquired by the foreign licenser, others competitively eliminated as a result of the cost advantages of the local subsidiaries of the MNEs stemming from their easier access to finance and technology. This became particularly apparent when the initially favourable demand weakened and profits began to be squeezed. Government responses to this development varied (some like Mexico were more nationalistic than others) but none were able to resist the growing penetration of the international firms.

This almost complete dominance of the emerging Latin American motor industries has resulted in the continuous outflow of foreign exchange in the form of profits, dividends, royalties, fees, the overpricing of imported intermediate inputs and the overseas purchase of machinery and equipment. Exports, on the other hand, have been limited, partly because of the high costs and prices referred to previously, and partly because of the restrictions imposed by parent companies on exports from local subsidiaries, and those imposed by foreign licensers on their licensees. Hence the motor industry, despite its import-substituting nature continues to contribute substantially towards the chronic balance of payments problems of the industrialising Latin American countries.

On the question of employment, the conclusion drawn is that as an import-substituting industry the motor industry has not had a major effect in displacing workers from other sectors. And while it is accepted that an appreciable number of jobs has been created, it is argued that the total is disappointing. Significantly, no attempt is made to blame this on the use of capital-intensive technology by the MNEs or to maintain that the foreign firms were producing the wrong products.

Finally, alternative patterns of development of an automotive industry are examined and approval given to the policies of Japan, the Soviet Union and Eastern Europe. (In Yugoslavia, however, 'The opportunity to develop an independent automotive industry has been passed over and the path of increased collaboration with foreign companies is being followed.')[3] Like Latin America, these countries pursued an inward-orientated strategy, but they did not make the mistake of admitting foreign capital. Abandoning ownership and control of the Latin American industry to the MNEs meant, 'The failure to develop a rational production structure, to develop exports, or to give priority to commercial vehicle production . . . Furthermore, tariff protection and favourable demand conditions in the early years of the development of the industry gave rise to high profits for foreign companies rather than providing a basis for internal accumulation as in Japan or the USSR. Put in a nutshell, these are all problems of dependent capitalist development.'[4]

Brazil:[5] *An Assessment*

Since much of the above criticism is concerned with the structure of the Latin American automotive industry and its denationalisation, Table 15.1 provides a good starting point. The eleven firms present in Brazil in 1956 were there because the Grupo Executivo da Industria Automobilistica (GEIA), the government body which initiated and planned the development of the industry chose them out of 17 applicants willing to undertake local production. If too many were allowed in, the responsibility lies with the GEIA. It is possible that there was US pressure to include Ford and General Motors — but for the rest? Of the

Table 15.1: Structural Change in Brazilian Motor Industry, 1956-1980

1956	1970	1980	**Unit Production 1979	Per Cent Share
1. Volkswagen (Germany)	Volkswagen	Volkswagen	542,677*	48.1
2. Vemag (Brazil)				
3. Simca (France)	Chrysler (US)			
4. International Harvester (US)				
5. Ford (US)	Ford	Ford	170,875	15.1
6. Willys Overland (US)				
7. FNM (Brazil)	Alfa Romeo (Italy)	Fiat (Italy)	134,866	12.0
8. General Motors (US)	General Motors	General Motors	207,682	18.4
9. Mercedes (Germany)	Mercedes	Mercedes	58,943	5.2
10. Toyota (Japan)	Toyota	Toyota	4,105	.3
11. Scania Vabis (Sweden)	Saab-Scania	Saab-Scania	3,363	.3
	Puma (Brazil)	Puma	3,609	.3
		Others	1,846	.1
		Total	1,127,966	100.0

*Includes Chrysler
**Source: SMMT.

two Brazilian companies, Fabrica Nacional de Motores (FNM) was
state-owned, its founding stimulated by the second world war to make
sure that essential products to keep industry going would not be cut
off. It produced commercial vehicles with technical assistance from
Alfa Romeo. 'Since no foreign or private domestic enterprise was in a
position to establish such an undertaking, a government firm was found
to be the only solution.'[6] The other Brazilian company, Vemag,
represented a joint venture between Novo Mundo a local financial
group, and the German firm, Auto Union. In short, the initial structure
of the industry as far as final production and assembly were concerned
left relatively little scope for denationalisation.

It is true that the subsequent concentration and other changes that
took place reflected developments in the international motor industry
– it could hardly be otherwise. There was, notably, Chrysler's entry
and exit, Ford's acquisition of Willys, and Volkswagen's purchase of
Auto Union which left Vemag without a source for new models and it
too sold out to the German company. But the industry structure was
also influenced by governmental decisions made in Brazil. The first
military government (1964) hived off FNM to Alfa Romeo, and the
State of Minas Gerais was responsible for introducing another contender for the mass market for cars when it initiated a joint venture
(state share 42 per cent) with Fiat. Had it not been for the latter development, Brazil would have ended up with three major producers
accounting for well over 90 per cent of the unit output – a fairly
rational structure given the size of the Brazilian market.

The charge of denationalisation has much more substance when it
comes to the suppliers of the vehicle manufacturers, the firms in the
parts and components sector. 'Unlike the early automobile industries
in the United States and in Europe, the Brazilian automobile industry
at its start already had a flourishing parts industry developed mainly
by local capital and management.'[7] This had come into being during
the second world war when Brazil was cut off from the US which had
supplied 90 per cent of the country's requirements for replacement
parts. However, it appears that many of these firms lacked the technology to move from replacement manufacturer to the mass production of original equipment with its more rigid specifications and
tolerances, and were handicapped in raising finance for expansion,
especially from international sources. At any rate, established foreign
components manufacturers moved in and it is now generally accepted
that they dominate this sector. The only available estimate of the
extent of this dominance comes from a document prepared for the US

State Department which claims that 78 per cent of the auto parts industry in Brazil was foreign-controlled in 1969.[8] To reach that figure a good many small Brazilian parts makers must have been eliminated.

So Brazil has a 'national' motor industry, one largely created by foreign MNEs and, for the most part, owned and controlled by them. From a production standpoint it has been a great achievement for a Third World country to move, in scarcely more than a generation, from an almost complete dependence on imported vehicles to being the world's ninth largest manufacturer with an annual output of over one million units. With the help of government incentives, the industry is becoming a significant exporter. Rather than restricting exports, foreign ownership has made it easier because of the extensive possibilities of internal trade within each of the MNE networks. As an import-substituting industry, it is responsible for tremendous savings in foreign exchange even though vehicle imports continued to exceed exports up until 1976. As regards employment, the vehicle manufacturers themselves have over 100,000 workers and their suppliers probably three times that figure so that some 400,000 new industrial jobs have been created. All in all, not a bad record.

Table 15.2: Brazilian Automotive Exports, 1976-1978 (US $ Millions)

	1976	1977	1978
Passenger vehicles	29.3	51.0	90.2
Passenger vehicles ckd	78.7	71.2	93.0
Trucks	63.1	76.7	115.3
Trucks ckd	33.1	11.4	26.1
Buses	25.9	22.9	34.9
Engines	77.6	173.6	218.6
Other Automotive Parts	224.9	316.0	438.2
Total	532.6	722.8	1,016.3

Source: Brazilian Trade Centre, London.

But the critics take the benefits for granted and point to the costs — the stream of profits, royalties and other foreign exchange payments to foreigners. With 'independencia' the profits from industrialisation would stay in Brazil, the GNP would be somewhat higher and there would be more of a surplus to provide a basis for further growth. This is as far as an industry study can go. Unfortunately it does not reach the heart of the matter. Whether or not the Brazilian entrepreneurial class could or could not have developed an independent motor industry with all the benefits of the existing one is really a red herring. In either case it would have made little difference to Brazil's political and economic structure or to the lives of the majority of the Brazilian people. And that is what the 'dependencia' school is on about. MNEs are attacked, not primarily on the basis of their economic performance, but because their presence is believed to strengthen and support a 'system' which exploits the mass of the population.

'And thereby hangs a tale.' It is a tale of Communism and Capitalism, of Social Justice, Democracy and Freedom, of Bureaucracy and Dictatorship (right and left), of Violence and Revolution, of Birth Rates and Death Rates, of Heroism and Self-Sacrifice, of Cowardice and Corruption, of Hope and Despair. It is also a tale that lies outside the scope of this book – thank God!

Nevertheless, something must be said concerning the distribution of income in Brazil and its consequences. Table 15.3 indicates how unequal it is and how the gap is growing between the rich and poor.

Table 15.3: Changes in Brazilian Income Distribution, 1960-1970 (Per Cent of Total Income Received)

	1960	1970	Change in Share 1960-1970
Richest 1%	11.7	17.8	+6.1
Next 4%	15.6	18.5	+2.9
Total Top 5%	27.3	36.3	+9.0
Bottom 80%	45.5	36.8	−8.7

Source: Peter Evans, *Dependent Development: The Alliance of Multinational, State, and Local Capital in Brazil* (Princeton University Press, Princeton, New Jersey, 1979), p. 97.

Commenting on this table Peter Evans writes:

In a decade during which the production of television sets tripled and the top 5 per cent of the population almost doubled their average income, the 80 million of the bottom remained stagnated at incomes averaging below $200 a year ... The rate of infant mortality in Sao Paulo, one of the most modern and heavily industrialised cities in the world, was 84 per 1000 live births in 1969, about a third higher than the rates for the entire nation of Argentina. The rate for

Recife, the largest and most advanced city in the northeast was 263.5 per 1000 in 1971, about 60 per cent higher than the rate for the rural population of Chad, which was the highest national rate recorded by the United Nations.[9]

In the same vein, the Economist Intelligence Unit described the Brazilian setup in 1975 as '. . . a regime where few people (even if they are lucky enough to work for a multinational firm) earn more than twice the official wage, which is less than enough to keep a wife and two children in food alone . . .'[10]

That distribution of income created an elite group which provided a sizable market in Brazil for automobiles and the other consumer durable goods common in more affluent countries. But if the inequality is not appreciably reduced, the scope for expanded domestic sales is now very limited. Unless the Brazilian car worker can expect, some day, to drive to work (as do his fellow workers in the factories owned by foreign MNEs in Australia, Canada and Belgium) it is hard to picture a profitable future, in the long run, for the MNEs in Brazil.

Strangely enough, the existence of a large motor industry has become a major factor in forcing the government to give priority to agriculture, the fundamental source of the inequality. The need for fuel to power the large and growing numbers of vehicles on the roads, coupled with the rising price of oil which cost the country $7 billion to import in 1979 (or almost half its export earnings), has convinced the government that home-produced alcohol must be substituted for oil. Brazil has the land and the sunshine to grow all the sugar cane, manioc (cassava), and perhaps other crops which may turn out to be suitable, to meet its needs. By 1985 the country expects to have more than 2 million alcohol cars on the road. To provide the fuel calls for an estimated expenditure of $15 billion and the building of one new optimum-sized distillation plant (capacity 120,000 litres a day) every four days during 1980-4. Each distillery requires 2.6 million tons of sugar cane a year and an average planted area of 12,500 acres. This will create considerable employment in rural areas and an infrastructure of roads and services which could attract further development, and it is hoped that in the long run this will redistribute income socially and regionally. The latter effect will be limited if production is carried out entirely by the large landholders on vast cane estates with hired labour. If ways could be found of bringing in to the programme large numbers of small farmers growing manioc (a cottage crop) on their own land, the prospect for agriculture and the future would be much brighter.

In the meantime, 250,000 alcohol-powered cars, buses, vans and mini-buses will roll off the assembly lines of the major producers in 1980 and the industry is committed to provide one-third of all new cars with alcohol-burning engines by 1985. Developing the engines has not been difficult. Relatively simple adjustments to the ordinary petrol engine make it operate efficiently using alcohol. After all Brazilian scientists developed cars which ran successfully on alcohol back in 1923, but with oil so much cheaper then the project was dropped. As for multi-fuel engines, a car was exhibited at the 1912 London Motor Show which could run on petrol, pure alcohol, or any good spirit such as gin, brandy or whisky!

India

Like Brazil, India followed a policy of import-substituting industrialisation but, unlike Brazil, it largely prevented the entry of foreign investment. As discussed in Chapter 7, India's motor industry was shaped for the most part by the government. The policy has been to create a self-sufficient, nationally-owned and controlled industry and in that it has been successful. Priority has been given to commercial vehicle production, with the output of private cars deliberately kept down. The number of manufacturers, the number of models and the frequency of model changes have been restricted, and all financial and technical collaboration agreements with foreign companies have been subject to government approval and normally are not to last longer than five years. The consequences of that policy are reflected in Table 15.4.

Table 15.4: Indian Vehicle Production, 1973 and 1979 (Units)

	1973		1979	
	Cars	CVs	Cars	CVs
Hindustan Motors	25,440	3,161	17,523	2,599
Jeep/Mahindra and Mahindra	13,071	1,299	12,340	3,084
Ashok Leyland	–	5,639	–	12,319
Telco	–	23,107	–	31,689
Premier Automobile	13,883	5,735	11,550	1,079
Standard	614	963	56	2,425
Tempo	–	5,005	–	6,509
Sunrise	–	–	104	–
Total	53,008	44,909	41,573	59,704

Source: SMMT.

As far as the passenger car sector is concerned, a very outdated, poor quality product is manufactured with 100 per cent local content at hopelessly uneconomic volumes. Of the two producers of any consequence, Hindustan Motors makes the Ambassador (a 1954 Morris Oxford) and Premier Automobile the Padmini (a Fiat 1100 of the late 1950s). In commenting on the quality of these cars, *Business India* notes that the four bores in the cylinder of the engine are sometimes of varying sizes and sums up the public's reaction to these cars by quoting an angry customer: 'The Indian car manufacturers exploit an overprotected market on the basis of a completely oligopolistic position. And if you want a car, there's no choice. The whole situation is absurd when you know that you are buying a car whose design is 25 or 30 years old; whose fuel consumption is 20 per cent higher than that of a small 10 year old European model; which has been built sloppily, and might break down in anything between 3 days and 3 months.'[11]

Clearly India's car producers lack the technical resources and the volume necessary to finance the development of new models. The government has considered various projects for a large-volume small-car plant and during 1970 held discussions with Fiat, Renault, Ford-US, Nissan and Toyo Kogyo. This was followed by an attempt to produce an entirely indigenous car promoted by the late Sanjay Gandhi, the Prime Minister's son. A large site was acquired in 1974 but no more than 20 cars were ever produced and the model failed to meet its design specification. The firm was dissolved in 1977.

Two years later the government again decided to seek foreign help in modernising its car industry. Local firms were given the go-ahead to enter collaboration agreements and Mahindra and Mahindra have received government approval for an agreement signed with Peugeot to obtain technology for a plant to manufacture modern diesel engines. The factory will have an initial capacity of 25,000 engines a year which will replace those now being made under licence from American Motors and used in the local production of Jeeps. Premier Automobiles has been negotiating with Fiat and Peugeot for the expertise to replace its Padmini with a more fuel-efficient model. The government has recently invited Renault to set up a plant to make small cars — exclusively for export. This was in response to a plan put forward earlier by Renault to make a passenger car in collaboration with Indian companies to be marketed in India only. Some compromise might be possible, but no Indian-based affiliate of an MNE could hope to compete in far-Eastern export markets against Japan without a substantial domestic market.

On the commercial vehicle side the situation is somewhat brighter. The largest producer, Telco (Tata Engineering and Locomotive

Company) makes buses and heavy trucks and has an installed annual
capacity of 36,000 units. It initially made vehicles in collaboration with
Daimler-Benz which had (and still holds) an 11.9 per cent financial
interest. The company's vehicles are completely indigenous and independently manufactured, and are sold under the Tata brand name,
with sales in more than 40 countries. Ashok-Leyland, in which BL
holds a 50.6 per cent stake, also produces buses and heavy trucks, and
it has an installed annual capacity of 12,500 units. The export of
buses, mostly to developing countries, has been successful but few trucks
have been sold abroad. Although Ashok-Leyland has its own research
and development department, the vehicles are based on parent company designs, and most of the technology comes from BL which
receives up to a maximum of $250,000 for each of its technical agree-
ments with the subsidiary. The latter now has an Indian as managing
director and seeks to operate with a good deal of autonomy. At times
this may run counter to the policy of the parent company. BL, for
example, wants to bring Ashok-Leyland into a world-wide agreement
whereby it would promote sales from its Indian operation through its
own distribution system. It believes the subsidiary would benefit from
the superior marketing and servicing it can provide in south-east-Asian
and African markets for which the Indian product is ideally suited. The
only other producer of any size is Bajaj Tempo which makes light
commercial vehicles. It too has a foreign associate — Daimler-Benz,
which holds a 25.9 per cent share in the company.

Demand for commercial vehicles exceeds capacity and continues to
grow at a rapid rate so that even though the present capacity is under-
utilised — primarily because of power shortages and supply difficulties
resulting from India's inadequate road system — the government is
anxious to expand production facilities. Plans have been approved to
increase Telco's capacity to 46,640 vehicles and Ashok-Leyland's to
27,500. MAN of West Germany is being allowed to enter a technical
and financial collaboration with Escorts of Delhi in a new joint venture,
Escorts-MAN, to make stationary and automotive diesel engines. Moreover, the Simpson group, which holds a licence to manufacture commercial vehicles, has been given permission to import a few hundred Ford
trucks for assembly in India. This collaboration with Ford is being
watched with some concern by the established manufacturers.

The development of an indigenous motor industry has necessarily
involved the establishment of Indian suppliers of parts and components
to the vehicle manufacturers. Here too there was much reliance on
foreign firms for technology, but the government's stipulated maximum

of 40 per cent shareholding in joint ventures ensured that control remained with the Indian partners. In 1974 there were almost 100 recorded collaborations between foreign companies with developed technologies and Indian producers, some financial and others on a purely technical level.[12] Most of these were in the ancillary sector and included such well-known names as Eaton, Dana, Repco, Dunlop, Girling, Autolite, Smith's Industries, Purolater, Bendix and Bosch. Each collaboration required government approval and it was said at the time that the authorities were getting more demanding, frowning on attempts to restrict markets or the use of know-how and setting limits to the payments that could be made for technology. So much so that doubts were expressed as to the profitability for foreign concerns in such agreements, and the possibility raised that they might only be willing in future to offer technology that was already obsolete.

India: An Assessment

It was inevitable that a country as large and populous as India would seek to meet its own automotive needs with domestic production. As a very poor country those needs were correctly seen to be for trucks and buses rather than for private cars, hence the priority given to commercial vehicles and the very limited resources allocated to the production of cars. Its import-substitution policy increased industrial employment directly by 158,000 jobs, and ensured that the country's needs for motor vehicles could be met without any cost to the balance of payments. The position for 1977-8 is given in Table 15.5

Table 15.5: India's Automotive Balance of Payments, 1977-1978 (US $ Millions)

Imports	
Vehicles	10.7
Parts and components	64.5
Payments abroad (dividends, royalties, etc.)*	7.8
Total	83.0
Exports	
Vehicles	36.3
Parts and components	63.3
Total	99.6

*Vehicle manufacturers only.
Source: Association of Indian Automobile Manufacturers (Rupee figures furnished converted at Rs 8 = US $).

Finally, India's policy of preference for technical rather than financial agreements and of limiting foreign ownership almost entirely to minority interests has made certain that nationals own and control the country's motor industry.

That said, it must be pointed out that the industry has been stagnating for a decade or more, and that enthusiastic plans for expansion tend to bog down in a morass of red tape and bureaucratic delays over licences for capital goods, for imports, and for approval for collaboration agreements, to say nothing of being overwhelmed by the more general problems of the Indian economy as a whole. Moreover, despite the general exclusion of foreign capital, the Indian industry remains heavily dependent on overseas firms for technology — and will remain so until the country develops a large and rapidly-growing market for cars and trucks and the ability to supply it internally. The present situation in the car sector is the extreme reflection of that dependence. Indeed, until India is ready to promote large-volume car production, that dependence could be greatly reduced, and significant savings in resources made, by annually importing two or three of the latest fuel-efficient models, say 20,000 to 40,000 in all depending on the state of the economy, and assembling them locally with up to 60 per cent local content.

It is very doubtful whether the performance of the industry would have been any better had foreign investment been encouraged. The characteristics of the economy appear to have been far more important than ownership, i.e., location-specific factors dominated ownership specific factors. If that is accepted then the Indian policy was the right one — a stagnant industry under national ownership is preferable to a stagnant industry owned by foreigners.

In a way this may answer the question implicitly raised at the beginning of this chapter, that is, did Brazil or India follow the right course as regards foreign investment and the development of their motor industries? Were they perhaps both right — given the political, social and economic factors at work in each during this phase in their history? Brazil went all out for economic growth and it encouraged MNE participation to achieve that goal. Its motor industry is now ten times the size of India's. Its gross domestic product, which was not much more than half that of India's in 1960, was nearly twice as large in 1976. Masses of its people remain in appalling poverty (as they do in India), but that increase in wealth and production capacity does mean that there is more to aim at for the forgotten 40 per cent of the population when they begin to make their presence felt.

Notes

1. Peter Evans, *Dependent Development: The Alliance of Multinational, State, and Local Capital in Brazil* (Princeton University Press, Princeton, New Jersey 1979), p. 290.

2. Rhys Owen Jenkins, *Dependent Industrialisation in Latin America: The Automotive Industry in Argentina, Chile and Mexico* (Praeger, New York, 1977).

3. Ibid., p. 247.

4. Ibid, pp. 247-8.

5. Note that Jenkins did not specifically deal with the Brazilian industry.

6. Evans, *Dependent Development*, p. 89.

7. E.F. Gibian, 'Problems Related to the Production and Supply of Automotive Components', *Establishment and Development of Automotive Industries in Developing Countries, Part II* (United Nations, New York, 1970), p. 56.

8. Evans, *Dependent Development*, table 3.2, pp. 114-15. Taken from Richard S. Newfarmer and Willard Mueller, *Multinational Corporations in Brazil and Mexico: Structural Sources of Economic and Non-Economic Power*, Report to the Subcommittee on Multinationals, Committee on Foreign Relations, US Senate (Washington, DC, 1975). That book gives Jasperson as the author of the estimate but does not cite his sources. The figure is roughly in line with three other estimates of the percentages of foreign capital in the transportation equipment industry given in Evans.

9. Evans, *Dependent Development*, pp. 96-7.

10. Economist Intelligence Unit, *Multinational Business*, 'Brazil Has Second Thoughts About the Multinationals', no. 3 (1975), p. 20. The article claims that foreign-controlled firms pay wages considerably above the average, an estimated 30 per cent more than their Brazilian competitors. The MNEs get no credit for this from their critics who accuse them of creating a labour elite and splitting the labour movement.

11. *Business India*, 8-21 January 1979, p. 43.

12. Economist Intelligence Unit, *Motor Business*, 'The Indian Motor Industry', no. 82 (2nd Quarter, 1975), pp. 41-51.

CONCLUSIONS

The answers to several of the questions raised in this book lies in the investment decisions which turned national firms into MNEs.

'Export if you can, invest abroad if you must' could have been the industry's motto. Throughout its entire history, almost all foreign direct investment decisions have been prompted by tariff barriers to exports. From the establishment of Ford-Canada in 1903 to the recent investments by Nissan and Toyota in Australia, this has been the pattern. With very few exceptions, where there were no trade barriers there was no foreign investment. But as countries sought to protect domestic industries from exports, or to encourage the development of local motor industries, the only way firms could retain markets or secure access to important potential markets was to invest in overseas production. In short, foreign direct investment in the automobile industry has almost always been defensive investment.

That conclusion applies also to Volkswagen's decision to invest in the US which was exceptional in that it was not prompted by a tariff but by other location-specific factors, namely, changes in relative wage and exchange rates. Without local production the US market would have been lost to lower-cost competitors. In contrast the Japanese manufacturers would much prefer to continue to export to America since there is no tariff barrier and the other location-specific factors favour production in Japan.

If tariffs almost invariably provided the motive for foreign investment, what were the ownership-specific factors which made that investment possible? Up until the second world war, Ford and General Motors were the only MNEs in the industry. Their competitive advantage lay not so much in superior automotive technology but in superior knowledge of mass production and marketing techniques, and in their size compared to their rivals in Europe. Since the war those advantages have been eroded by the rapid growth of European and Japanese firms, but superior knowledge and size still serve to explain the success of foreign subsidiaries in developing countries, be they American, European or Japanese.

What the theory of foreign investment cannot account for is the cross investment that has occurred between America and Europe in recent years. It is hard to believe that Opel, for example, has cost advantages over Volkswagen while at the same time Volkswagen of America has cost advantages over General Motors in the production of similar products. It may be that the cost disadvantages of producing abroad have been exaggerated or that they disappear over time. If Opel's costs were roughly the same as Volkswagen, then 'superiority' would not have to be brought in to explain foreign investment. Such investment could merely be part of a competitive process leading to increased output or improved (or differentiated) products and techniques, which would be countered in due course by Volkswagen. Similarly, the success of Volkswagen of America and of Japanese exports to the US is being met (at long last) by fuel-efficient, small cars produced by the American companies. This ties in with the product cycle theory.

Factor cost and demand conditions in the US led to the mass production of automobiles at a time when they were more or less handmade luxury products in European countries. American exports to Europe and elsewhere were so successful that tariffs were imposed which in turn prompted foreign investment by the US companies. After the second world war, mass markets developed in Europe and Japan for small cars, cheaper to buy and to run than the American models. The pattern of exports, tariffs and foreign investment was repeated, creating European and Japanese MNEs. Finally, the narrowing of the wage gap between America and the other major producing countries, together with the fuel crisis has meant that similar factor cost and demand conditions now exist in all of them. Consequently the American producers can be expected to meet the foreign competitors with their own differentiated small cars.

There are, however, few signs to support phase III of the product cycle where, in a mature industry with a standardised product, oligopolistic competition drives the surviving firms to reduce costs by investing in low-wage developing countries. Home investment still dominates MNE spending on productive capacity and less than 10 per cent is being allocated to developing countries.

The cost pressures are there but they are taking the form of forcing the MNEs to rationalise and integrate production in optimum-sized plants and to economise on research, development and engineering expenditure by producing 'world cars'. The 'international sourcing of components' means just that and is not a euphemism for the wholesale shifting of production to low-wage countries. As sources of supply for parts, components and finished vehicles, their contributions have been modest and as easily explained by host country pressure and incentives to export as by low costs.

Which brings balance of payments considerations into the investment decision. The rationalisation and integration of world-wide
networks, including the siting of new optimum-sized plants, inevitably
means a great increase in specialisation and 'internal' trade. It appears
that the long-run interests of the MNE will be best served by allocating
investment so that the trade is as complementary as possible, imposing
no continuing burden on the balance of payments of any sizable
country in which the MNE is established as a manufacturer. In other
words, huge world-wide sales cannot be sustained without world-wide
production — in widely scattered optimum-sized units. If this is right
the Japanese producers cannot hope to flood the world with exports
much longer. The argument also implies that the cost of production
does not vary a great deal from country to country provided the scale
of production is right. But how else explain General Motor's decision to
produce one of its new engines in Australia, Brazil, Austria and Japan,
and to supply its European subsidiaries from the first three countries?

This internationalisation of production within the MNE networks
calls for sophisticated planning and complex logistics, hence tight
control by the parent company. The structure strongly implies that the
MNE will seek to 'internalise' the operations and therefore will prefer
wholly-owned subsidiaries, although joint ventures may be acceptable
if managerial control rests with the MNE. Licensing is likely to be
confined to firms which are not part of the 'team', small assemblers
catering solely for their home markets, and to 'buy back' deals with
East European countries where the supply conditions are precisely
stated in the agreement.

This development means, of course, the end of 'national' motor
industries. Already it makes more sense to speak of the European
motor industry than of the British, French, German, Italian or Swedish
industries. The US industry has become the North American industry
following the US-Canada Automotive Agreement which formally led
to complete integration. Informally, Mexico is rapidly becoming part
of the North American industry. Europe and North America in turn
have growing links with South America and to a lesser extent with Asia
and Africa.

It might have been expected that this internationalisation would
have been opposed by national governments anxious to preserve their
'own' motor industries, but this has not happened. Home governments
have accepted it without protest, perhaps reassured because control of
the world-wide enterprise remains with their nationals. Host govern-

ments have even encouraged integration, notably Canada through the Automotive Agreement with the US, Britain in its attitude to Chrysler-UK, Spain, in legislation preparing the way for entry into the EEC, and developing countries in pushing subsidiaries to export. The battle of the century, MNEs vs the nation-state, has turned out to be a non-event as far as the motor industry is concerned.

Not that the MNE has been given a free hand. The nation-state is not without bargaining power, and the inevitable problem of how a purely national political unit can safeguard its interests in dealing with an international business organisation remains for home as well as host countries. As does the question of the impact of MNEs on the world community as a whole.

Home Countries

The characteristics of MNEs indicated in Part Two strongly suggests that concern over the policies of home-based MNEs has been largely mis-placed. The defensive nature of their overseas investment means that it has a favourable effect on the home balance of payments. Exports are higher than they otherwise would be. It is true that the home country might be supplied from lower-cost foreign subsidiaries but in practice the use made of captive imports has been restricted in amount and confined to a time when the only alternative was higher imports from foreign MNEs. The American firms clearly intend to meet the US demand for their new world cars from their factories in America. The trade effects then of the foreign investment are favourable. So too, of course, are the effects of the money flows associated with that invest-ment, effects which are reinforced by the practices of financing most overseas investment from the retained profits of foreign subsidiaries and by borrowing locally.

If exports are stimulated more than imports then the employment effects of the foreign investment must be positive. It is not a question of producing vehicles abroad which could be produced at home. The export market is closed to home produced cars and trucks, but invest-ment in that market brings with it demand for home country machinery and equipment as well as for parts and components for some consider-able time, and this creates jobs that would not otherwise exist.

But in a competitive world, jobs also depend on maintaining techno-logical superiority, and fears have been expressed that investments abroad using home technology will undermine its superiority. As long as the great bulk of research and development expenditure takes place in parent companies, as it does, these fears seem groundless. One need only ask the rhetorical question — where are the world cars of the 1980s being designed and developed, incorporating the latest in car electronics? And to assist in this task, parent companies are seconding the best people from their foreign subsidiaries in a sort of short-term brain drain from the periphery to the centre.

On the question of ownership and control, the home government has less to worry about than do host governments. Ownership of the MNE rests predominantly with nationals and its top decision-making body consists almost entirely of nationals. In all sorts of ways this makes for an affinity between firm and government which would be impossible in the case of foreign-owned and controlled companies. Nevertheless, governments do not always see eye to eye with private business organisations, and the MNE controls facilities outside the home country's jurisdiction which might be used in ways which conflict with government policies. Just as purely domestic firms will exploit loopholes in laws and regulations to increase profits or to reduce the taxes they pay, so too will the MNE, and the internationalisation of the motor industry with its large scale intra-company trade presents it with more and bigger loopholes. Putting questions such as these to one side (and a determined government can perhaps close the loopholes) relations between the state and its own MNEs are close and generally harmonious. The above analysis suggests why this is so.

Host Countries (Developed)

Every national motor industry has grown up behind tariff barriers. The ownership of the surviving firms in each country has depended on its policy regarding foreign direct investment and the competitiveness of its indigenous producers. The consequences can be looked at in terms of the top ten manufacturers. The US has three, due entirely to the superior competitiveness of its firms prior to the second world war. Of the rest, Japan and Italy excluded foreign investment and they have two and one respectively. France, which saw some foreign investment but had a climate basically hostile to foreign companies, has two. The UK and Canada, both of which encouraged foreign investment, have none. Germany is the only country which permitted foreign investment yet managed to develop 'world class' companies of its own, two in this case. The lesson is clear, but 'bygones are forever bygones' and times change.

The general elimination of tariffs has exposed 'national' motor industries to greatly increased competition. It is one of the contentions of this book that no industrialised country is going to allow its domestic motor industry to disappear, that it aims to sustain automotive employment as best it can and to export at least enough to cover imports. Hence, the financial support given by governments, not only to firms owned by nationals, e.g., Chrysler-US, BL, Peugeot-Citroen, Renault, Alfa Romeo, but also to foreign subsidiaries, e.g., Chrysler-UK, Chrysler-Canada and Volvo Car BV. Hence, too, the willingness to accept regional integration as a necessary step for survival.[1] Most striking of all is the willing acceptance of foreign investment by the US and the spectacle of its government, automotive trade union and firms pleading with Japan to invest in America.

Host Countries (Developing)

It has been said, and often repeated, that the basic principles of the automobile have been widely known and have changed little over the years, that the industry is not a high technology industry, and that its products and production processes have become standardised. Nevertheless, no developing country has proved capable of independently designing and developing a motor car or of producing one in volume. (Even the Soviet Union had to buy a modern design and the know-how to produce it on a large scale from Fiat.) India is probably the only developing country whose nationals are capable of producing and selling a unique truck in world markets. In short, Third World nations have been (and still are) dependent on the MNEs for automotive technology.

That technology could theoretically have been obtained by means of licences or via direct foreign investment. The latter was almost invariably chosen outside the socialist bloc. A number of reasons for this choice might be cited. No capable entrepreneurial groups willing to undertake the task, shortage of engineers and managers with the ability of absorbing the new knowledge and adapting it to local conditions, a largely untrained and unskilled workforce, an absence of suppliers of basic materials, parts and components, a shortage of capital, or a refusal by MNEs to grant licences. On the positive side, governments may have believed that the needed technology would be transferred more quickly and efficiently by MNEs with an investment stake in the success of an industry regarded as a crucial part of their industrialisation programme. Whatever the explanation, the Hyundai Motor Company of South Korea is the only firm in a developing country which has successfully produced cars in volume relying entirely on licences, hiring foreign designers and managers and borrowing from abroad. Successful so far, but the sole exception to the rule.

Assuming that without the foreign investment the vast majority of developing countries would have had no motor industry, then the economic benefits of that investment would seem to have been considerable. Obviously employment was increased. The balance of payments effect was favourable, since the investment was in an import-saving industry so that the trade effects swamped the adverse money flows in the form of profits, etc. As an industry with many backward and forward linkages, the external economies associated with the foreign investment must have been considerable, raising the overall level of technology and acting as a stimulant to industrialisation and economic growth generally.

And yet much dissatisfaction exists in many developing countries with the industry's performance and it has been subject to a chorus of attacks, some aimed specifically at the vehicle producers and some at MNEs in general. It is useful to separate the critics into two groups; those who broadly accept the 'system' and whose charges might be met by policy changes or 'reforms' without basically altering it, and those who reject the 'system' and whose recommendations can only be effected by a fundamentally different political, economic and social regime.

Of major importance in the first category are the structural problems which have arisen out of the conditions of production in the motor industry and its pattern of oligopolistic competition. High cost, inefficient industries have resulted from small-scale production and insistence on a high local content. The small-scale production was brought about by a limited domestic market, fragmented by MNEs anxious to secure shares in all potentially significant markets. Competition between them was very slow in eliminating any of the rivals so that the faulty structure has been perpetuated.

Only a half dozen or so developing countries have, or can hope to have in the coming decade, an annual demand of 200,000 cars (including van and jeep derivatives). Yet some such figure is considered to be the minimum efficient scale for the complete manufacture of just one basic, but conventional, car. Fewer countries still have a market large enough to support more than one manufacturer. A monopoly *might* be efficient but is considered undesirable. Developing countries continue to want a motor industry of their own, but they are much more aware now of these problems than they were twenty or even ten years ago. And steps can and are being taken to reduce if not to eliminate these structural difficulties.

Developing countries which are just beginning to move into manufacture can restrict the number of producers and models, and can encourage standardisation amongst component suppliers. They can establish a regional motor industry, as the Andean Pact countries are attempting to do, selecting a few manufacturers for the whole region and planning the specialisation and exchange of models and components to get longer production runs, with final assembly taking place in each country. Complementation within MNE networks can achieve similar results. For some of the smaller countries, assembly with something like 50 per cent local content may be the best policy for cars, combined with domestic production of truck and bus chassis. But even assembly should be ruled out for countries with annual markets of less than 10,000 cars and 5,000 commercial vehicles since such assembly is not only inefficient but also usually costs more in foreign exchange than imports of built-up vehicles. In short, the structural problems can largely be overcome and most developing countries can hope to meet the bulk of their automotive needs without a great waste in resources or a heavy foreign exchange cost.

There remains the difficult and emotional question of ownership and control which lies at the heart of foreign investment. Foreign ownership means that (whatever the import savings may be) actual money flows are negative because of the stream of profits and other payments going abroad, that decisions will be made by the parent company regarding new investment, product policy and trade which may not be in the country's interest; or worse that the local subsidiary, as part of a profit-seeking international organisation, may be used to exploit the host nation.

Fears such as these have been behind the trend away from wholly-owned subsidiaries to joint ventures in recent years in the motor industry, with the host government as one of the partners and the MNE holding perhaps only a minority share, albeit a large one. This has obvious advantages for the host country – local capital which might have been borrowed by the MNE is converted into equity and the state and local shareholders receive part of the profits. How much local control goes with the local ownership is debatable. The logic of the MNE calls for a closely-knit world organisation, operated for the benefit of the group as a whole, and the belated willingness to accept joint ventures suggests a dawning realisation that control remains with the management and that the local partners are much more likely to be allies than antagonists.

More promising from the standpoint of control is the use of the state's sovereign power to negotiate entry terms with the MNE and to pass laws and regulations affecting its behaviour. The level of technology can be raised and overall industrialisation fostered by insisting that MNEs establish training schemes for operatives, groom nationals for top management positions in the subsidiary and buy parts and components from locally-owned suppliers. Priority may be given to trucks and buses. Profits may be taxed, kept down by price controls or lowering tariffs, limits placed on profit remissions, royalties and other payments and export requirements laid down. All these measures have been tried in the motor industry.

As for controlling the use of transfer prices to evade the host government's attempts to limit profits and their remission to the parent company, Sanjaya Lall, who has made a critical study of transfer pricing, has this to say:

> The automobile industry is not, however, a particularly difficult case to tackle as far as transfer pricing is concerned. It is not a high technology industry. There is a substantial amount of inter-firm trade. Costs of production are easy to discover and fixed costs are not particularly difficult to allocate since there is little R & D, components are fairly standardised and produced by large numbers of sub-contractors, and innovation is not particularly risky. This is not to say that TNCs cannot manipulate transfer prices in the absence of special regulatory measures, only that there are few problems *in principle* for a government which is determined to control the practice. The case falls into the group where remedies are possible mainly by the collection of information.[2]

However, all talk of local control of MNE subsidiaries is dismissed as nonsense by the second group of critics, those who reject the 'system'. For them, asking local capitalists and/or a local capitalist state to control foreign investment for the benefit of the mass of the population is like asking jackals to control lions for the benefit of grazing antelopes. Only a socialist revolutionary regime can tame the 'agents of imperialism'. Only such a regime can bring about the radical redistribution of income and the reorganisation of industry required to meet the basic needs of the masses. No longer will the 'wrong' products be produced using the 'wrong' technology.

On this last point, it is notable that no Communist country has contributed any ideas on a truly low-cost vehicle for developing countries, or evolved labour-intensive technologies for the production of existing vehicles. Even China seems ready to join the Soviet Union and several of the East European countries in replacing outmoded designs and methods with the best MNE models to be obtained under licence, together with the latest techniques for producing them. It would seem that as far as the motor industry is concerned, the wrong product and the wrong technology turn out to be right when the regime is Left.

World

> Whether we like it or not Africa, Asia, Latin America are going all out into the industrial age . . .
> If we want to share in these markets, rich and vast as they some day surely will be . . . we are going to have to go in with our capital, tools and know-how and help them get the things they want.
> (Henry Ford II, Spring 1961)[3]

If the nations of the world manage to realise in time that there is no alternative to peace and thus avoid the insanity of a nuclear war, then the world's most pressing problem will most certainly be mass poverty in the developing countries and the growing gap between the rich and poor nations. The enormity and urgency of that problem enables us to give some practical meaning to the hazy concept 'world welfare' and to say that any appreciable contribution towards solving it represents an improvement in world welfare. It seems fair to say that the MNEs in the motor industry have made such a contribution.

As an import-substituting industry and one that acts as a catalyst for economic growth, the motor industry has been a key element in the industrialisation programmes of developing countries. Lacking the knowledge and resources to establish such an industry, with its complicated relationships with numerous supplying industries and its need for a distribution and service network, they induced the MNE to perform the task, in most cases via direct foreign investment. There followed a rapid buildup of production capacity and an impressive transfer of technology, a process which is continuing. Moreover, sizable exports of automotive products are beginning to be shipped back to the developed countries and this trade seems bound to increase. This is of vital importance since the future economic growth of developing countries very much depends on their ability to sell growing amounts of manufactures in the markets of the rich. The MNE networks provide such outlets for automotive exports, outlets which would not otherwise exist.

Nevertheless a few words of warning are in order. MNEs are profit-making organisations, not charities. They have much to offer developing countries, but it is up to the governments of those countries, singly and collectively, to make sure that they deliver.

It is important to stress that this gradual shift in the location of the industry is inevitable and is not taking place at the expense of home countries. This is partly because control remains with the MNE's parent company, and partly because of the ability to offset the lure of low wages in developing countries with greater capital-intensive production at home. In short, car making in high-wage, developed countries does have a future. But economic and political pressures on the MNEs from various quarters have produced a situation in which the future growth of the motor industry will take place in the developing countries, with output in the home countries more or less stabilised at existing levels. 'A moment's thought will make clear why the future must see nation after nation taking over its own work of supply. And we ought to be glad to help the work along.'

Notes

1. Regional integration and 'world cars' make the case much weaker for putting political pressure on MNE subsidiaries to carry out research and development.
2. Sanjaya Lall, 'Transfer Pricing and Developing Countries: Some Problems of Investigation', *World Development*, vol. 7 (1979), pp. 66-7. Not entirely agreeing with the premises on which this conclusion is based, i.e. the characteristics of the motor industry, I am not quite so optimistic about the ability of governments to control transfer pricing.
3. M. Wilkins and F.E. Hill, *American Business Abroad: Ford on Six Continents* (Wayne State University Press, Detroit, 1964), p. 414.

SELECTED BIBLIOGRAPHY

Books

Baranson, J. *Automotive Industries in Developing Countries* (World Bank Staff Occasional Papers Number Eight, 1969)
—— *Technology and the Multi-nationals* (Lexington Books, Lexington, Mass. 1978)
Behrman, J.N. *The Role of the International Companies in Latin American Integration: Autos and Petrochemicals* (Lexington Books, Lexington, Mass. 1972)
Behrman, J.N. and Wallender, H. *Transfers of Manufacturing Technology Within Multinational Enterprises* (Ballinger Publishing Co, Cambridge, Mass. 1976)
Bhaskar, K. *The Future of the World Motor Industry* (Kogan Page, London, 1980)
Bloomfield, G. *The World Automotive Industry* (David & Charles, Newton Abbot, 1978)
Buckley, P.J. and Casson, M. *The Future of the Multinational Enterprise* (Macmillan, London, 1976)
Donner, F.G. *The World-wide Industrial Enterprise* (McGraw-Hill, New York, 1967)
Dunning, J.H. (ed.) *Economic Analysis and the Multinational Enterprise* (Allen & Unwin, London, 1974)
—— (ed.) *International Investment* (Penguin, London, 1972)
Evans, P. *Dependent Development: The Alliance of Multinational, State and Local Capital in Brazil* (Princeton University Press, Princeton, NJ, 1979)
Ginsberg, H. and Abernathy, W.J. (eds.) *Government, Technology and the Future of the Automobile* (McGraw-Hill, New York, 1980)
Hartnett, L. *Big Wheels and Little Wheels* (Gold Star Publications, Australia, 1973)
Hodges, M. *Multinational Corporations and National Government* (Saxon House, Farnborough, 1974)
Hood, N. and Young, S. *The Economics of Multinational Enterprise* (Longman, London, 1979)
Hu, Y.S. *The Impact of US Investment in Europe: A Case Study of the Automotive and Computer Industries* (Praeger, New York, 1973)
Jackson, R.A. (ed.) *The Multinational Corporation and Social Policy.*

Special Reference to General Motors in South Africa (Praeger, New York, 1974)

Jenkins, R.O. *Dependent Industrialisation in Latin America: The Automotive Industry in Argentina, Chile and Mexico* (Praeger, New York, 1977)

Kindleberger, C.P. *American Business Abroad: Six Lectures on Direct Investment* (Yale University Press, New Haven, Conn. 1969)

—— (ed.) *The International Corporation* (MIT Press, Cambridge, Mass. 1970)

Lall, S. and Streeten, P. *Foreign Investment, Transnationals and Developing Countries* (Macmillan, London, 1977)

Lloyd, I. *Rolls-Royce: The Years of Endeavour* (Macmillan, London, 1978)

Nevins, A. *Ford: The Times, the Man, the Company* (Charles Scribner's Sons, New York, 1954)

Nevins, A. and Hill, F.E. *Ford, Expansion and Challenge 1914-1933* (Charles Scribner's Sons, New York, 1957)

Rakovic, P. *Development of the Automotive Industry in Developing Countries in Cooperation with Industries in the Developed Countries* (UNIDO, Vienna, ID/WG 136/4, 13 October 1972)

Rhys, D.G. *The Motor Industry: An Economic Survey* (Butterworths, London, 1972)

Sloan, A.P. Jr *My Years With General Motors* (McFadden Books, New York, 1965)

Stubbs, P. *The Australian Motor Industry* (Cheshire Publishing, Melbourne for the Institute of Applied Economic and Social Research, University of Melbourne, 1972)

Turner, G. *The Leyland Papers* (Eyre & Spottiswoode, London, 1971)

Turner, L. *Multinational Companies and the Third World* (Allen Lane, London, 1974)

Vernon, R. *Sovereignty at Bay* (Basic Books, London, 1971)

White, L.J. *The Automobile Industry Since 1945* (Harvard University Press, Cambridge, Mass. 1971)

Wilkins, M. and Hill, F.E. *American Business Abroad: Ford on Six Continents* (Wayne State University Press, Detroit, 1964)

Wyatt, R.J. *The Motor Car for the Million: The Austin Seven 1922-1929* (London, 1968)

Journals and Articles

Caves, R.E. 'International Corporations: The Industrial Economics of Investment', *Economica*, vol. 38 (1971)

Dunning, J.H. 'Trade, Location of Economic Activity and the MNE: A Search for an Eclectic Approach' in Ohlin, B., Hesselborn, P. and Wijkman, P.M. (eds.) *The International Location of Economic Activity* (Macmillan, London, 1977)

Hymer, S. 'The Multinational Corporation and the Law of Uneven Development' in Bhagwati, J. *Economics and the World Order* (Macmillan, New York, 1972)

Johnson, H. 'Survey of the Issues' in Drysdale, P. (ed.) *Direct Foreign Investment in Asia and Pacific* (Australian National University Press, Canberra, 1972)

Lall, S. 'Transfer Pricing by Multinational Firms', *Oxford Bulletin of Economics and Statistics*, vol. 35, no. 3 (1973)

—— 'Transfer Pricing and Developing Countries: Some Problems of Investigation', *World Development*, vol. 7 (1979)

Vernon, R. 'International Investment and International Trade in the Product Cycle', *Quarterly Journal of Economics*, vol. 80 (1966)

—— 'The Product Cycle Hypothesis in a New International Environment', *Oxford Bulletin of Economics and Statistics*, vol. 41, no. 4 (November 1979)

White, L.J. 'The American Automobile Industry and the Small Car 1945-1970', *Journal of Industrial Economics* (April 1972)

Official Publications

Central Policy Review Staff *The Future of the British Car Industry* (HMSO, London, 1975)

Industries Assistance Commission *Passenger Motor Vehicles Etc.* (Australian Government Printing Service, Canberra, 1974)

Parliament (Commons) *Fourteenth Report of the Expenditure Committee, Session 1974-75, The Motor Vehicle Industry* (HMSO, London, 1975)

—— *Eighth Report From the Expenditure Committee, Session 1975-76, Public Expenditure on Chrysler, UK Ltd.* (HMSO, London, 1976)

United Nations Department of Economic and Social Affairs *Multinational Corporations in World Development*, E.73.11.A.11 (UN,

New York, 1973)

—— *The Impact of Multinational Corporations in the Development Process and on International Relations*, Report of the Group of Eminent Persons, E.74.11.A.5 (UN, New York, 1974)

United Nations Economic and Social Council *Transnational Corporations in World Development: A Re-examination*, Commission on Transnational Corporations, 4th session, EC.10/38 (UN, New York, 1978)

United Nations Industrial Development Organisation *Establishment and Development of Automotive Industries in Developing Countries*, Report and Proceedings of Seminar held in Karlovy Vary, Czechoslovakia 24 February-14 March 1969 (UN, New York, 1970)

—— *The Motor Vehicle Industry* (UN, New York, 1972)

—— *The Manufacture of Low-cost Vehicles in Developing Countries* (UN, New York, 1978)

INDEX

Agnelli, Giovanni 195
Agnelli, Umberto 144-5
Alfa Romeo 120, 148-9, 194, 259-60, 275
American Motors 99, 136, 194, 265; and Renault 137, 139, 160-1; in Australia 118; in Canada 69-70, 245; in Mexico 121-2
Andean Pact countries 153
Argentina 119-21, 124-5, 153, 163
Ashok Leyland 264, 266; see also BL
Austin Motor Company 83, 110
Australia 81-2, 115-19, 163, 251-4; Japanese investment in 141
Australian Motor Industries (AMI) 118
Austrian Daimler Company 63; see also Daimler-Benz
Austro-Fiat 63, 84
Authi, 126, 188
Auto Union 260

Bajaj Tempo 264, 266
balance of payments 124-5, 166, 168, 245-6, 273, 275, 277; and investment decisions 162, 239-41, 272; see also foreign direct investment
Baranson, Jack 213
Barber, John 220
Bayerische Motoren Werke (BMW) 194
Belgium 104-6, 163
Benn, Wedgwood 227-8
BL 142, 194, 266, 275; and Honda 149; see also British Leyland
Borgward 121-2
Bourke, William O. 195
Brazil 119-20, 124-5, 153, 163, 255-64, 268
British Leyland 102, 104, 114, 130; balance of payments 233; comparative UK performance 220-6; employment 234; in Australia 118, 141, 188, 252; in India 128; in Italy 103, 188; in Spain 126, 188; nationalisation of 188-9, 227-8; need to integrate 188, 226, 231, 236; R & D co-operation 235; see also BL
British Motor Corporation (BMC) 118, 126, 251; see also British

Motor Holdings
British Motor Holdings (BMH), merger with Leyland Motors 188
Bulgaria 165, 170
Burke-Hardke Bill 180

Caldwell, Philip 173
Canada 163, 245-6, 250; auto pact with US 246-50
captive imports 100-1; see also UK, US
Central Policy Review Staff, Report 200-2, 229
Chile 129-30
China 173-6
Chrysler 71, 94-5, 97-8, 114, 194-5, 242; acquisitions, European 104, 107; and IMF 183; captive imports 222-4; foreign imports, response to 99-101; foreign investment, pre-war 71-2, 85; in Argentina 121, 140-1, 190; in Australia 251-2, 254; in Brazil 120, 141, 183, 190, 259; in Canada 69-70, 245, 275; in China 175; in France 108; in Latin America 122, 141; in Philippines 154; in Spain 108, 126; integration, Europe 146; link with Mitsubishi 111-12; sale of overseas assets 138, 141, 243; see also Chrysler-UK
Chrysler-UK 108, 146; and UK government 227-30, 243n11; balance of payments 233-4; comparative performance 221-6; employment 234; establishment 227; sale to Peugeot-Citroen 231; see also Talbot-UK
Citroen 86, 102, 114, 130; and Fiat 147; overseas 84, 104-5, 121, 171, 175; see also Peugeot
Cole, Edward N. 100
Communist countries and MNEs 165-78; China 173-6; Poland 168-9, 170, 172-3; reasons for relationship 176-7; Soviet Union 169-70, 172; Yugoslavia 165-8, 170-2
complementation see integration

285

Europe 146, 190; and Communist
countries 171; in Europe 147, 149,
226, 235
Philippines 153-4
Poland 163, 166, 168-70, 172-3
Portugal 104, 150-1
Premier Automobiles 264-5
product cycle theory 28-31, 155,
162-3, 239, 242, 244n23-24, 271

Quick, John 175

Rakovic, Prvslav 165
Rebhan, Herman 181
regional integration *see* integration
Renault 102, 110, 114-15, 130, 160-1,
194, 210, 265; and Communist
countries 169-70, 175; in
Argentina 121; in Australia 118;
in Europe 84, 104-5, 126, 147-51,
235; in Mexico 121-2, 140, 161; in
US 135, 137, 139, 239, 241; link
with American Motors 160; link
with Volvo 147
Research and Development 159, 161,
202, 266; European MNEs pool
costs 235; location of 49-50,
235-6, 274, 280n1
Reuther, Victor 179
Rhys, Owen Jenkins 256, 269n5
Ricardo, John 190
Rolls-Royce 82-3
Romania 170-2
Rootes 107, 110
Russia *see* Soviet Union
Ryder Committee 189, 228

Saab-Scania 104, 120, 148, 194, 259
Scania-Vabis *see* Saab-Scania
Seddon-Atkinson 138
Siam di Tella 121
Sloan, Alfred P. Jr 76-7
Sociedad Española de Automóviles
de Turismo (SEAT) 126, 140, 149-50
Société Industrielle de Mechanique
et Carrosserie Automobile (SIMCA)
84, 104, 107, 259; *see also* Chrysler,
Fiat
Sorenson, Charles E. 80
sourcing, international 154-8, 162,
271
South Africa 129
South Korea 163, 209-10; *see also*
Hyundai Motor Company
Soviet Union 72-3, 163, 165, 169-70,
172

Spain 126-7, 150, 163
Standard Motor Products of India
264
Steyr-Daimler-Puch 142, 147
Stokes, Lord 227
Suzuki 194
Sweden 163, 181

Taiwan 206-7
Talbot-UK 221-3, 226, 234; *see also*
Chrysler-UK
tariffs 238, 270-1, 275; Australian
252-4; Canadian 64-9;
European 75-6, 79, 85, 96,
102-6; Japanese 112; US 241
Tata Engineering and Locomotive
Company (TELCO) 128, 264-6
technology 203, 211-18; and wages
209, 211-12
technology transfer 49, 63, 203-11,
275-6; cost 207-8
Townsend, Lynn 98
Toyo Kogyo 111-12, 134, 194, 196,
210, 265
Toyota 110, 114, 154, 161, 194,
205-6; in Australia 118, 141, 251,
253; in Brazil 113, 120, 259; in
Europe 104, 140, 150; in US
135-6, 139, 241; *see also*
Japanese MNEs
trade unions 179-86
transfer prices 21-2, 278, 280n2
Turnbull, George 208, 210-11,
219n14

UNIC 147; *see also* Fiat
United Auto Workers (UAW) 180,
186, 186n6, 191
United Kingdom (UK) 163, 220-37;
assessment of MNEs 231-6;
captive imports 221-2; exports
221-5; integration 225-6, effects
232-6, government response
226-31; profitability 225;
prospects 236-7
United Nations, reports on MNEs
47, 58-9
United Nations Industrial Development Organisation (UNIDO) 202-3
United States (US) 69, 96, 133, 163,
237-44; and Japan 110-12, 133-5;
auto pact with Canada 273, *see
also* Canada; foreign investment in
63-4, 241-2; vehicle imports 99-101,
134
United States MNEs 97, 107-8, 115;